LIFELINES 3

LIFELINES

LETTERS FROM FAMOUS PEOPLE ABOUT THEIR FAVOURITE POEM

Compiled by

Ralph Croly
Caroline Dowling
Gareth McCluskey

Edited by Niall MacMonagle

Foreword by Eavan Boland

Town House, Dublin

First published in Ireland in 1997 by
Town House and Country House
Trinity House
Charleston Road
Ranelagh, Dublin 6
Ireland

This selection copyright © Wesley College, Dublin, 1997

Foreword copyright © Eavan Boland, 1997

Preface copyright © Ralph Croly, Caroline Dowling and Gareth McCluskey, 1997

Letters copyright © the individual contributors, 1997

All rights reserved. No part of this publication may be reproduced, stored in a retrieval system, or transmitted in any form or by any means, electronic, mechanical, photocopying, recording or otherwise, without prior permission in writing from the publishers.

British Library Cataloguing in Publication Data. A catalogue record for this book is available from the British Library.

ISBN: 1-86059-049-7 (pbk)
ISBN: 1-86059-058-6 (hbk)

Cover illustration: *The Red Madras Headdress* by Henri Matisse. Courtesy of The Barnes Foundation, USA.

Typesetting: Red Barn Publishing, Skibbereen
Printed in Ireland by ColourBooks Ltd, Dublin

For the children of the Third World

The mass and majesty of this world, all
That carries weight and always weighs the same,
Lay in the hands of others; they were small
And could not hope for help . . .
                                                W H Auden

1.3 billion out of a world population of 5.5 billion (80% of the world's population live in developing countries) live in absolute poverty — 'a condition of life so degraded by disease, illiteracy, malnutrition, and squalor as to deny its victims basic human necessities.'
— from *Masters of Illusion: The World Bank and the Poverty of Nations* by Catherine Caufield (Macmillan 1997)

CONTENTS

Foreword	x		
Preface	xiii		
	page		
Arthur Miller	1	Kevin Casey	52
Joanna Trollope	1	John Boland	53
P J Lynch	2	Marilyn Taylor	54
Michael Aspel	3	John Major	55
Stephen Brennan	5	Kathleen Jamie	60
John Burnside	7	David Wheatley	61
Carol Shields	8	Betty Boothroyd	62
Colum McCann	8	Lara Harte	62
Colm Tóibín	9	Brídóg Ní Bhuachalla	63
Philip Davison	11	Philip Casey	64
Eamonn Sweeney	12	Marian Keyes	65
Eileen Battersby	13	John F Deane	66
Elizabeth Jolley	15	Denise Levertov	67
Gordon Snell	17	Andy Pollak	71
Valerie Goulding	18	Peter Sirr	73
Harry Clifton	19	Trevor Sargent	76
Josephine Hart	21	Andrea Corr	77
Oscar Hijuelos	22	Penelope Fitzgerald	78
Tobias Hill	26	Aidan Mathews	79
Ivy Bannister	27	Marie Foley	81
Jane Ray	28	Roz Cowman	82
Jill Paton Walsh	29	Brian Fallon	83
Niamh Bhreathnach	30	James Ryan	85
Jon Silkin	31	Gary Lineker	87
Alex Ferguson	33	Frank Ronan	88
Dermot Healy	35	Frank Kermode	89
Paul Brady	37	Brenda Maddox	90
David Whyte	38	Roddy Doyle	91
Brendan Howlin	39	Anne Robinson	92
Dave Smith	40	Eugene Lambert	94
Dermot Bolger	44	Harry Secombe	96
Angela Bourke	46	Feargal Quinn	97
Betty Ann Norton	50	Declan McGonagle	98
		Áine Ní Ghlinn	99
		Mary Gordon	101
		Katharine Whitehorn	103
		Ronnie Corbett	104
		Terry Eagleton	105
		Barbara Trapido	106

Michael Schmidt	107	Katy Hayes	165
Robert Welch	109	Brendan O'Carroll	168
Selima Hill	110	Tony Roche	168
Soinbhe Lally	111	Fionnuala Ní Chiosáin	169
Catherine Byrne	111	Pauline Stainer	170
Justin Quinn	113	Joyce Carol Oates	171
Michael Scott	114	Andrew Hamilton	172
Kerry Hardie	115	Anne Haverty	173
Siobhán Parkinson	116	Tom Courtenay	174
Gerard Beirne	117	John Kelly	175
Iggy McGovern	118	Eamon Delaney	176
Orla Melling	119	Barry Castle	177
Rodney Rice	121	Barbara Windsor	178
Lia Mills	122	Tom Mac Intyre	179
Ita Quilligan	124	Melvyn Bragg	180
Patrick Chapman	125	Mike McCormack	181
Sebastian Faulks	126	Myrtle Allen	183
Aisling Foster	128	Michael Hartnett	184
Harold Pinter	131	Catherine Cookson	185
Miriam O'Callaghan	131	Michael Gorman	187
John Hughes	134	Fergal Keane	188
Terry Prone	135	Richard Dawkins	189
Marie Heaney	136	Kate Atkinson	190
Desmond O'Grady	136	Tony Kushner	190
A N Wilson	140	Molly McCloskey	193
Pat Boran	143	Rolf Harris	194
Michael Mortell	145	Declan Hughes	196
Tim Robinson	146	Matthew Dempsey	197
Pauline McLynn	146	Mildred Fox	197
Mary Rose Binchy	148	Michael Curtin	198
Melanie Rae Thon	149	Hayden Carruth	199
Michael Smurfit	149	Charles Handy	200
Susan Wicks	153	Bernard O'Donoghue	201
Will Self	155	Brian Ashton	202
Mary Ryan	156	Eimear Quinn	203
Aengus Finucane	157	Tony Blair	204
Martin Drury	158	Elaine Crowley	204
Robert Ayling	159	Conor McPherson	205
Tom Stoppard	163	Peter Reading	206

Susan McKenna-Lawlor	207	*Notes on the contributors*	267
Eamonn Lawlor	208		
John Harris	209	*Index of poets and their works*	272
Robert Dunbar	211		
Frank McCourt	213		
Lesley Joseph	214	*Index of poem titles*	280
Michael Mullen	215	*Index of first lines*	284
Beryl Bainbridge	216		
Tony Keily	217	*Contributors to the first Lifelines*	288
Anita Groener	228		
Glenn Patterson	229	*Contributors to Lifelines 2*	289
Jessie Lendennie	230		
Stephen Pearce	231		
Frank McDonald	232	*Acknowledgements*	290
Martin McDonagh	235		
Jeremy Clarkson	239		
Michael McDowell	239		
Louis de Paor	244		
William Wall	247		
Austin McQuinn	248		
Paul Carson	251		
Seamus Hosey	252		
Tom Garvin	253		
Patricia McKenna	255		
Richard Wilson	256		
Nora Owen	256		
Mary Finan	257		
Michael Parkinson	257		
Jonathan Rhys Meyers	258		
Pauline Quirke	259		
Philip Castle	260		
Antonia Logue	263		

FOREWORD

I have been an admirer of this project since it began. In fact, when the first volume of poems — edited by Wesley students, chosen and commented on by various people, and all in an excellent and deserving cause — was published, I was almost taken aback by the charm, elegance and readability of the book. What's more, my own surprise surprised me. Like all working poets, anthologies have been a part of my life. Yet my relation to them, and I have no idea how representative this is, has never been simple. Most of them have almost no organising principle. Poems turn up in them randomly, scattered across their pages according to some non-specific agenda of taste or history. They create problems rather than solve them. They erase by fiat and preserve by diktat. By and large, I have come to feel about them as I do about family photograph albums. You have to trawl doggedly and patiently through far too many lost moments and inconclusive occasions to find the one perfect representation.

But this is different. These books have a design. They have a purpose and they get a result. What's more, somehow Ralph, Caroline and Gareth have enhanced the original version of both, so that the structure appears as fresh and convincing as ever, instead of just seeming a tired repetition. I have no idea of how this is done, and yet nothing appears like formula here. On the other hand, the form of this book resembles the others: public figures, from every part of the working community, have been asked for a favourite poem, and to give a reason for their choice. Artists, politicians, activists of all kinds have selected the poems, justified their selection and written back to the editors with both projects completed.

So what makes this different from the usual anthology? The answer to that question seems to me important. In giving it, I'll try — however inaccurately — to define some of the unease I feel about elements of the ethos surrounding contemporary poetry, which also has to do with my real appreciation of this book.

To return to my harsh words about anthologies, my resistance to them has to do with the fact that they so often reverse the process by which poetry is treasured, remembered and handed on from generation to generation. They substitute individual whim for the slow, measured communal sifting of poems. And yet that sifting is crucial. Take a poem like 'Dead Man's Dump' by Isaac Rosenberg, which Jon Silkin has chosen here. The poem is about the catastrophic violence of the First World War. About what Jon Silkin eloquently calls 'the spiritual problems of what killing each other entails'. I have remembered one line from the poem for years. *Will they come? Will they ever come?* But somehow the rest of it disappeared. Now here it is, with its powerful argument and discordant cadences, re-joining the line I remembered.

Therefore, so far from being an ordinary anthology, this book mirrors the almost-secret and yet definitive process by which poems are handed on. Take this poem, one reader says to another. Join the rest of it up to the single line you have half-remembered. And so a poem becomes a talisman, and a talisman becomes a treasure.

This makes an enchanting, readable book. But the enchantment shouldn't obscure the fact that this book also offers us a serious, interesting insight into the less glamorous, more democratic and, finally, more reliable way of handing on poetry. The difference between this book, with its personal selections and much-loved choices, and the average anthology, is the difference between a tradition and a canon. A tradition leads us towards the communal centre. A canon leads us away from it. The fact that so many poems here have been the loved companions of those who choose them tells us something about memory and association. It shows how obstinately poetry sets itself into feeling and recall. It also does something to recover the close affinities between music and poetry, because a lot of the poems here have been remembered by those who love them in the same way that a melody is remembered; something so woven into the associative fabric of their existence that it has become more life than literature.

Of course, that means that we're not likely to find too much Milton here, or Spenser or Crabbe or Bunting. By and large, the poems in this book have wheels and handles. They fit in the overhead compartment. They are the carry-ons of the poetry world. They are portable and manageable, which accounts for the fact that they tend not to get lost so easily.

This book, then, is just as engaging as the others — which is saying a great deal. The wonderful mixture of choice, memory and chance has lost none of its charm. Government ministers and priests and poets and actors and activists reveal themselves through poems. And the poems reveal ourselves to ourselves as part of this continuing process. Like everyone else who will read this book, I trust the choices here. They are too personal, quirky and definite to be anything but true. And this touches on one of the great pleasures of it all. Turning the pages, we ask ourselves why does this or that person, who we think of as hard-headed and practical, treasure and defend this or that poem, which seems so lyrical and other-worldly? Is this a voyeuristic or journalistic question? The very opposite, I think.

I congratulate the editors of the book, Ralph, Caroline and Gareth. To their commitment and the hours they spent on it we owe the final result. I congratulate Wesley, which has hosted this marvellous project, and Niall MacMonagle, who has fostered it. I hope, and suspect, that it will continue and strengthen, and there will be more books like this. I hope that I and other readers get more chances to be surprised into the kind of curiosity which makes us trace the advocacy to the poem, the reason to the rationale, the river to its source, till we find ourselves, all at once, at the magic heart of the original eco-system of poetry: its oldest habitat. The human spirit.

Eavan Boland
Dundrum
1997

PREFACE

The *Lifelines* project which some Fifth Year students began in 1985 here in Wesley College has enjoyed enormous success. And the royalties have helped in a small way to alleviate the suffering in the Developing World. We hope that *Lifelines 3*, the latest book in the series, will prove as big a success as its predecessors. We were delighted to see the interest and the willingness of the contributors to this book and it was very exciting to see who responded as the replies poured in.

Lifelines has moved with the times — some of the letters in this volume came as e-mails and faxes and we and fellow Wesley students typed up the replies. We sent *Lifelines 3* to the publishers on disk.

We would like to thank most sincerely everybody who so generously contributed to the project: those who chose the poems and wrote the letters, those who helped with the keying in of the text, Eavan Boland for writing the Foreword and Niall MacMonagle, our English teacher, who oversaw the project.

Finally, thank you, the reader, for supporting this worthwhile cause and we hope that you will find this book as interesting and as enjoyable as the other two.

Ralph Croly
Caroline Dowling
Gareth McCluskey

Wesley College
Dublin

Entries 1 to 223 appeared in *Lifelines*, which was published by Town House and Country House in 1992, and entries 224 to 418 appeared in *Lifelines 2*, published by Town House and Country House in 1994.

ARTHUR MILLER

10 February 1997

How about 'The Diviner' by Heaney?

   Cut from the green hedge a forked hazel stick . . .

The poem evokes the magic of the creative person, the one who knows without knowing, who is in touch with hidden, ultimate things. And in so few words!

Arthur Miller

The Diviner

Cut from the green hedge a forked hazel stick
That he held tight by the arms of the V:
Circling the terrain, hunting the pluck
Of water, nervous, but professionally

Unfussed. The pluck came sharp as a sting.
The rod jerked down with precise convulsions,
Spring water suddenly broadcasting
Through a green aerial its secret stations.

The bystanders would ask to have a try.
He handed them the rod without a word.
It lay dead in their grasp till nonchalantly
He gripped expectant wrists. The hazel stirred.

Seamus Heaney (b.1939)

JOANNA TROLLOPE

20 January 1997

Dear Ralph, Caroline and Gareth,

Here is my choice for the new Lifelines. *I think it's a wonderful idea and I hope it's a huge success.*

With very best wishes,

Yours sincerely,
Joanna Trollope

Heaven-Haven

A nun takes the veil

> I have desired to go
>   Where springs not fail,
> To fields where flies no sharp and sided hail
>   And a few lilies blow.
>
> And I have asked to be
>   Where no storms come,
> Where the green swell is in the havens dumb,
>   And out of the swing of the sea.

Gerard Manley Hopkins (1844–1889)

I think we all hope to get to some kind of heaven, somewhere, and this expression of it seems to me not only peaceful but also poignant, which makes it very human. I also like the pictures in it.

P J LYNCH   421

5 February 1997

Dear Ralph, Caroline and Gareth,

Thank you for inviting me to contribute to Lifelines 3.

Adrian Mitchell is one of my favourite poets. He writes wonderful poems on a huge range of subjects in plain yet magical language. I love his funny poems, but the one I have chosen is one of his most sad.

He wrote 'Especially When It Snows' for Boty Goodwin, his adopted daughter, who died in 1995 when she was just 29 years old. I find this a most beautiful poem, full of love and tenderness and grief.

I knew Boty, so this poem is particularly moving for me.

Wishing you every success with the book.

Yours sincerely,
P J Lynch

Especially When It Snows
(for Boty)

especially when it snows
and every tree
has its dark arms and widespread hands
full of that shining angelfood

especially when it snows
and every footprint
makes a dark lake
among the frozen grass

especially when it snows darling
and tough little robins
beg for crumbs
at golden-spangled windows

ever since we said goodbye to you
in that memorial garden
where nothing grew
except the beautiful blank-eyed snow

and little Caitlin crouched to say goodbye to you
down in the shadows

especially when it snows
and keeps on snowing

especially when it snows
and down the purple pathways of the sky
the planet staggers like King Lear
with his dead darling in his arms

especially when it snows
and keeps on snowing

Adrian Mitchell (b.1932)

MICHAEL ASPEL 422

Thames Television
4 February 1997

Dear Ralph, Caroline and Gareth,

Thanks for your letter. I hope the latest Lifelines *will be a sell-out. I don't know if my choice will merit inclusion.*

I find the last verse of Henry Wadsworth Longfellow's 'The Day Is Done' very comforting — particularly in the middle of a difficult day with many tedious hours stretching ahead. It conjures up a beautiful image, too.

> And the night shall be filled with music,
> And the cares that infest the day
> Shall fold their tents, like the Arabs,
> And as silently steal away.

Best wishes,
Michael Aspel

The Day Is Done

The day is done, and the darkness
    Falls from the wings of Night,
As a feather is wafted downward
    From an eagle in his flight.

I see the lights of the village
    Gleam through the rain and the mist,
And a feeling of sadness comes o'er me
    That my soul cannot resist:

A feeling of sadness and longing,
    That is not akin to pain.
And resembles sorrow only
    As the mist resembles the rain.

Come, read to me some poem,
    Some simple and heartfelt lay,
That shall soothe this restless feeling,
    And banish the thoughts of day.

Not from the grand old masters,
    Not from the bards sublime,
Whose distant footsteps echo
    Through the corridors of Time.

For, like strains of martial music,
    Their mighty thoughts suggest
Life's endless toil and endeavour;
    And to-night I long for rest.

Read from some humbler poet,
    Whose songs gushed from his heart,
As showers from the clouds of summer,
    Or tears from the eyelids start;

Who, through long days of labour,
    And nights devoid of ease,
Still heard in his soul the music
    Of wonderful melodies.

Such songs have power to quiet
    The restless pulse of care,
And come like the benediction
    That follows after prayer.

Then read from the treasured volume
    The poem of thy choice,
And lend to the rhyme of the poet
    The beauty of thy voice.

And the night shall be filled with music,
And the cares that infest the day
Shall fold their tents, like the Arabs,
And as silently steal away.

Henry Wadsworth Longfellow (1807–1882)

STEPHEN BRENNAN   423

Gate Theatre
Dublin
9 January 1997

I was first introduced to the works of Dylan Thomas by my late father, and have been a devoted fan ever since. However, I was introduced to this particular poem by my colleague and fellow Romantic Macdara Ó Fatharta, who, when speaking its opening lines, reminded me that the Celtic use of the English language, both written and spoken, is magical, mystical and unique. Ride now, through the hills and valleys of this remarkable magician's life.

I hope the above will suffice. Best of luck with your publication.

Best wishes,
Stephen Brennan

Lament

When I was a windy boy and a bit
And the black spit of the chapel fold,
(Sighed the old ram rod, dying of women),
I tiptoed shy in the gooseberry wood,
The rude owl cried like a telltale tit,
I skipped in a blush as the big girls rolled
Ninepin down on the donkeys' common,
And on seesaw sunday nights I wooed
Whoever I would with my wicked eyes,
The whole of the moon I could love and leave
All the green leaved little weddings' wives
In the coal black bush and let them grieve.

When I was a gusty man and a half
And the black beast of the beetles' pews,
(Sighed the old ram rod, dying of bitches),
Not a boy and a bit in the wick-
Dipping moon and drunk as a new dropped calf,
I whistled all night in the twisted flues,
Midwives grew in the midnight ditches,

And the sizzling beds of the town cried, Quick! —
Whenever I dove in a breast high shoal,
Wherever I ramped in the clover quilts,
Whatsoever I did in the coal-
Black night, I left my quivering prints.

When I was a man you could call a man
And the black cross of the holy house,
(Sighed the old ram rod, dying of welcome),
Brandy and ripe in my bright, bass prime,
No springtailed tom in the red hot town
With every simmering woman his mouse
But a hillocky bull in the swelter
Of summer come in his great good time
To the sultry, biding herds, I said,
Oh, time enough when the blood creeps cold,
And I lie down but to sleep in bed,
For my sulking, skulking, coal black soul!

When I was a half of the man I was
And serve me right as the preachers warn,
(Sighed the old ram rod, dying of downfall),
No flailing calf or cat in a flame
Or hickory bull in milky grass
But a black sheep with a crumpled horn,
At last the soul from its foul mousehole
Slunk pouting out when the limp time came;
And I gave my soul a blind, slashed eye,
Gristle and rind, and a roarers' life,
And I shoved it into the coal black sky
To find a woman's soul for a wife.

Now I am a man no more no more
And a black reward for a roaring life,
(Sighed the old ram rod, dying of strangers),
Tidy and cursed in my dove cooed room
I lie down thin and hear the good bells jaw —
For, oh, my soul found a sunday wife
In the coal black sky and she bore angels!
Harpies around me out of her womb!
Chastity prays for me, piety sings,
Innocence sweetens my last black breath,
Modesty hides my thighs in her wings,
And all the deadly virtues plague my death!

Dylan Thomas (1914–1953)

JOHN BURNSIDE 424

Ralph, Caroline, Gareth,

Thanks for your letter about Lifelines. *I am pleased to be invited to take part in No 3.*

I enclose a choice of poem, and a few lines on why I chose it. I hope it will be of use to you, and good wishes with the project.

Sincerely,
John Burnside

It's impossible — for me, at least — to choose a single favourite poem. There are so many fine poems to consider, some justly famous, others unfairly neglected. Still, one poet to whose work I keep returning is Michael Longley, one of the finest lyric poets of our century. In choosing 'Household Hints', I do not intend to say that this is the 'best' of his work; rather that, for mostly personal reasons, it's a poem that lives in my mind, nourishes me and enriches my notions of home.

Household Hints

Old clothes have hearts, livers that last longer:
The veils, chemises, embroidered blouses
Brought back to life in suds and warm water,
Black lace revived by black tea, or crape
Passed to and fro through steam from a kettle.

So look on this as an antique nightdress
That has sleepwalked along hundreds of miles
Of rugs and carpets and linoleum,
Its clean hem lifted over the spilt milk
And ink, the occasional fall of soot.

This places you at a dressing-table,
Two sleeves that float into the looking-glass
Above combs and brushes, mother-of-pearl,
Tortoiseshell, silver, the discreet litter
Of your curling papers and crimping pins.

Though I picked it up for next to nothing
Wear this each night against your skin, accept
My advice about blood stains and mildew,
Cedar wood and camphor as protection
Against moths, alum-water against fire,

For I have been bruised like the furniture
And am more than a list of household hints,
The blackleader of stoves and bootscrapers,
Mender of sash cords, the mirror you slip
Between sheets to prove that the bed is damp.

Michael Longley (b.1939)

CAROL SHIELDS

Winnipeg
Manitoba
Canada
22 January 1997

Dear Ralph, Caroline and Gareth,

First, I congratulate you on this wonderful project. Second, I thank you for giving me a chance to think about what my favourite poem really is; there are so many. But I've always loved the American poet Emily Dickinson and her elliptical, eccentric and truthful work. There was, and is, no one like her. In a sense, she remakes language, using verbs for nouns, adjectives for verbs, and she establishes rhythms that are vigorous, startling and utterly original. Her poems offer the remarkable compression that the best and most directly affecting poetry possesses. Poetry should go off like a flashbulb, and her poems do. Here's one of my favourites.

Tell all the Truth but tell it slant —
Success in Circuit lies
Too bright for our infirm Delight
The Truth's superb surprise

As Lightning to the children eased
With explanation kind
The Truth must dazzle gradually
Or every man be blind —

Emily Dickinson (1830–1886)

With best wishes to all concerned in this effort,
Carol Shields

COLUM McCANN

25 January 1997

Dear Ralph, Caroline and Gareth,

Congratulations on a splendid idea and a very worthwhile project. I take off my proverbial hat to you.

I'm delighted to be able to send on one of my favourite poems. I decided that, rather than picking something well-known, I'd go for a more obscure poet — Wendell Berry, a writer/farmer from Kentucky. (Another one of his poems which you might enjoy is the tiny political lyric called 'The Mad Farmer's Liberation Song': Instead of reading Chairman Mao/I think I'll go and milk my cow)!

Anyway, enclosed is my favourite poem of Berry's and my response to it.

With very best wishes for you and your project,

Yours sincerely,
Colum McCann

A Meeting

In a dream I meet
my dead friend. He has,
I know, gone long and far,
and yet he is the same
for the dead are changeless.
They grow no older.
It is I who have changed,
grown strange to what I was.
Yet I, the changed one,
ask: 'How you been?'
He grins and looks at me.
'I been eating peaches
off some mighty fine trees.'

Wendell Berry (b.1934)

Wendell Berry is a farmer who lives in the farmlands of Kentucky. Once — while I was travelling across the United States on a bicycle — I carried his poems with me for thousands of miles. (Other poets I carried in my pannier bags were Dylan Thomas, Gary Snyder, Jim Harrison and Seamus Heaney.) Late at night I would learn the poems off by heart. The rhythms have clicked with me ever since. I think this particular poem, 'A Meeting', is sad, wise, funny, poignant and just unspeakably beautiful.
I recently read it at a funeral service for a friend of mine — strangely enough, not far from the service, a man was out on the street selling peaches. He was grinning at the world.

COLM TÓIBÍN

Dear Ralph, Caroline and Gareth,

Thank you for asking me to select a poem. I do so with pleasure. This is called 'Málaga' and it is by Pearse Hutchinson. I wish you and your venture every success.

Yours with all best wishes,
Colm Tóibín

I love how sensuous this poem is, how steeped it is in the pleasure of sights and smells. I love how the complex diction plays against the ballad rhythms and the simple rhyme scheme. It seems to me to be a quintessential Irish poem because I can hear in its rhythms the sound of a Gaelic poem, and I can feel the sense of wonder and joy and release of someone being in the south of Europe who is used to the north. It is a poem that never fails to make me feel happy and glad to be alive.

Málaga
(for Sammy Sheridan)

The scent of unseen jasmine on the warm night beach.

The tram along the sea-road all the way from town
through its wide open sides drank unseen jasmine down.
Living was nothing all those nights but that strong flower,
whose hidden voice on darkness grew to such mad power
I could have sworn for once I travelled through full peace
and even love at last had perfect calm release
only by breathing in the unseen jasmine scent,
that ruled us and the summer every hour we went.

The tranquil unrushed wine drunk on the daytime beach.
Or from an open room all that our sight could reach
was heat, sea, light, unending images of peace;
and then at last the night brought jasmine's great release —
not images but calm uncovetous content,
the wide-eyed heart alert at rest in June's own scent.

In daytime's humdrum town from small child after child
we bought cluster on cluster of the star flower's wild
white widowed heads, re-wired on strong weed stalks they'd
    trimmed
to long green elegance; but still the whole month brimmed
at night along the beach with a strong voice like peace;
and each morning the mind stayed crisp in such release.

Some hint of certainty, still worth longing I could teach,
lies lost in a strength of jasmine down a summer beach.

Pearse Hutchinson (b.1927)

PHILIP DAVISON

6 February 1997

Dear Ralph, Caroline and Gareth,

Thank you for inviting me to contribute to Lifelines 3. *My choice of poem is* 'somewhere i have never travelled, gladly beyond', *by E E Cummings. It seems we never have doubts about what we are drawn to in others, but have only the vaguest notion of what others see in us. This poem does more than illuminate the power of attraction. Somehow, it suggests, though we may fail to seize the moment, there is still cause for celebration — and perhaps the moment has not yet passed.*

Very best wishes for the new volume. Lifelines *is an outstanding initiative.*

Yours sincerely,
Philip Davison

somewhere i have never travelled,gladly beyond
any experience,your eyes have their silence:
in your most frail gesture are things which enclose me,
or which i cannot touch because they are too near

your slightest look easily will unclose me
though i have closed myself as fingers,
you open always petal by petal myself as Spring opens
(touching skilfully,mysteriously)her first rose

or if your wish be to close me,i and
my life will shut very beautifully,suddenly,
as when the heart of this flower imagines
the snow carefully everywhere descending;

nothing which we are to perceive in this world equals
the power of your intense fragility:whose texture
compels me with the colour of its countries,
rendering death and forever with each breathing

(i do not know what it is about you that closes
and opens;only something in me understands
the voice of your eyes is deeper than all roses)
nobody,not even the rain,has such small hands

E E Cummings (1894–1962)

EAMONN SWEENEY

7 January 1997

Dear Ralph, Caroline and Gareth,

Thanks very much for asking me to pick my favourite poem for Lifelines; it's a great honour. Thinking about which poem I'd pick if I was ever asked is, like choosing my top ten records for Desert Island Discs *or selecting a World football team to play Mars in the Inter-Galactic Cup, something I've thought of many a night when it would have been more in line to be doing some work.*

The fact is that every time I pick a favourite poem, it's different. So this choice reflects what I think tonight, it would have been another poem yesterday and it will be another one tomorrow. The reason I've answered you this quickly is to end the torment of choosing just one poem. Already, I'm thinking of the poems by Paul Durcan, Seamus Heaney and Robert Lowell among others which I could have picked.

The poem I've gone for is 'Iola, Kansas' by the American poet Amy Clampitt from her collection Westward. *It strikes a chord with me for many reasons. It evokes the mind-numbing atmosphere of the long-distance bus-ride (and reminds me of the trek from London to Holyhead when I was too broke to travel back to Ireland any other way except by bus and ferry). It paints a great picture of the neglected heartland of America. And, in the end, it celebrates the unifying joy which seemingly minor pleasures can bring to people's hearts. I love this poem.*

Thanks again for asking me for a contribution and best of luck with the anthology. I think the work done by the Lifelines *people over the past few years has been admirable. Keep it going and best of luck in the future to the three of you.*

Yours sincerely,
Eamonn Sweeney

Iola, Kansas

Riding all night, the bus half empty, toward the interior,
among refineries, trellised and turreted illusory cities,
the crass, the indispensable wastefulness of oil rigs
offshore, of homunculi swigging at the gut of a continent:

the trailers, the semis, the vans, the bumper stickers,
slogans in day-glo invoking the name of Jesus, who knows
what it means: the air waves, the brand name, the backyard
Barbie-doll barbecue, graffiti in video, the burblings,

the dirges: *heart like a rock, I said Kathy I'm lost,*
the scheme is a mess, we've left Oklahoma, its cattle,
sere groves of pecan trees interspersing the horizonless
belch and glare, the alluvium of the auto junkyards,

we're in Kansas now, we've turned off the freeway,
we're meandering, as again night falls, among farmsteads,
the little towns with the name of a girl on the watertower,
the bandstand in the park at the center, the churches

alight from within, perpendicular banalities of glass
candy-streaked purple-green-yellow (who is this Jesus?),
the strangeness of all there is, whatever it is, growing
stranger, we've come to a rest stop, the name of the girl

on the watertower is Iola: no video, no vending machines,
but Wonder Bread sandwiches, a pie: 'It's boysenberry,
I just baked it today', the woman behind the counter
believably says, the innards a purply glue, and I eat it

with something akin to reverence: free refills from
the Silex on the hot plate, then back to our seats,
the loud suction of air brakes like a thing alive, and
the voices, the sleeping assembly raised, as by an agency

out of the mystery of the interior, to a community —
and through some duct in the rock I feel my heart go out,
out here in the middle of nowhere (the scheme is a mess)
to the waste, to the not knowing who or why, and am happy.

Amy Clampitt (1920–1994)

EILEEN BATTERSBY 430

I am so sorry I have been so slow. But poetry offers such a vast store and I can only suggest now that perhaps fate had deliberately had a hand, and the delay meant Fergus could be honoured and remembered in your wonderful book.

Regards,
Eileen Battersby

Selecting a favourite poem is as difficult as choosing a favourite piece of music, such is the diversity of music and poetry. Also, so much depends on the mood of a given moment. Poetry may not be quite as emotive as music, but it is a form of music, just as music is poetry — which is why I have at times offered Mozart's Great Mass in C, *or*

Beethoven's Violin Concerto as my favourite poem. However much I might complain about having to whittle down a vast list of personal favourite poems, it is extremely pleasing to be asked, particularly for a cause as big-hearted as this project. What to choose? Work by Thomas Hardy, Shakespeare, John Donne, Akhmatova, Louis MacNeice, Mandelstam, Heaney, Wallace Stevens, Ovid, Robert Frost or Derek Mahon? Having pondered over so many poems for so long, having tested the patience of the Lifeline *compilers as I constantly changed my mind or mood, from Elizabethan sonnet, to Keats, to Emily Dickinson, to Austin Clarke, my mind was made up for me by a tragic event — the death of a greatly beloved and respected colleague, Fergus Pyle, a former editor of the* Irish Times *and one of the most remarkable individuals I have ever known, a man of immense personal charm, exuberance and daunting intellectual range. He died on April 11 after a short, viciously cruel two-month illness. Since then, lines from* Richard II *continue to run through my mind:*

> For God's sake let us sit upon the ground
> and tell sad stories of the death of kings

Richard's powerful, moving, exasperated lament is, of course, concerned with kingship and the swift betrayals which result in the loss of power. A betrayal of life caused Fergus's death, and for anyone who knew him, he was a king. He was also very, very human, a committed European who loved art, music, history, ideas and life itself. Not even the most eloquent elegy seems sufficient.

Few poets match art and life as well as that most human of writers, Philip Larkin, who worked in the library of Queen's University Belfast, a city whose tragic history was recorded and analysed so brilliantly by Fergus Pyle in his reports from there. Although I had considered selecting Dylan Thomas's dramatically defiant ode, 'And Death Shall Have No Dominion'*, it is Larkin's thoughtful meditation,* 'And Now The Leaves Suddenly Lose Strength'*, which best catches the atmosphere of numbed loss, more accurately perhaps than any epic or elegy. This poem, with its theme of day's end, winter's arrival and life's passing, expresses, for me, some sense of the emptiness left by the death of a dear friend.*

For Fergus Pyle (1935–1997).

And Now the Leaves Suddenly Lose Strength

And now the leaves suddenly lose strength.
Decaying towers stand still, lurid, lanes-long,
And seen from landing windows, or the length
Of gardens, rubricate afternoons. New strong
Rain-bearing night-winds come: then
Leaves chase warm buses, speckle statued air,
Pile up in corners, fetch out vague broomed men
Through mists at morning.

And no matter where goes down,
The sallow lapsing drift in fields
Or squares behind hoardings, all men hesitate
Separately, always, seeing another year gone —
Frockcoated gentleman, farmer at his gate,
Villein with mattock, soldiers on their shields,
All silent, watching the winter coming on.

3 November 1961

Philip Larkin (1922–1985)

['And Now the Leaves Suddenly Lose Strength' was also chosen by Maura Treacy in *Lifelines 2*.]

ELIZABETH JOLLEY

Dear Ralph, Caroline and Gareth,

I like this part of Wordsworth's 'Prelude' because he is showing the development of conscience by parallels with natural scenery. Also, beautiful language.

Yours sincerely,
Elizabeth Jolley

from The Prelude
Book I. Childhood and School-Time [1805 version]

The mind of Man is fram'd even like the breath
And harmony of music. There is a dark
Invisible workmanship that reconciles
Discordant elements, and makes them move
In one society. Ah me! that all
The terrors, all the early miseries
Regrets, vexations, lassitudes, that all
The thoughts and feelings which have been infus'd
Into my mind, should ever have made up
The calm existence that is mine when I
Am worthy of myself! Praise to the end!
Thanks likewise for the means! But I believe
That Nature, oftentimes, when she would frame
A favor'd Being, from his earliest dawn
Of infancy doth open up the clouds,
As at the touch of lightning, seeking him
With gentlest visitation; not the less,
Though haply aiming at the self-same end,
Does it delight her sometimes to employ
Severer interventions, ministry
More palpable, and so she dealt with me.

One evening (surely I was led by her)
I went alone into a Shepherd's Boat,
A Skiff that to a Willow tree was tied
Within a rocky Cave, its usual home.
'Twas by the shores of Patterdale, a Vale
Wherein I was a Stranger, thither come
A School-boy Traveller, at the Holidays.
Forth rambled from the Village Inn alone
No sooner had I sight of this small Skiff,
Discover'd thus by unexpected chance,
Than I unloos'd her tether and embark'd.
The moon was up, the Lake was shining clear
Among the hoary mountains; from the Shore
I push'd, and struck the oars and struck again
In cadence, and my little Boat mov'd on
Even like a Man who walks with stately step
Though bent on speed. It was an act of stealth
And troubled pleasure; not without the voice
Of mountain-echoes did my Boat move on,
Leaving behind her still on either side
Small circles glittering idly in the moon,
Until they melted all into one track
Of sparkling light. A rocky Steep uprose
Above the Cavern of the Willow tree
And now, as suited one who proudly row'd
With his best skill, I fix'd a steady view
Upon the top of that same craggy ridge,
The bound of the horizon, for behind
Was nothing but the stars and the grey sky.
She was an elfin Pinnace; lustily
I dipp'd my oars into the silent Lake,
And, as I rose upon the stroke, my Boat
Went heaving through the water, like a Swan;
When from behind that craggy Steep, till then
The bound of the horizon, a huge Cliff,
As if with voluntary power instinct,
Uprear'd its head. I struck, and struck again,
And, growing still in stature, the huge Cliff
Rose up between me and the stars, and still,
With measur'd motion, like a living thing,
Strode after me. With trembling hands I turn'd,
And through the silent water stole my way
Back to the Cavern of the Willow tree.
There, in her mooring-place, I left my Bark,
And, through the meadows homeward went, with grave
And serious thoughts; and after I had seen
That spectacle, for many days, my brain
Work'd with a dim and undetermin'd sense
Of unknown modes of being; in my thoughts

There was a darkness, call it solitude,
Or blank desertion, no familiar shapes
Of hourly objects, images of trees,
Of sea or sky, no colours of green fields;
But huge and mighty Forms that do not live
Like living men mov'd slowly through the mind
By day and were the trouble of my dreams.

William Wordsworth (1770–1850)

GORDON SNELL 432

18 January 1997

Dear Editors,

Thank you for asking me to submit a poem I like for Lifelines 3. *I have chosen W H Auden's poem* 'Lullaby'.

I first read this poem when I was around 17, and have liked it ever since. It is melodiously lyrical, while still having the quirky and startling array of words that's typical of Auden's style. It manages to be robust and optimistic in the midst of a melancholy view of the transient nature of life.

The best of success to your excellent project.

Sincerely,
Gordon Snell

Lullaby

Lay your sleeping head, my love,
Human on my faithless arm;
Time and fevers burn away
Individual beauty from
Thoughtful children, and the grave
Proves the child ephemeral:
But in my arms till break of day
Let the living creature lie,
Mortal, guilty, but to me
The entirely beautiful.

Soul and body have no bounds:
To lovers as they lie upon
Her tolerant enchanted slope
In their ordinary swoon,
Grave the vision Venus sends
Of supernatural sympathy,
Universal love and hope;
While an abstract insight wakes
Among the glaciers and the rocks
The hermit's carnal ecstasy.

Certainty, fidelity
On the stroke of midnight pass
Like vibrations of a bell
And fashionable madmen raise
Their pedantic boring cry:
Every farthing of the cost,
All the dreaded cards foretell,
Shall be paid, but from this night
Not a whisper, not a thought,
Not a kiss nor look be lost.

Beauty, midnight, vision dies:
Let the winds of dawn that blow
Softly round your dreaming head
Such a day of welcome show
Eye and knocking heart may bless,
Find our mortal world enough;
Noons of dryness find you fed
By the involuntary powers,
Nights of insult let you pass
Watched by every human love.

January 1937

W H Auden (1907–1973)

VALERIE GOULDING

Dear Friends,

I was very pleased to receive your letter inviting me to send you my favourite poem. This one as you will see was written by Christopher Nolan when he was only fourteen years old. He is totally paralysed and can only be moved in a wheelchair. Apart from this he is unable to speak but he is able by moving his head to just manage a typewriter. He has written other poems but this is his first poem and from my point of view most interesting.

I hope that like me you will find it a wonderful effort being written by a completely crippled boy. I hope that you will admire his work. As you can imagine, he is truly a wonderful man.

Good luck to the three of you with the other poems.

Yours,
Valerie Goulding
The Hon Lady Goulding, LL D.

Christopher Nolan's Tribute to a Friend

Slowly, slowly, slowly,
Love wishes as love does;
Pealing bragging bells of faith
In the sobbing place of woe,
Fostering, lovely hope, asleep,
Offended, and heart-worn,
Giving measle-spotted help
To a handicap man forlorn.
Castigating gospel stories
Of Samaritan special help,
She diligently sought an answer,
Kathleen found time, told well;
Capitalising on caring people
Offering monetary help, 'twixt
Love and serene suffering,
They built a bridge to health;
Now, celestial glory 'waits them,
Graciously foretold, by One who
Raised the crippled man Divinely,
In Capernaum — so long ago.

Christopher Nolan (b.1966)

Written 3 September 1980, aged 14 years
Winner of 1987 Whitbread Book of the Year Award

HARRY CLIFTON

6 February 1997

Dear Ralph, Caroline and Gareth,

Years ago, when I worked in Africa and Asia, I used to wonder how the ethical (Third World Aid Programmes) and the aesthetic (lyric poetry) could be reconciled without compromise to either. The brilliance of Lifelines *is that it somehow manages to do this, and I'm honoured to be part of it.*

Here are two poems that speak to me now, at a time in my life when, as Eliot says in the 'Four Quartets', 'You must go by a way in which there is no ecstasy'. The keynote of both is continuity, humble persistence, and the realisation that, as Eliot again says, 'we are only undefeated / Because we have gone on trying'. I hope they mean as much to you and your readers as they do to me.

Every good wish for the continuity of your great project.

Salut,
Harry Clifton

Dear Folks

Just a line to remind my friends that after much trouble
Of one kind and another I am back in circulation.
I have recovered most of my heirlooms from the humps of
    rubble
That once was the house where I lived in the name of a nation.
And precious little I assure you was worth mind storage:
The images of half a dozen women who fell for the unusual,
For the Is that Is and the laughter-smothered courage,
The poet's. And I also found some crucial
Documents of sad evil that may yet
For all their ugliness and vacuous leers
Fuel the fires of comedy. The main thing is to continue,
To walk Parnassus right into the sunset
Detached in love where pygmies cannot pin you
To the ground like Gulliver. So good luck and cheers.

Patrick Kavanagh (1904–1967)

Swami Anand

In Kosbad during the monsoons
there are so many shades of green
your mind forgets other colours.

At that time
I am seventeen, and have just started
to wear a sari every day.
Swami Anand is eighty-nine
            and almost blind.
His thick glasses don't seem to work,
they only magnify his cloudy eyes.
Mornings he summons me
      from the kitchen
and I read to him until lunch time.

One day he tells me
'you can read your poems now'
I read a few, he is silent.
Thinking he's asleep, I stop.
But he says, 'continue'.
I begin a long one
in which the Himalayas rise
            as a metaphor.

Suddenly I am ashamed
to have used the Himalayas like this,
ashamed to speak of my imaginary mountains
to a man who walked through
      the ice and snow of Gangotri
          barefoot
a man who lived close to Kangchenjanga
   and Everest clad only in summer cotton.
I pause to apologise
but he says 'just continue'.

Later, climbing through
      the slippery green hills of Kosbad,
Swami Anand does not need to lean
on my shoulder or his umbrella.
I prod him for suggestions,
ways to improve my poems.
He is silent a long while,
then, he says
      'there is nothing I can tell you
          except continue.'

Sujata Bhatt (b.1956)

JOSEPHINE HART   435

6 February 1997

Dear Ralph Croly, Caroline Dowling and Gareth McCluskey,

I have great pleasure in replying to your letter concerning Lifelines 3.

My favourite poem is Four Quartets *by T S Eliot. I believe it to be in poetic terms the towering masterpiece of the Twentieth Century. It is open to many interpretations. Perhaps that is its genius. To me it is the journey of the human soul, from hope to despair . . .*

   Let me disclose the gifts reserved for age
   To set a crown upon your lifetime's effort.

   . . . And the awareness
   Of things ill done and done to others' harm
   Which once you took for exercise of virtue.

to the wonderfully uplifting last lines:

   And all shall be well and
   All manner of thing shall be well
   When the tongues of flame in-folded
   Into the crowned knot of fire
   And the fire and the rose are one.

My favourite lines in the entire poem are, however,

> Footfalls echo in the memory
> Down the passage which we did not take
> Towards the door we never opened
> Into the rose-garden.

Few lines of literature are as evocative of the extraordinarily complex nature of Time. I hope this is of some use to you. I wish you every success in your endeavours.

Yours, with respect and admiration,
Josephine Hart

from *Four Quartets*
from Little Gidding (1947)

IV
The dove descending breaks the air
With flame of incandescent terror
Of which the tongues declare
The one discharge from sin and error.
The only hope, or else despair
   Lies in the choice of pyre or pyre —
   To be redeemed from fire by fire.

Who then devised the torment? Love.
Love is the unfamiliar Name
Behind the hands that wove
The intolerable shirt of flame
Which human power cannot remove.
   We only live, only suspire
   Consumed by either fire or fire.

T S Eliot (1888–1965)

[The publishers were unable to obtain permission to print the complete poem.]

OSCAR HIJUELOS

NYC
7 February 1997

Dear Sirs and Ms Dowling,

In response to your query about a contribution to Lifelines 3, *I submit the following:*

Although there are many poets who I have come to deeply admire over the years — Yeats, T S Eliot, Neruda, Nazim Hikmet, Osip Mandelbaum, Ted Hughes, Walt Whitman, William Blake and innumerable others — a poet, if I can call him that, whom I have always loved reading was a newspaper man named Don Marquis who published a form of comic light verse, 'poetry' that spoofed the formlessness of Cummings and such notions as the afterlife, reincarnation, and (generally) the travails of life in America during the first quarter of this century. Free form verse told from the viewpoint of a cock-roach and cat, Archy and Mehitabel, the cat dictating and the cock-roach typing it out and never able to press down the 'caps' key, so that, like Cummings, everything came out lower case. It is not deep stuff, nor particularly beautiful, and it does not have much literary value, but I started to draw inspiration from Mr Marquis's work at a time when I had first considered writing myself, in college. He made the process and product seem fun, and even though I have since learned that serious work is never quite the 'fun' or exhilarating in the way we imagine it as young people, I am still fond of the work.

Now before you pass out, I proffer these few of the master's lines. This is from a poem entitled 'mehitabel in the catacombs':

> paris france
> i would
> fear greatly for the morals
> of mehitabel the cat if she had any
> the kind of life she
> is leading is too violent
> and undisciplined for words
> she and the disreputable
> tom cat who claims to have
> been francois villon
> when he was on earth
> before have taken up their
> permanent abode in the catacombs
> whence they sally
> forth nightly on excursions
> of the most undignified nature . . .

What can I say? This won't change the world and it's not Shakespeare but I'm glad that it was around.

With best wishes for your endeavor — and hoping that this will be suitable to your purposes —

Oscar Hijuelos

mehitabel in the catacombs

paris france
i would
fear greatly for the morals
of mehitabel the cat if she had any
the kind of life she
is leading is too violent
and undisciplined for words
she and the disreputable
tom cat who claims to have
been francois villon
when he was on earth
before have taken up their
permanent abode in the catacombs
whence they sally
forth nightly on excursions
of the most undignified nature
sometimes they honor
with their presence the cafes
of montparnasse and the boul mich
and sometimes they
seek diversion in the cabarets
on top of the butte
of montmartre
in these localities
it has become the fashion
among the humans
to feed beer to these
peculiar cats and they dance
and caper when they have
become well alcoholized
with this beverage
swinging their tails and
indulging in raucous feline
cries which they evidently
mistake for a song
it was my dubious
privilege to see them
when they returned to their
abode early yesterday morning
flushed as you might say
with bocks and still
in a holiday mood
the catacombs of paris are
not lined with the bones
of saints and martyrs
as are those of rome
but nevertheless these cats

should have more respect
for the relics of mortality
you may not believe me
but they actually danced and
capered among
the skeletons while the cat
who calls himself
francois villon gave forth
a chant of which the following
is a free translation

outcast bones from a thousand biers
click us a measure giddy and gleg
and caper my children dance my dears
skeleton rattle your mouldy leg
this one was a gourmet round as a keg
and that had the brow of semiramis
o fleshless forehead bald as an egg
all men s lovers come to this

this eyeless head that laughs and leers
was a chass daf once or a touareg
with golden rings in his yellow ears
skeleton rattle your mouldy leg
marot was this one or wilde or a wegg
who dropped into verses and down the abyss
and those are the bones of my old love meg
all men s lovers come to this

these bones were a ballet girl s for years
parbleu but she shook a wicked peg
and those ribs there were a noble peer s
skeleton rattle your mouldy leg
and here is a duchess that loved a yegg
with her lipless mouth that once drank bliss
down to the dreg of its ultimate dreg
all men s lovers come to this

prince if you pipe and plead and beg
you may yet be crowned with a grisly kiss
skeleton rattle your mouldy leg
all men s lovers come to this
                                         archy

Don(ald) Marquis (1878–1937)

TOBIAS HILL 437

15 February 1997

Dear Ralph, Caroline and Gareth,

Sorry this has taken a few weeks — your letter went pinballing all over the OUP departments, and reached me today.

Lifelines *sounds great. If I had to take one poem to a desert island it'd probably be a Shakespeare, but that's a bit predictable. Here's another.*

Jalaluddin Rumi was a war refugee in Asia 750 years ago — poverty was something he understood well. I love his work, although it concerns me for the same reason I love it: that, after seven centuries, his poetry still has the capacity to surprise and excite us. Rumi's poetry is as generous, lucid and intelligent as anything written today, and that seems to be both wonderful and disturbing.

I'll stick in two poems — I'd prefer 'Unmarked Boxes' if you've room; the quatrain is just in case you're running short of page.

Thanks for writing to me, good luck with the book, and I hope you enjoy the poems!

Tobias

Quatrain 1078

Think that you're gliding out from the face of a cliff
like an eagle. Think that you're walking
like a tiger walks by himself in the forest.
You're most handsome when you're after food.

Spend less time with nightingales and peacocks.
One is just a voice, the other only colour.

Mevlana Jalaluddin Rumi (1207–1273)
Translated by Moyne and Banks

Unmarked Boxes

Don't grieve. Anything you lose comes round
in another form. The child weaned from mother's milk
now drinks wine and honey mixed.

God's joy moves from unmarked box to unmarked box,
from cell to cell. As rainwater, down into flowerbed.
As roses, up from the ground.
Now it looks like a plate of rice and fish,
now a cliff covered with vines,
now a horse being saddled.
It hides within these,
until one day it cracks them open.

Part of us leaves the body when we sleep
and changes shape. You might say, 'Last night
I was a cypress tree, a small bed of tulips,
a field of grapevines.' Then the vision goes away.
You're back in the room.
I don't want to make anyone fearful.
Here's what's behind what I say.

Tatatumtum tatadum tumtum.
There's the light gold of wheat in the sun
and the gold of bread made from that wheat.
I have neither. I'm only talking about them,

as a town in the desert looks up
at stars on a clear night.

Mevlana Jalaluddin Rumi (1207–1273)
Translated by Moyne, Banks, Arberry and Nicholson

IVY BANNISTER 438

31 January 1997

Dear Ralph and Caroline and Gareth,

I'm delighted to be involved in Lifelines 3. *I've enclosed a copy of the poem I like: Maxine Kumin's 'Woodchucks'. Also enclosed, of course, are the reasons for my choice.*

Best wishes with your excellent project,
Ivy Bannister

I like 'Woodchucks' because it's funny in a black sort of way. It perfectly captures the armchair liberal, whose principles are instantaneously gutted at the first whiff of personal inconvenience. There's a lovely visual quality here. I can see it all: the busy jaws of the woodchucks, their sweet faces, their sudden violent deaths.

It is certainly my favourite poem on the morning after an orgy of slug-bait laying, when — with horrified guilt — I inspect the ghastly slime of dead and dying snails. All murdered by me! Gentle, unassuming me! A startling thought.

Kumin's transition from particular to universal is seamless. Her point about the addictiveness of violence terrifies. The speaker really gets into the killing with her cheery 'O one-two-three'. By the end of the poem, she's hooked, utterly hooked — 'cocked and ready day after day after day' — and dreaming of murder by night. And how many of us, in our hearts, are capable of the same?

Magnificent.

Woodchucks

Gassing the woodchucks didn't turn out right.
The knockout bomb from the Feed and Grain Exchange
was featured as merciful, quick at the bone
and the case we had against them was airtight,
both exits shoehorned shut with puddingstone,
but they had a sub-sub-basement out of range.

Next morning they turned up again, no worse
for the cyanide than we for our cigarettes
and state-store Scotch, all of us up to scratch.
They brought down the marigolds as a matter of course
and then took over the vegetable patch
nipping the broccoli shoots, beheading the carrots.

The food from our mouths, I said, righteously thrilling
to the feel of the .22, the bullets' neat noses.
I, a lapsed pacifist fallen from grace
puffed with Darwinian pieties for killing,
now drew a bead on the littlest woodchuck's face.
He died down in the everbearing roses.

Ten minutes later I dropped the mother. She
flipflopped in the air and fell, her needle teeth
still hooked in a leaf of early Swiss chard.
Another baby next. O one-two-three
the murderer inside me rose up hard,
the hawkeye killer came on stage forthwith.

There's one chuck left. Old wily fellow, he keeps
me cocked and ready day after day after day.
All night I hunt his humped-up form. I dream
I sight along the barrel in my sleep.
If only they'd all consented to die unseen
gassed underground the quiet Nazi way.

Maxine Kumin (b.1925)

JANE RAY

24 January 1997

Dear Ralph, Caroline and Gareth,

Thank you so very much for inviting me to send you my favourite poem — I am very honoured.

The poem I have chosen isn't actually my favourite — I have many favourites for different reasons. But this poem which I only discovered recently, set to music by David Bedford, is so tender that it always moves me.

Even Now

Even now, the fragrance of your hair
Has brushed my cheek; and once in passing by
Your hand upon my hand lay tranquilly;
What things unspoken trembled in the air.

Ah might it be, that just by touch of hand
Or speaking silence, shall the barrier fall;
And you will come with no more words at all,
Come into my arms and understand.

Ernest Dowson (1867–1900)

Hope that's OK — very best of luck with your book and thankyou again for including me. I would love to buy a copy when it's published — would you let me know?

Best wishes,
Jane Ray

JILL PATON WALSH 440

20 January 1997

Dear Ralph, Caroline and Gareth,

Gerald Manley Hopkins's 'Spring and Fall: to a young child' is a deep favourite of mine. It catches life's sadness, and a certain serenity about it. I have written two novels for which these lines are the epigram; they are called Goldengrove Unleaving. *My own daughter is called Margaret after the girl in this poem.*

Spring and Fall
to a young child

Márgarét, are you gríeving
Over Goldengrove unleaving?
Léaves, líke things of man, you
With your fresh thoughts care for, can you?
Ah! ás the heart grows older
It will come to such sights colder,
By and by nor spare a sigh
Though worlds of wanwood leafmeal lie;
And yet you *will* weep, and know why.

Now no matter, child, the name:
Sórrow's spríng's áre the same.
Nor mouth had, no nor mind, expressed
What heart heard of, ghost guessed:
It ís the fate man was born for;
It is Margaret you mourn for.

Gerald Manley Hopkins (1844–1889)

I wish you every good luck with the project in such a good cause,

Yours faithfully,
Jill Paton Walsh

NIAMH BHREATHNACH 441

Oifig an Aire Oideachais
(Office of the Minister for Education)
Sráid Maoilbhríde
(Marlborough Street)
Baile Átha Cliath 1
(Dublin 1)
30 January 1997

Dear Friends,

Thank you for your letter in relation to your plans to publish Lifelines 3 *and I congratulate you on your initiative.*

My favourite poem is 'Spring and Fall: to a young child', by Gerard Manley Hopkins.

Hopkins is a favourite poet of mine because he had uniqueness of style which gives a freshness and vitality to his poetry. For me, this particular poem captures a very real sense of the transition from childhood to adulthood — Spring to Fall. In the Romantic tradition Hopkins uses nature as a means to express his theme. The imagery of nature, combined with Hopkins's unique rhythmic style, make this a poem which never fails to please when read silently or aloud.

Thank you for asking me to contribute to Lifelines 3 *and I wish you every success with its publication.*

With kind regards,
Yours sincerely,
Niamh
Niamh Bhreathnach, TD
Minister for Education

['Spring and Fall' was also Jill Paton Walsh's choice. The poem can be found on page 29.]

JON SILKIN 442

Stand Magazine
5 February 1997

Dear Ralph, Caroline and Gareth,

You have asked me for a few lines for Lifelines; *here they are:*

Earth! have they gone into you?
Somewhere they must have gone,

And flung on your hard back
Is their souls' sack,
Emptied of God-ancestralled essences.

This comes from 'Dead Man's Dump' by Isaac Rosenberg, a poet killed in the First World War who, even more than the Christian Wilfred Owen, attempted to consider the spiritual problems of what killing each other entails. These lines engage with this, I believe.

Yours,
Jon Silkin

Dead Man's Dump

The plunging limbers over the shattered track
Racketed with their rusty freight,
Stuck out like many crowns of thorns,
And the rusty stakes like sceptres old
To stay the flood of brutish men
Upon our brothers dear.

The wheels lurched over sprawled dead
But pained them not, though their bones crunched,
Their shut mouths made no moan,
They lie there huddled, friend and foeman,
Man born of man, and born of woman,
And shells go crying over them
From night till night and now.

Earth has waited for them
All the time of their growth
Fretting for their decay:
Now she has them at last!
In the strength of their strength
Suspended — stopped and held.

What fierce imaginings their dark souls lit
Earth! have they gone into you?
Somewhere they must have gone,
And flung on your hard back
Is their souls' sack,
Emptied of God-ancestralled essences.
Who hurled them out? Who hurled?

None saw their spirits' shadow shake the grass,
Or stood aside for the half used life to pass
Out of those doomed nostrils and the doomed mouth,
When the swift iron burning bee
Drained the wild honey of their youth.

What of us, who flung on the shrieking pyre,
Walk, our usual thoughts untouched,
Our lucky limbs as on ichor fed,
Immortal seeming ever?
Perhaps when the flames beat loud on us,
A fear may choke in our veins
And the startled blood may stop.

The air is loud with death,
The dark air spurts with fire
The explosions ceaseless are.
Timelessly now, some minutes past,
These dead strode time with vigorous life,
Till the shrapnel called 'an end!'
But not to all. In bleeding pangs
Some borne on stretchers dreamed of home,
Dear things, war-blotted from their hearts.

A man's brains splattered on
A stretcher-bearer's face;
His shook shoulders slipped their load,
But when they bent to look again
The drowning soul was sunk too deep
For human tenderness.

They left this dead with the older dead,
Stretched at the cross roads.
Burnt black by strange decay,
Their sinister faces lie
The lid over each eye,
The grass and coloured clay
More motion have than they,
Joined to the great sunk silences.

Here is one not long dead;
His dark hearing caught our far wheels,
And the choked soul stretched weak hands
To reach the living world the far wheels said,
The blood-dazed intelligence beating for light,
Crying through the suspense of the far torturing wheels
Swift for the end to break,
Or the wheels to break,
Cried as the tide of the world broke over his sight.

Will they come? Will they ever come?
Even as the mixed hoofs of the mules,
The quivering-bellied mules,
And the rushing wheels all mixed
With his tortured upturned sight,
So we crashed round the bend,
We heard his weak scream,
We heard his very last sound,
And our wheels grazed his dead face.

Isaac Rosenberg (1890–1918)

ALEX FERGUSON 443

The Manchester United Football Club plc
9 January 1997

Dear Ralph, Caroline and Gareth,

Many thanks for your letter concerning your poetry project. My favourite poem is by the famous Scottish poet, Robbie Burns, and is called 'To a Mouse'.

To a Mouse
On turning her up in her nest with the plow, November, 1785

Wee, sleekit, cow'rin' tim'rous beastie,
Oh, what a panic's in thy breastie!
Thou need na start awa' sae hasty,
        Wi' bickering brattle!
I wad be laith to rin an' chase thee
        Wi' murd'ring pattle!

I'm truly sorry man's dominion
Has broken Nature's social union,
An' justifies that ill opinion
        Which makes thee startle
At me, thy poor, earth-born companion,
        An' fellow mortal!

I doubt na, whiles, but thou may thieve;
What then? poor beastie, thou maun live!
A daimen-icker in a thrave
                'S a sma' request:
I'll get a blessin' wi' the lave,
                And never miss 't!

Thy wee-bit housie, too, in ruin!
Its silly wa's the win's are strewin'!
An' naething, now, to big a new ane,
                O' foggage green!
An' bleak December's winds ensuin',
                Baith snell an' keen!

Thou saw the fields laid bare and waste,
An' weary winter comin' fast,
An' cozie here, beneath the blast,
                Thou thought to dwell,
Till crash! the cruel coulter passed
                Out-through thy cell.

That wee-bit heap o' leaves an' stibble
Has cost thee mony a weary nibble!
Now thou's turn'd out, for a' thy trouble,
                But house or hald,
To thole the winter's sleety dribble,
                An' cranreuch cauld!

But Mousie, thou art no thy lane,
In proving foresight may be vain:
The best-laid schemes o' mice an' men
                Gang aft a-gley,
An' lea'e us nought but grief an' pain,
                For promised joy.

Still thou art blest compared wi' me!
The present only toucheth thee:
But och! I backward cast my e'e
                On prospects drear!
An' forward though I canna see,
                I guess an' fear!

Robbie Burns (1759–1796)

Yours sincerely,
Alex Ferguson

DERMOT HEALY

Dear Folk,

Thank you for your letter. The poems I like best are anonymous — the name of the author has been written away by time so no autobiography clings weighing the text down, with all kinds of Hi-fal-la.

The other type of poems I like are songs, or maybe songs that are not considered poems. 'Donal Og' could have been a song once, but 'Frankie and Johnny' still is, and, best of all, is anonymous, despite the fact that it's comparatively recent.

Good luck with the enterprise,
Dermot Healy

Frankie and Johnny

Frankie and Johnny were lovers.
O my Gawd how they did love!
They swore to be true to each other,
As true as the stars above.
He was her man but he done her wrong.

Frankie went down to the hock-shop,
Went for a bucket of beer,
Said: 'O Mr Bartender
Has my loving Johnny been here?
He is my man but he's doing me wrong.'

'I don't want to make you no trouble,
I don't want to tell you no lie,
But I saw Johnny an hour ago
With a girl named Nelly Bly,
He is your man but he's doing you wrong.'

Frankie went down to the hotel,
She didn't go there for fun,
'Cause underneath her kimona
She toted a 44 Gun.
He was her man but he done her wrong.

Frankie went down to the hotel.
She rang the front-door bell,
Said: 'Stand back all you chippies
Or I'll blow you all to hell.
I want my man for he's doing me wrong.'

Frankie looked in through the key-hole
And there before her eye
She saw her Johnny on the sofa
A-loving up Nelly Bly.
He was her man; he was doing her wrong.

Frankie threw back her kimona,
Took out a big 44,
Root-a-toot-toot, three times she shot
Right through that hardware door.
He was her man but he was doing her wrong.

Johnny grabbed up his Stetson,
Said: 'O my Gawd Frankie don't shoot!'
But Frankie pulled hard on the trigger
And the gun went root-a-toot-toot.
She shot her man who was doing her wrong.

'Roll me over easy,
Roll me over slow,
Roll me over on my right side
'Cause my left side hurts me so.
I was her man but I done her wrong.'

'Bring out your rubber-tired buggy,
Bring out your rubber-tired hack;
I'll take my Johnny to the graveyard
But I won't bring him back.
He was my man but he done me wrong.

'Lock me in that dungeon,
Lock me in that cell,
Lock me where the north-east wind
Blows from the corner of Hell.
I shot my man 'cause he done me wrong.'

It was not murder in the first degree,
It was not murder in the third.
A woman simply shot her man
As a hunter drops a bird.
She shot her man 'cause he done her wrong.

Frankie said to the Sheriff,
'What do you think they'll do?'
The Sheriff said to Frankie,
'It's the electric-chair for you.
You shot your man 'cause he done you wrong.'

Frankie sat in the jail-house,
Had no electric fan,
Told her sweet little sister:
'There ain't no good in a man.
I had a man but he done me wrong.'

Once more I saw Frankie,
She was sitting in the Chair
Waiting for to go and meet her God
With the sweat dripping out of her hair.
He was a man but he done her wrong.

This story has no moral,
This story has no end,
This story only goes to show
That there ain't no good in men.
He was her man but he done her wrong.

Anonymous

PAUL BRADY 445

19 January 1997

Dear Ralph, Caroline and Gareth,

Thanks for your letter. Enclosed is a poem of my choice and a few lines to accompany it. I hope it is along the lines of what you are looking for.

Best wishes with your project. I hope you make 'Loadsamoney'.

Yours with pleasure,
Paul Brady

Liebes-Lied

Wie soll ich meine Seele halten, daß
sie nicht an deine rührt? Wie soll ich sie
hinheben über dich zu andern Dingen?
Ach gerne möcht ich sie bei irgendwas
Verlorenem im Dunkel unterbringen
an einer fremden stillen Stelle, die
nicht weiterschwingt, wenn deine Tiefen schwingen.
Doch alles, was uns anrührt, dich und mich,
nimmt uns zusammen wie ein Bogenstrich,
der aus zwei Saiten *eine* Stimme zieht.
Auf welches Instrument sind wir gespannt?
Und welcher Geiger hat uns in der Hand?
O süßes Lied.

Rainer Maria Rilke (1875–1926)

Lovesong

How should I keep my soul in bounds, that it
May not graze against yours? How should I raise
It over you to other things above it?
Ah, if only I knew of someplace lost
That lies in darkness, I would gladly leave it
There in a strange and silent place, somewhere
Where all your depths may swing, and will not move it.
But all the things that touch us, me and you,
Take us together like a stroking bow
As from two strings it draws a voice along.
Upon what instrument have we been spanned?
And who the fiddler has us in his hand?
O sweet the song.

Translated by Andy Gaus

This beautiful little poem shows the fragility of the lover's state in the midst of that wild and unpredictable calling. The certainty that risk involves pain but that nothing is gained without risking comes through soft and clear.

The abandoning of ourselves to whatever sound the fiddler makes of our union is surely the only way to learn how to love?

DAVID WHYTE

25 January 1997

Dear Caroline, Gareth and Ralph,

Thank-you for your letter and request for a favourite poem. This one by Seamus Heaney I have by heart, as a touchstone of faith in the act of writing. 'The Railway Children' is the kind of poem every poet comes to write at least once in their life, as an act of remembrance and faith in their own instinctual way of being in the world. The poet returns to childhood not to become a child again but to remember the original nature of that belonging, and through speech bring it to life again in the temple of their adult body. The poem is a deep loving metrical act of memory and rehabilitation, the black lines of the wires like lovely freehand presaging the writer's determination to write his way courageously into the world he sees around him. The imagery is dense and lovely. The swallows are brief musical notes perching on lines united by the stave of the telegraph poles. The final image is ancient but necessary to every contemporary life, the act of laying down the burden of a large encrusted self in order to slip through into the great self of the world.

... and ourselves
So infinitesimally scaled

We could stream through the eye of a needle.

Sincerely,
David Whyte

The Railway Children

When we climbed the slopes of the cutting
We were eye-level with the white cups
Of the telegraph poles and the sizzling wires.

Like lovely freehand they curved for miles
East and miles west beyond us, sagging
Under their burden of swallows.

We were small and thought we knew nothing
Worth knowing. We thought words travelled the wires
In the shiny pouches of raindrops,

Each one seeded full with the light
Of the sky, the gleam of the lines, and ourselves
So infinitesimally scaled

We could stream through the eye of a needle.

Seamus Heaney (b.1939)

BRENDAN HOWLIN   447

Oifig an Aire
(Office of the Minister)
An Roinn Comhshaoil
(Department of the Environment)
Baile Átha Cliath 1
(Dublin 1)
20 January 1997

Dear Ralph, Caroline and Gareth,

Thank you for writing to me concerning your worthy project. I regret the delay in replying.

You ask a most difficult question — my favourite poem. To tell the truth I have many depending on my mood and focus of the time.

Over Christmas and indeed in recent months I have read a great deal about 1798 in preparation for the 200 anniversary celebrations due in 1998 which will of course focus on my home county of Wexford.

I have walked Oulart Hill, Vinegar Hill and other associated sites in recent times which put me in mind of Seamus Heaney's poem 'Requiem for the Croppies'. It evokes for me a remembrance which brings the sites, the fields, the hedges and the hills to life.

I attach a copy of the poem. I hope that it might be of interest/use to you in completing your project.

With every good wish,
Brendan Howlin

Requiem for the Croppies

The pockets of our great coats full of barley —
No kitchens on the run, no striking camp —
We moved quick and sudden in our own country.
The priest lay behind ditches with the tramp.
A people, hardly marching — on the hike —
We found new tactics happening each day:
We'd cut through reins and rider with the pike
And stampede cattle into infantry,
Then retreat through hedges where cavalry must be thrown.
Until, on Vinegar Hill, the fatal conclave.
Terraced thousands died, shaking scythes at cannon.
The hillside blushed, soaked in our broken wave.
They buried us without shroud or coffin
And in August the barley grew up out of the grave.

Seamus Heaney (b.1939)

DAVE SMITH 448

The Southern Review
24 January 1997

Dear Friends,

Thank you for asking me to give you the name of a favorite poem. I think you meant a poem by another author and so have enclosed one, though perhaps not my favorite tomorrow or the next day, and attached a small comment. In the event you wanted a favorite poem of my own, I have also enclosed that with a small comment. Of course, I'd prefer not to use my own poem. I do wish you the best of luck with your project and hope that I will be able to purchase a copy when it appears.

Sincerely,
Dave Smith

Robert Penn Warren's 'Little Boy and Lost Shoe' is one of my favorite poems because it expresses a range of emotions between a parent and a small child, and does so in language that is both elegant and curiously plain. Any parent fears the unknown which will prove dangerous to the child, yet the parent knows the child must go forth into the big world. That journey is the world of fable and mortal consequence. Nothing is more frightening than being lost in the looming, often hostile world. Warren's poem makes me feel that fear grow and throb even as it attends to responsibility for a missing shoe.

Little Boy and Lost Shoe

The little boy lost his shoe in the field.
Home he hobbled, not caring, with a stick whipping goldenrod.
Go find that shoe — I mean it, right now!
And he went, not now singing, and the field was big.

Under the sky he walked and the sky was big.
Sunlight touched the goldenrod, and yellowed his hair,
But the sun was low now, and oh, he should know
He must hurry and find that shoe, or the sun will be down.

Oh, hurry, boy, for the grass will be tall as a tree.
Hurry, for the moon has bled, but not like a heart, in pity.
Hurry, for time is money and the sun is low.
Yes, damn it, hurry, for shoes cost money, you know.

I don't know why you dawdle and do not hurry.
The mountains are leaning their heads together to watch.
How dilatory can a boy be, I ask you?

                                Off in Wyoming,
The mountains lean. They watch. They know.

Robert Penn Warren (1905–1988)

Of all my poems, I have a continuing fondness for 'The Roundhouse Voices'. Perhaps this is because it is a funeral elegy for a favorite uncle. Or perhaps because the speaker's journey back to a family place, where he doesn't live, is a sort of reunion with the past. Or perhaps because it features a railroad roundhouse, and I have always loved the railroads that provided employment for generations of my family. Or perhaps because it is a poem about language and stories that can't be entirely contained in language. Or perhaps because my publisher thought the Mick was the Pope and not the great baseball player, Mickey Mantle, my boyhood hero. Or perhaps because the poem took me eleven years to finish.

The Roundhouse Voices

In full flare of sunlight I came here, man-tall but thin
as a pinstripe, and stood outside the rusted fence
with its crown of iron thorns while
the soot cut into our lungs with tiny diamonds.
I walked through houses with my grain-lovely slugger
from Louisville that my uncle bought and stood
in the sun that made its glove soft on my hand
until I saw my chance to crawl under and get past
anyone who would demand a badge and a name.

The guard hollered that I could get the hell from there quick
when I popped in his face like a thief. All I ever wanted
to steal was life and you can't get that easy
in the grind of a railyard. *You can't catch me
lardass, I can go left or right good as the Mick,*
I hummed to him, holding my slugger by the neck
for a bunt laid smooth where the coal cars
jerked and let me pass between tracks
until, in a slide on ash, I fell safe and heard
the wheeze of his words: *Who the hell are you, kid?*

I hear them again tonight Uncle, hard as big brakeshoes,
when I lean over your face in the box of silk. The years
you spent hobbling from room to room alone crawl
up my legs and turn this house to another
house, round and black as defeat, where slugging
comes easy when you whip the gray softball over
the glass diesel globe. Footsteps thump on the stairs
like that fat ball against bricks and when I miss
I hear you warn me to watch the timing, to keep
my eyes on your hand and forget the fence,

hearing also that other voice that keeps me out and away
from you on a day worth playing good ball. Hearing
Who the hell . . . I see myself, like a burning speck
of cinder come down the hill and through a tunnel
of porches like stands, running on deep ash,
and I give him the finger, whose face still gleams
clear as a B & O headlight, just to make him get up
and chase me into a dream of scoring at your feet.
At Christmas that guard staggered home sobbing,
the thing in his chest tight as a torque wrench.
In the summer I did not have to run and now

who is the one who dreams of a drink as he leans over
tools you kept bright as a first-girl's promise? I
have no one to run from or to, nobody to give
my finger to as I steal his peace. Uncle, the light
bleeds on your gray face like the high barbed wire

shadows I had to get through and maybe you don't remember
you said to come back, to wait and you'd show me
the right way to take a hard pitch
in the sun that shudders on the ready man. I'm here

though this is a day I did not want to see. In the roundhouse
the rasp and heel-click of compressors is still,
soot lies deep in every greasy fingerprint.
I called you from the pits and you did not come up
and I felt the fear when I stood on the tracks
that are like stars which never lead us
into any kind of light and I don't know who'll
tell me now when the guard sticks his blind snoot
between us: take off and beat the bastard out.
Can you hear him over the yard, grabbing his chest,
cry out *Who the goddamn hell are you, kid?*

I gave him every name in the book, Uncle, but he caught us
and what good did all those hours of coaching do?
You lie on your back, eyeless forever, and I think
how once I climbed to the top of a diesel and stared
into that gray roundhouse glass where, in anger,
you threw up the ball and made a star
to swear at greater than the Mick ever dreamed.
It has been years but now I know what followed there
every morning the sun came up, not light
but the puffing bad-bellied light of words.

All day I have held your hand, trying to say back that life,
to get under that fence with words I lined
and linked up and steamed into a cold room
where the illusion of hope means skin torn in boxes
of tools. The footsteps come pounding into words
and even the finger I give death is words
that won't let us be what we wanted, each one
chasing and being chased by dreams in a dark place.
Words are all we ever were and they did us
no damn good. Do you hear that?

Do you hear the words that, in oiled gravel, you gave me
when you set my feet in the right stance to swing?
They are coal-hard and they come in wings
and loops like despair not even the Mick
could knock out of this room, words softer
than the centers of hearts in guards or uncles,
words skinned and numbed by too many bricks.
I have had enough of them and bring them back here
where the tick and creak of everything dies
in your tiny starlight and I stand down
on my knees to cry, *Who the hell are you, kid?*

Dave Smith (b.1942)

DERMOT BOLGER

12 January 1997

Dear Editors,

I write to you with a guilty conscience as I was asked to contribute to Lifelines 2 and the question of my favourite poem so perplexed me that I missed all the deadlines involved.

One is inclined to try to think of the best poem you ever read, which is really an impossible question, because poems are like snares waiting to trap you at certain moments of your life. Like good jokes told at a bad time, they often pass you by, whereas at another moment of your life they would leap from the page to transfix you.

So the poem I have finally picked is not the best poem I have ever read and nor is the poet, for that matter, a major figure — although, if he had been allowed to live, perhaps he might well have become one. But he was vitally important to me when I was the age that you are now, when I was finishing secondary school and looking out, both excitedly and somewhat fearful, at the adult world, utterly uncertain as to what course my life would take.

Back then there were no Writers-in-Schools schemes, the explosion of Irish writing now occurring could not have even been guessed at, and there wasn't even a public library in the suburb of Finglas where I grew up. I had never read a modern poet and had little notion that such people existed (and even less notion that if you threw a rock over your shoulder in Dublin you were likely to hit one).

All I knew was that I wished to write poems and that this desire and practice was regarded as odd locally. Adolescence is confusing at the best of times and poetry made me feel especially isolated. At such times of great loneliness (I mainly lived alone in a house by myself from the age of fifteen) you reach for any straw which makes you feel less alone or less foolish and so at the age of fifteen I stumbled upon the poetry of Francis Ledwidge.

Ledwidge had been born in great poverty in Slane, County Meath. His father died when he was very young and his mother had to slave in the fields to keep him and his younger brother Joe with him in her small cottage there. After school he helped her, working for local farmers, but at the age of fourteen it seemed that a new life was opening up for him when she managed to apprentice him to a Dublin grocer in Rathfarnham. But Ledwidge was so homesick there that one night he was moved to write his first poem, 'Behind the Closed Eye', and was so exhilarated and awed by this experience that he secretly packed his clothes and walked the thirty-five miles home to Slane that night, arriving home at dawn to find his young brother already awake, instinctively knowing that something special was happening.

I was moved by the idea of a poem being powerful enough to change the course of somebody's life and even more so when I discovered that Ledwidge had rested at every milestone along that road home. Because, near my house in Finglas, one of those self-same milestones had somehow survived the planners and still existed. I would walk there late at night and sit where Ledwidge had sat, at much the same age as me, equally fearful and uncertain about his future, but knowing (as his fingers touched that hand-written poem in his pocket) that poetry would be the centre of his life from now on.

Ledwidge worked as a farm boy, a labourer, a road-mender and a miner, among other jobs in the years that followed, perpetually writing poems of often intense beauty in those free moments he had. He only lived to see one book of his poems in print before being killed in the first world war in his late twenties. Yet today he is still read and remembered by so many and the street benches in Slane do not refer to the powerful family who owned the great castle there, but simply read 'Ledwidge Country'.

It would be nice if I could say that 'Behind the Closed Eye' was a great poem and I have picked it here. It's not, however, and the one I have picked (and the one I recite in my mind every time I pass through Slane) is one written by him much later, on his last visit home from the war before his death in fact. It is an elegy on the death of a local Slane boy, Jack Tiernan, who had worked at driving cattle for a local farmer just as Ledwidge himself once had, and whom Francis used to meet on his morning walks.

Only a few months after this was written Ledwidge himself was dead and now the older I get the more I read it as an elegy for the young Francis Ledwidge himself, for that child who rested on a milestone in the village of Finglas with nothing before him except the dark country road and a return to bleak poverty, but with his life transformed by the gift of poetry.

Yours sincerely,
Dermot Bolger

A Little Boy in the Morning

He will not come, and still I wait.
He whistles at another gate
Where angels listen. Ah, I know
He will not come, yet if I go
How shall I know he did not pass
Barefooted in the flowery grass?

The moon leans on one silver horn
Above the silhouettes of morn,
And from their nest-sills finches whistle
Or stooping pluck the downy thistle.
How is the morn so gay and fair
With his whistling in its air?

The world is calling, I must go.
How shall I know he did not pass
Barefooted in the shining grass?

Francis Ledwidge (1887–1917)

ANGELA BOURKE

An Coláiste Ollscoile
Baile Átha Cliath
Roinn na Nua-Ghaeilge
30 January 1997

Dear Ralph, Caroline and Gareth,

I'm sorry, but I have to send you two poems.

I started to read Elizabeth Bishop's poetry after I found 'The Moose', chosen by Derek Mahon, in the first Lifelines. *I love the simplicity of her language, and the way she arranges it so beautifully, on the page and for the ear, to make it say exactly what she means. 'In the Waiting Room' is as true to the child she was in February 1918 as to the adult she was when writing it. As she remembers the vertiginous effect of losing herself in reading, the poem marks a moment of shock, when she understood something profound about being a girl, and a woman, and living in the developed world.*

The second poem is by Nuala Ní Dhomhnaill, who writes in Irish. It's about the Irish language: how delicate it is, and yet how flexible and strong; how suitable for carrying hopes and dreams. I like its brevity, and the way it manages to be what it's about: words woven together to convey a meaning, just as the cradle his mother wove from plants growing nearby conveyed Moses safely over water. The plants mentioned here, though, are Irish, with names which themselves are full of poetry, like coigeal na mban sí, *'the fairy-woman's spindle', for 'bulrush'. Writing in a lesser-used language is like putting a message in a bottle and throwing it out to sea: you can only hope it will be read and understood. Many people around the world have read this poem in translation, and been moved by it, and still it's untranslatable.*

Thank you very much for inviting me to be part of this wonderful project.

Gura fada buan sibh!
Angela Bourke

In the Waiting Room

In Worcester, Massachusetts,
I went with Aunt Consuelo
to keep her dentist's appointment
and sat and waited for her
in the dentist's waiting room.
It was winter. It got dark
early. The waiting room
was full of grown-up people,
arctics and overcoats,
lamps and magazines.
My aunt was inside
what seemed like a long time
and while I waited I read
the *National Geographic*
(I could read) and carefully
studied the photographs:
the inside of a volcano,
black, and full of ashes;
then it was spilling over
in rivulets of fire.
Osa and Martin Johnson
dressed in riding breeches,
laced boots, and pith helmets.
A dead man slung on a pole
— 'Long Pig,' the caption said.
Babies with pointed heads
wound round and round with string;
black, naked women with necks
wound round and round with wire
like the necks of light bulbs.
Their breasts were horrifying.
I read it right straight through.
I was too shy to stop.
And then I looked at the cover:
the yellow margins, the date.

Suddenly, from inside,
came an *oh!* of pain
— Aunt Consuelo's voice —
not very loud or long.
I wasn't at all surprised;
even then I knew she was
a foolish, timid woman.
I might have been embarrassed,
but wasn't. What took me
completely by surprise
was that it was *me*:

my voice, in my mouth.
Without thinking at all
I was my foolish aunt,
I — we — were falling, falling,
our eyes glued to the cover
of the *National Geographic*,
February, 1918.

I said to myself: three days
and you'll be seven years old.
I was saying it to stop
the sensation of falling off
the round, turning world
into cold, blue-black space.
But I felt: you are an *I*,
you are an *Elizabeth*,
you are one of *them*.
Why should you be one, too?
I scarcely dared to look
to see what it was I was.
I gave a sidelong glance
— I couldn't look any higher —
at shadowy gray knees,
trousers and skirts and boots
and different pairs of hands
lying under the lamps.
I knew that nothing stranger
had ever happened, that nothing
stranger could ever happen.
Why should I be my aunt,
or me, or anyone?
What similarities —
boots, hands, the family voice
I felt in my throat, or even
the *National Geographic*
and those awful hanging breasts —
held us all together
or made us all just one?
How — I didn't know any
word for it — how 'unlikely' . . .
How had I come to be here,
like them, and overhear
a cry of pain that could have
got loud and worse but hadn't?

The waiting room was bright
and too hot. It was sliding
beneath a big black wave,
another, and another.

Then I was back in it.
The War was on. Outside,
in Worcester, Massachusetts,
were night and slush and cold,
and it was still the fifth
of February, 1918.

Elizabeth Bishop (1911–1979)

Ceist na Teangan

Cuirim mo dhóchas ar snámh
i mbáidín teangan
faoi mar a leagfá naíonán
i gcliabhán
a bheadh fite fuaite
de dhuilleoga feileastraim
is bitiúman agus pic
bheith cuimilte lena thóin

ansan é a leagadh síos
i measc na ngiolcach
is coigeal na mban sí
le taobh na habhann,
féachaint n'fheadaraís
cá dtabharfaidh an sruth é,
féachaint, dála Mhaoise,
an bhfóirfidh iníon Fharoinn?

Nuala Ní Dhomhnaill (b.1952)

The Language Issue

I place my hope on the water
in this little boat
of the language, the way a body might put
an infant

in a basket of intertwined
iris leaves,
its underside proofed
with bitumen and pitch,

then set the whole thing down amidst
the sedge
and bulrushes by the edge
of a river

only to have it borne hither and thither,
not knowing where it might end up;
in the lap, perhaps,
of some Pharaoh's daughter.

Translated by Paul Muldoon (b.1951)

BETTY ANN NORTON

27 January 1997

Dear Ralph, Caroline and Gareth,

Thank you for your letter and invitation to choose my favourite poem for Lifelines. I am pleased to be associated with this excellent anthology.

It is difficult to choose a favourite poem which is 'a poem for all seasons', but 'Dublin' by Louis MacNeice is a poem I return to again and again. It captures the essence of Dublin, Dublin of the Danes, of the Pale, of Swift, of the Civil War, of O'Casey and Joyce. For me it is a journey through time. It is an elegant poem, its shape on the page echoes Georgian windows, and it is full of images, tastes and smells — a poem to savour.

Every good wish with your publication.

Yours sincerely,
Betty Ann Norton

Dublin
from The Closing Album

Grey brick upon brick,
Declamatory bronze
On sombre pedestals —
O'Connell, Grattan, Moore —
And the brewery tugs and the swans
On the balustraded stream
And the bare bones of a fanlight
Over a hungry door
And the air soft on the cheek
And porter running from the taps
With a head of yellow cream
And Nelson on his pillar
Watching his world collapse.

This was never my town,
I was not born nor bred
Nor schooled here and she will not
Have me alive or dead
But yet she holds my mind
With her seedy elegance,
With her gentle veils of rain
And all her ghosts that walk
And all that hide behind
Her Georgian façades —
The catcalls and the pain,
The glamour of her squalor,
The bravado of her talk.

The lights jig in the river
With a concertina movement
And the sun comes up in the morning
Like barley-sugar on the water.
And the mist on the Wicklow hills
Is close, as close
As the peasantry were to the landlord,
As the Irish to the Anglo-Irish,
As the killer is close one moment
To the man he kills,
Or as the moment itself
Is close to the next moment.

She is not an Irish town
And she is not English,
Historic with guns and vermin
And the cold renown
Of a fragment of Church latin,
Of an oratorical phrase.
But oh the days are soft,
Soft enough to forget
The lesson better learnt,
The bullet on the wet
Streets, the crooked deal,
The steel behind the laugh,
The Four Courts burnt.

Fort of the Dane,
Garrison of the Saxon,
Augustan capital
Of a Gaelic nation,
Appropriating all
The alien brought,
You give me time for thought
And by a juggler's trick
You poise the toppling hour —
O greyness run to flower,
Grey stone, grey water,
And brick upon grey brick.

Louis MacNeice (1907–1963)

['Dublin' was also the choice of Charles Brady in *Lifelines 2*.]

KEVIN CASEY 452

4 January 1997

Dear Ralph, Caroline and Gareth,

Thank you for inviting me to contribute to the next volume of Lifelines.

It is an honour to do so. I have greatly admired the diverse literary richness of the earlier volumes and the manner in which the proceeds have helped to alleviate suffering in the Third World.

Hilaire Belloc, like his friend and contemporary G K Chesterton, is no longer a fashionable figure, but the energy of 'The Winged Horse', the sheer exuberance and joy of its many rhythms, has made it very special to me since I first came across it many years ago. It is not a great poem but it has those difficult to define qualities that make it unforgettable.

Yours sincerely,
Kevin Casey

The Winged Horse

It's ten years ago today you turned me out o' doors
To cut my feet on flinty lands and stumble down the shores
And I thought about the all-in-all, oh more than I can tell!
But I caught a horse to ride upon and I rode him very well,
He had flames behind the eyes of him and wings upon his side
And I ride, and I ride!

I rode him out of Wantage and I rode him up the hill,
And there I saw the Beacon in the morning standing still,
Inkpen and Hackpen and southward and away
High through the middle airs in the strengthening of the day,
And there I saw the channel-glint and England in her pride
And I ride, and I ride!

And once a-top of Lambourne down towards the hill of Clere
I saw the Host of Heaven in rank and Michael with his spear,
And Turpin out of Gascony and Charlemagne the Lord
And Roland of the marshes with his hand upon his sword
For the time he should have need of it, and forty more beside
And I ride, and I ride!

For you that took the all-in-all, the things you left were three.
A loud voice for singing and keen eyes to see
And a spouting well of joy within that never yet was dried!
And I ride.

Hilaire Belloc (1870–1953)

JOHN BOLAND

20 January 1997

Dear Ralph, Caroline and Gareth

Thank you for your invitation to contribute to the splendid Lifelines *series. A favourite poem? Out of hundreds of favourites, I'm especially reluctant to leave aside Marvell's 'To His Coy Mistress', Gray's 'Elegy', Browning's 'A Toccata of Galuppi's', Matthew Arnold's 'The Buried Life', Emily Dickinson's 'I Cannot Live With You', Yeats's 'Adam's Curse', James Elroy Flecker's 'The Old Ships', Wallace Stevens's 'Sunday Morning', Edward Thomas's 'And You, Helen', Patrick Kavanagh's 'Advent' . . . I could go on and on.*

However, Philip Larkin it has to be. His cadences have sung in my imagination for so long that I could hardly choose otherwise. But which Larkin? There are the great, terrifying poems about death ('The Old Fools', 'The Building', 'Aubade'), there are the famous squibs ('Annus Mirabilis', 'This Be the Verse'), there are less-known masterpieces ('No Road', 'Deceptions'), and then there are the poems to which Ted Hughes referred when he said, 'I like all of Philip Larkin, but the sadder he is the better I like him.'

I'll opt for one of these. It's called 'Love Songs in Age', and among the reasons it means so much to me is that, like the woman in the poem, my mother used to play the piano in her younger years. In the third stanza, Larkin writes about how that 'much-mentioned brilliance, love' promises 'to solve, and satisfy, and set unchangeably in order'. The promise isn't fulfilled here, and the poet seems to suggest that perhaps it never can be, yet the poem itself, through its lyrical beauty and formal perfection, sets something unchangeably in order.

John Boland

Love Songs in Age

She kept her songs, they took so little space,
    The covers pleased her:
One bleached from lying in a sunny place,
One marked in circles by a vase of water,
One mended, when a tidy fit had seized her,
    And coloured, by her daughter —
So they had waited, till in widowhood
She found them, looking for something else, and stood

Relearning how each frank submissive chord
    Had ushered in
Word after sprawling hyphenated word,
And the unfailing sense of being young
Spread out like a spring-woken tree, wherein
    That hidden freshness sung,
That certainty of time laid up in store
As when she played them first. But, even more,

The glare of that much-mentioned brilliance, love,
    Broke out, to show
Its bright incipience sailing above,
Still promising to solve, and satisfy,
And set unchangeably in order. So
    To pile them back, to cry,
Was hard, without lamely admitting how
It had not done so then, and could not now.

Philip Larkin (1922–1985)

MARILYN TAYLOR   454

7 January 1997

Dear Ralph, Caroline and Gareth,

Thank you for your letter requesting my favourite poem for Lifelines 3. *I'm delighted to have been asked, both because I am a poetry lover, and also because I am most impressed with the practical help you are giving in your contribution to Third World aid.*

My favourite poem is 'The Wanderer', by W H Auden (I enclose a copy). Although it is based on an ancient Saxon poem, it evokes the emotions and sadness of leaving home in a way that will be familiar to every modern emigrant and expatriate, or anyone who has ever had to leave loved ones and woken, homesick, in a strange place. In language that is both powerful and tender, W H Auden allows the wanderer to speak to us across the centuries, and reminds us that the human condition is universal.

Best of luck with your valuable work,

Yours sincerely,
Marilyn Taylor

The Wanderer

Doom is dark and deeper than any sea-dingle.
Upon what man it fall
In spring, day-wishing flowers appearing,
Avalanche sliding, white snow from rock-face,
That he should leave his house,
No cloud-soft hand can hold him, restraint by women;
But ever that man goes
Through place-keepers, through forest trees,
A stranger to strangers over undried sea,
Houses for fishes, suffocating water,
Or lonely on fell as chat,
By pot-holed becks
A bird stone-haunting, an unquiet bird.

There head falls forward, fatigued at evening,
And dreams of home,
Waving from window, spread of welcome,
Kissing of wife under single sheet;
But waking sees
Bird-flocks nameless to him, through doorway voices
Of new men making another love.

Save him from hostile capture,
From sudden tiger's leap at corner;
Protect his house,
His anxious house where days are counted
From thunderbolt protect,
From gradual ruin spreading like a stain;
Converting number from vague to certain,
Bring joy, bring day of his returning,
Lucky with day approaching, with leaning dawn.

W H Auden (1907–1973)

JOHN MAJOR

10 Downing Street
London
21 February 1997

Dear Ralph, Caroline and Gareth,

The Prime Minister has asked me to thank you for your recent letter and to let you know that the many calls on his time make it impossible to reply personally.

I therefore hope you don't mind if I answer your question for you. Mr Major enjoys a number of poems but amongst his favourites are 'The Jackdaw of Rheims' *from the* Ingoldsby Legends *by the Reverend R H Barham and* 'If' *by Rudyard Kipling.*

Yours sincerely,
Simon Qasim
Correspondence Secretary

If

If you can keep your head when all about you
    Are losing theirs and blaming it on you;
If you can trust yourself when all men doubt you,
    But make allowance for their doubting too;
If you can wait and not be tired by waiting,
    Or being lied about, don't deal in lies,
Or being hated, don't give way to hating,
    And yet don't look too good, nor talk too wise:

If you can dream — and not make dreams your master;
    If you can think — and not make thoughts your aim;
If you can meet with Triumph and Disaster
    And treat those two impostors just the same;
If you can bear to hear the truth you've spoken
    Twisted by knaves to make a trap for fools,
Or watch the things you gave your life to, broken,
    And stoop and build 'em up with worn-out tools:

If you can make one heap of all your winnings
    And risk it on one turn of pitch-and-toss,
And lose, and start again at your beginnings
    And never breathe a word about your loss;
If you can force your heart and nerve and sinew
    To serve your turn long after they are gone,
And so hold on when there is nothing in you
    Except the Will which says to them: 'Hold on!'

If you can talk with crowds — and keep your virtue,
    Or walk with Kings — nor lose the common touch,
If neither foes nor loving friends can hurt you,
    If all men count with you, but none too much;
If you can fill the unforgiving minute
    With sixty seconds' worth of distance run,
Yours is the Earth and everything that's in it,
    And — which is more — you'll be a Man, my son!

Rudyard Kipling (1865–1936)

The Jackdaw of Rheims
from *The Ingoldsby Legends*

The Jackdaw sat on the Cardinal's chair!
Bishop and abbot and prior were there;
   Many a monk, and many a friar,
   Many a knight, and many a squire,
With a great many more of lesser degree,
In sooth a goodly company;
And they served the Lord Primate on bended knee.
Never, I ween, was a prouder seen,
Read of in books, or dreamt of in dreams,
Than the Cardinal Lord Archbishop of Rheims!

In and out through the motley rout,
That little Jackdaw kept hopping about;
Here and there like a dog in a fair,
Over comfits and cates, and dishes and plates,
Cowl and cope,
   and rochet and pall,
Mitre and crosier!
   he hopp'd upon all!

With saucy air, he perch'd on the chair
Where, in state, the great Lord Cardinal sat
In the great Lord Cardinal's great red hat;
And he peer'd in the face
Of his Lordship's Grace,
With a satisfied look, as if he would say,
'We two are the greatest folks here today!'

And the priests, with awe,
As such freaks they saw,
Said, 'The Devil must be in that little Jackdaw!'
The feast was over, the board was clear'd.
The flawns and the custards had all disappear'd.

And six little singing-boys — dear little souls!
In nice clean faces, and nice white stoles,
Came, in order due, two by two,
Marching that grand refectory through!
A nice little boy held a golden ewer,
Emboss'd and fill'd with water, as pure
As any that flows between Rheims and Namur,
Which a nice little boy stood ready to catch
In a fine golden hand-basin made to match.
Two nice little boys, rather more grown,
Carried lavender-water, and eau de Cologne;
And a nice little boy had a nice cake of soap,
Worthy of washing the hands of the Pope.
One little boy more a napkin bore,
Of the best white diaper, fringed with pink,
And a Cardinal's Hat mark'd in 'permanent ink'.

The great Lord Cardinal turns at the sight
Of these nice little boys dress'd all in white:
From his finger he draws his costly turquoise;
And, not thinking at all about little Jackdaws,
Deposits it straight by the side of his plate,
While the nice little boys on his Eminence wait;
Till, when nobody's dreaming of any such thing,
That little Jackdaw hops off with the ring!

There's a cry and a shout,
And a deuce of a rout,
And nobody seems to know
What they're about,
But the monks have their pockets
All turn'd inside out;
The friars are kneeling,
And hunting, and feeling
The carpet, the floor,
And the walls,
And the ceiling.

The Cardinal drew
Off each plum-colour'd shoe,
And left his red stockings
Exposed to the view;
He peeps, and he feels
In the toes and the heels;
They turn up the dishes,
They turn up the plates,
They take up the poker
And poke out the grates,
They turn up the rugs,
They examine the mugs:
But, no! No such thing:
They can't find THE RING!

And the Abbot declared that, 'when nobody twigg'd it,
Some rascal or other had popp'd in, and prigg'd it!'

The Cardinal rose with a dignified look,
He call'd for his candle, his bell, and his book!
In holy anger, and pious grief,
He solemnly cursed that rascally thief!
He cursed him at board, he cursed him in bed;
From the sole of his foot to the crown of his head;
He cursed him in sleeping, that every night
He should dream of the devil, and wake in a fright;
He cursed him in eating, he cursed him in drinking,
He cursed him in coughing, in sneezing, in winking;
He cursed him in sitting, in standing, in lying;
He cursed him in walking, in riding, in flying,
Never was heard such a terrible curse!

But what gave rise to no little surprise
Nobody seem'd one penny the worse!

The day was gone, the night came on,
The monks and the friars they search'd till dawn;
When the Sacristan saw, on crumpled claw,
Come limping a poor little lame Jackdaw!
No longer gay, as on yesterday;
His feathers all seem'd to be turn'd the wrong way;
His pinions droop'd — he could hardly stand,
His head was as bald as the palm of your hand;
His eye so dim so wasted each limb,
That, heedless of grammar, they all cried, 'THAT'S HIM!
That's the scamp that has done this scandalous thing!
That's the thief that has got my Lord Cardinal's Ring!'
The poor little Jackdaw when the monks he saw,
Feebly gave vent to the ghost of a caw;
And turn'd his bald head, as much as to say,
'Pray, be so good as to walk this way!'
Slower and slower he limp'd on before,
Till they came to the back of the belfry door,
Where the first thing they saw, midst the sticks and the straw,
Was the RING in the nest of that little Jackdaw!

Then the great Lord Cardinal
Call'd for his book,
And off that terrible curse he took;
The mute expression
Served in lieu of confession,
And, being thus coupled
With full restitution,
The Jackdaw got
Plenary absolution!
When those words were heard,
That poor little bird
Was so changed in a moment,
'Twas really absurd,
He grew sleek, and fat;
In addition to that;
A fresh crop of feathers
Came thick as a mat!

He hopp'd now about with a gait devout;
At Matins, at Vespers, he never was out;
And, so far from any more pilfering deeds,
He always seem'd telling the Confessor's beads.

If anyone lied, or if anyone swore,
Or slumber'd in prayer-time and happen'd to snore,
That good Jackdaw would give a great 'Caw!'
As much as to say, 'Don't do so any more!'

While many remark'd, as his manners they saw,
That they 'never had known such a pious Jackdaw!'
He long lived the pride of that country side.
And at last in the odour of sanctity died;
When, as words were too faint
His merits to paint,
The Conclave determined to make him a Saint;
And on newly-made Saints and Popes, as you know,
It's the custom, at Rome, new names to bestow,
So they canonized him by the name of Jim Crow!

Richard Harris Barham (1788–1845)

KATHLEEN JAMIE

Dear Editors,

Thank you for your request re Lifelines.

I would choose 'Encounter', *by the Polish poet Czeslaw Milosz.*

I have tried several times to do as you ask and write a few lines about this poem, but they are too clumsy, and only detract from the poem's astonishing clarity. I would rather keep quiet.

With best wishes for your venture,
Kathleen Jamie

Encounter

We were riding through frozen fields in a wagon at dawn.
A red wing rose in the darkness.

And suddenly a hare ran across the road.
One of us pointed to it with his hand.

That was long ago. Today neither of them is alive,
Not the hare, nor the man who made the gesture.

O my love, where are they, where are they going
The flash of a hand, streak of movement, rustle of pebbles.
I ask not out of sorrow, but in wonder.

Czeslaw Milosz (b.1911)
Translated by Czeslaw Milosz and Lillian Vallee

DAVID WHEATLEY

6 January 1997

Dear Ralph, Caroline and Gareth

Thank you for your kind invitation to contribute to Lifelines 3. *If there is one figure more than any other who incarnates the force and mystery of poetry for me it is Friedrich Hölderlin (1770–1843), and I would like to nominate as my choice the seventh section of his great elegy 'Brot und Wein'. How can the poet intercede, he asks, between suffering humanity and the unknowable gods?*

Yours sincerely,
David Wheatley

Brot und Wein

7
Aber Freund! wir kommen zu spät. Zwar leben die Götter,
    Aber über dem Haupt droben in anderer Welt.
Endlos wirken sie da und scheinens wenig zu achten,
    Ob wir leben, so sehr schonen die Himmlischen uns.
Denn nicht immer vermag ein schwaches Gefäß sie zu fassen,
    Nur zu Zeiten erträgt göttliche Fülle der Mensch.
Traum von ihnen ist drauf das Leben. Aber das Irrsal
    Hilft, wie Schlummer, und stark machet die Not und die
    Nacht,
Bis daß Helden genug in der ehernen Wiege gewachsen,
    Herzen am Kraft, wie sonst, ähnlich den Himmlischen sind.
Donnernd kommen sie drauf. Indessen dünket mir öfters
    Besser zu schlafen, wie so ohne Genossen zu sein,
So zu harren, und was zu tun indes und zu sagen,
    Weiß ich nicht, und wozu Dichter in dürftiger Zeit?
Aber sie sind, sagst du, wie des Weingotts heilige Priester,
    Welche von Lande zu Land zogen heiliger Nacht.

Friedrich Hölderlin (1770–1843)

Bread and Wine

But, my friend, we have come too late. True, the gods are living,
but above our heads, up there in a different world. Endlessly
there they are active and — so much do the Heavenly spare us
— little they seem to care whether we live or not. For not
always a fragile vessel can hold them, only at times can men
bear the plenitude of the divine. Henceforth our life is a dream

about them. But to wander astray helps, like sleep, and need and Night make us strong, until heroes enough have grown in the iron cradle, and hearts, as before, resemble the Heavenly in strength. Thundering then they come. Meanwhile it sometimes seems better to me to sleep than to be utterly without companions as we are, to be always waiting like this, and what's to be done or said in the meantime, I do not know, and what is the use of poets at a time of dearth? But they are, you say, like those holy priests of the wine-god who travelled from country to country in holy Night.

Translated by Michael Hamburger (b.1924)

BETTY BOOTHROYD 458

Speaker's Office
House of Commons
London
5 February 1997

Dear Mr Croly, Miss Dowling and Mr McCluskey,

Madam Speaker has asked me to thank you for your recent letter and to reply on her behalf.

The Speaker has asked me to say that her favourite poem is 'If' by Rudyard Kipling. Madam Speaker has asked me to send you a copy of the poem, which she feels speaks for itself.

The Speaker wishes you every success in your endeavours.

Yours sincerely,
Trudy Myers
Correspondence Manager

['If' was the choice of Fay Weldon in Lifelines 2. It was also John Major's choice in this volume. The poem can be found on page 56.]

LARA HARTE 459

27 January 1997

Dear Ralph, Caroline and Gareth,

I was delighted to be asked to participate in **Lifelines 3,** *and I'm sure it'll be a great success. Here is my favourite poem and a short piece explaining why.*

My favourite poem is 'Rupert the Bear', by Celia de Fréine. Celia happens to be my mother and in Paris I brought her to a Louise Bourgeois exhibition. A lot of the sculptures were life-size cells with old-fashioned laboratory equipment inside. They reminded her of a Rupert annual she had as a child and inspired this poem.

Yours sincerely,
Lara Harte

Rupert the Bear

She used to have the same nightmare
as a child and knew exactly what caused it —
a page in her Rupert book, the page showing
the laboratory of the wicked professor
who had kidnapped Rupert. She was not afraid
of the professor himself, and the nightmare
was not about being kidnapped. It was his array
of sterile apparatus that frightened her —
vials and cylinders, funnels and globes.
She dreamt that she was vapourised by them,
trapped in a cloud of green steam that puffed
endlessly back and forth. Years later
she came across a similar system
in a junk shop. Without upsetting
a single cobweb, she brought it home and
assembled it on a worm-eaten bench
in a lean-to at the bottom of her garden.

Celia de Fréine

BRÍDÓG NÍ BHUACHALLA   460

Rannóg na gClár Gaeilge
Radio Telefís Éireann
31 January 1997

A chairde,

I was delighted to get your letter re: Lifelines 3. *The collected edition is on my beside locker and it gives me many hours of enjoyment and pleasure.*

I have always appreciated and loved poetry and it is very difficult to mention a favourite poet or poem, but I will try. One Saturday a few years ago the Irish Times *published the following poem, 'Rag Doll' by Phil MacCarthy.*

Rag Doll

Straw-haired. Patchworked. I am
the rag doll you threaten to lose.
Each time, you push me

into the dark under the bed
to see if I'll be lost
when you turn blindly groping

cobwebs. Sometimes you slap me
on the face and warn
that I have to be good. Once,

you even tried to strangle me,
the vice grip of your small fingers
on my throat so fierce, tears

dripped from your eyes. At night
I sleep next to you on the pillow.
Your eyelashes brush my cheek.

Soon I'll be gone forever.
Neither of us will know
exactly how it happened.

Catherine Phil MacCarthy (b.1954)

For some strange reason it affected me deeply — I cut it out, covered it with cellophane and it stands beside the mirror in my bedroom. I read it most days and it never ceases to amaze and stir me or provoke some reaction, related to childhood, lost days and friends. Most importantly, it says to me not to take those close to me for granted.

Go néirí leis an deá-obair agus gura fada buan sibh i mbun an deá obair.

Le meas mór,
Brídóg Ní Bhuachalla

PHILIP CASEY

26 January 1997

Dear Ralph, Caroline, Gareth,

Many thanks for asking me to contribute to Lifelines. *I'm flattered and honoured to do so, and would like to congratulate you on undertaking such a mammoth task, and to wish you well.*

There are so many poems which mean a great deal to me that I have a personal anthology, for easy reference. Among old favourites are included poems by Brecht, Rilke, Lorca, Frank O'Hara, Herbert (the

Pole), Jack Spicer, and that's mentioning just a few of the foreigners. As for the Irish, well, there's an even longer list and many of the poets are my friends. So it's a very difficult choice. One of the reasons which helped me decide is that Pearse Hutchinson will be seventy in 1997, and I would like to celebrate his **Barnsley Main Seam** as among the most beautiful books of poetry published in many years, a triumphant vindication of a lifetime dedicated to the poet's art. This book represents for me the culmination of what Kavanagh called the journey 'from simplicity through complexity to simplicity'. Its individual poems speak simply, yet profoundly, out of a deeply experienced life. I'm choosing 'Until', as I think it epitomises what I think of the book as a whole.

All the best in your great endeavour.

Sincerely,
Philip Casey

Until
een fenster is alles
   — Paul van Ostaijen

The way an old man from his window looks out at the beauty
 of nature
   grass, trees, creatures
    the beauty surviving the horror
is not the same way that a young man
 looks out the window and goes out the door and enters
his own full nature and every nature and goes on living them all
 crushed insect, predator's prey: not surviving, not surviving
but the young man still living it all
 living it up and living through it all
  dancing or crawling every minute of it until
   he sits looking out of a window

Pearse Hutchinson (b.1927)

MARIAN KEYES   462

12 January 1997

Dear Ralph, Caroline and Gareth,

Thank you very much for your letter asking me to contribute to Lifelines 3. I'm honoured to be asked and delighted to be part of such a worthy project. My favourite poem — and has been for as long as I can remember — is 'The Wayfarer', the very last poem that Pádraig Pearse wrote, shortly before he was executed.

It conveys with exquisite poignancy how laughably short our little lives are. And I also find it fascinating to be given a glimpse into his head at such a unique, terrible time — it's almost like having a type of bizarre live video link-up with the past.

I'm deeply moved by the courage shown in the poem, by Pearse's unflinching acceptance of his fate, as he already mourns his own passing.

I wish you great success with the venture and thanks again for asking me to contribute.

Yours sincerely,
Marian Keyes

The Wayfarer

The beauty of the world hath made me sad,
This beauty that will pass;
Sometimes my heart hath shaken with great joy
To see a leaping squirrel in a tree,
Or a red lady-bird upon a stalk,
Or little rabbits in a field at evening,
Lit by a slanting sun,
Or some green hill where shadows drifted by
Some quiet hill where mountainy man hath sown
And soon would reap; near to the gate of Heaven;
Or children with bare feet upon the sands
Of some ebbed sea, or playing on the streets
Of little towns in Connacht,
Things young and happy.
And then my heart hath told me:
These will pass,
Will pass and change, will die and be no more,
Things bright and green, things young and happy;
And I have gone upon my way
Sorrowful.

Pádraig Pearse (1879–1916)

JOHN F DEANE

The Dedalus Press
14 January 1997

Dear Students,

Thankyou for asking me to contribute to your great task. I hope the enclosed is suitable.

I wish you success.
John F Deane

Heron I

St Simon Heron,
standing, standing, standing
upon his offshore pillar,

suddenly, subtly
dips his head to drink,
Three, then a fourth,
and more times, that legato
arabesque of the neck,
the small head almost a serpent's,
smoothly one with its flexible stem.
Body and tall legs
move not an inch.
                Hunger,
thirst, fulfillment
are ripples that lap his surface;
his patience absorbs them.
Time does not pass, for him;
it is the lake, and full, and still,
and he has all of it, and wades to strike
when he will upon his fish.

Denise Levertov (b.1923)

My favourite poem of all would be Hopkins's 'Wreck of the Deutschland' but it would take most of your book; Hopkins's 'Windhover' moves me deeply, too, but this poem by Denise Levertov contains with its simple accuracy almost as much as the 'Windhover' does; after the witty comparison of the heron to St Simon Stylites, the totally apt description, loving and detailed, you come to realise that the heron has merged perfectly with its world, is master of it and one with its patient obedience to its own laws. The poem envies such natural harmony with the world; the poem, in its perfection, is in harmony with the world. I long to know, and do not (yet) know, such harmony!

DENISE LEVERTOV   464

3 February 1997

The reasons why I am choosing 'A Tree Telling of Orpheus' are both subjective and objective. The writing of it was a memorable experience for me, since I felt I had left my own 'me-ness' and entered into tree-consciousness. Any act of creative imagination that is not focused on the self does this in some degree, but this was a particularly sustained and intense example of that act of imagination. That's the subjective reason for my choice. The objective one is that — no doubt as a result of the quality of the experience — this poem seems to me to be perhaps the most precise, musical, and fully articulated example of the 'organic form' I have always pursued; its linebreaks and indentations result in a full score, musically speaking, and audiences are always responsive to its music and drama when I read it.

I also like the way in which the experience of notating the tree's Orpheus-enchanted journey led me to unforeseen images that echo Christian images of conversion, hope and resurrection, which I perceived only after the poem was written.

Denise Levertov

A Tree Telling of Orpheus

White dawn. Stillness.   When the rippling began
    I took it for sea-wind, coming to our valley with rumors
    of salt, of treeless horizons. But the white fog
didn't stir; the leaves of my brothers remained outstretched,
unmoving.
        Yet the rippling drew nearer — and then
my own outermost branches began to tingle, almost as if
fire had been lit below them, too close, and their twig-tips
were drying and curling.
           Yet I was not afraid, only
        deeply alert.

I was the first to see him, for I grew
    out on the pasture slope, beyond the forest.
He was a man, it seemed: the two
moving stems, the short trunk, the two
arm-branches, flexible, each with five leafless
                twigs at their ends,
and the head that's crowned by brown or gold grass,
bearing a face not like the beaked face of a bird,
    more like a flower's.
                He carried a burden made of
some cut branch bent while it was green,
strands of a vine tight-stretched across it. From this,
when he touched it, and from his voice
which unlike the wind's voice had no need of our
leaves and branches to complete its sound,
                came the ripple.
But it was now no longer a ripple (he had come near and
stopped in my first shadow) it was a wave that bathed me
    as if rain
           rose from below and around me
        instead of falling.
And what I felt was no longer a dry tingling:

I seemed to be singing as he sang, I seemed to know
what the lark knows; all my sap
was mounting towards the sun that by now
had risen, the mist was rising, the grass
was drying, yet my roots felt music moisten them
deep under earth.

He came still closer, leaned on my trunk:
the bark thrilled like a leaf still-folded.
Music! There was no twig of me not
trembling with joy and fear.

Then as he sang
it was no longer sounds only that made the music:
he spoke, and as no tree listens I listened, and language
came into my roots
out of the earth,
into my bark
out of the air,
into the pores of my greenst shoots
gently as dew
and there was no word he sang but I knew its meaning.
He told of journeys,
of where sun and moon go while we stand in dark,
of an earth-journey he dreamed he would take some day
deeper than roots . . .
He told of the dreams of man, wars, passions, griefs,
and I, a tree, understood words — ah, it seemed
my thick bark would split like a sapling's that
grew too fast in the spring
when a late frost wounds it.

Fire he sang,
that trees fear, and I, a tree, rejoiced in its flames.
New buds broke forth from me though it was full summer.
As through his lyre (now I knew its name)
were both frost and fire, its chords flamed
up to the crown of me.
I was seed again.
I was fern in the swamp.
I was coal.

And at the heart of my wood
(so close I was to becoming man or a god)
there was a kind of silence, a kind of sickness,
something akin to what men call boredom,
something
(the poem descended a scale, a stream over stones)
that gives to a candle a coldness
in the midst of its burning, he said.

It was then,
             when in the blaze of his power that
                                  reached me and changed me
             I thought I should fall my length,
that the singer began
                   to leave me.   Slowly
                  moved from my noon shadow
                                            to open light,
words leaping and dancing over his shoulders
back to me
                  rivery sweep of lyre-tones becoming
        slowly again
                  ripple.

And I
        in terror
                  but not in doubt of
                                  what I must do

    in anguish, in haste,
                        wrenched from the earth root after root,
the soil heaving and cracking, the moss tearing asunder —
and behind me the others: my brothers
forgotten since dawn. In the forest
they too had heard,
and were pulling their roots in pain
out of a thousand years' layers of dead leaves,
        rolling the rocks away,
                        breaking themselves
                                            out of
                                            their depths.
You would have thought we would lose the sound of the lyre,
                        of the singing
so dreadful the storm-sounds were, where there was no storm,
                  no wind but the rush of our
        branches moving, our trunks breasting the air.
                  But the music!
                           The music reached us.

Clumsily,
        stumbling over our own roots,
                                  rustling our leaves
                                            in answer,
    we moved, we followed.

All day we followed, up hill and down.
                                  We learned to dance,
for he would stop, where the ground was flat,
                                  and words he said
taught us to leap and to wind in and out
around one another in figures the lyre's measure designed.

The singer
            laughed till he wept to see us, he was so glad.
                                            At sunset
we came to this place I stand in, this knoll
with its ancient grove that was bare grass then.
            In the last light of that day his song became
farewell.
        He stilled our longing.
        He sang our sun-dried roots back into earth,
watered them: all-night rain of music so quiet
                                    we could almost
            not hear it in the
                        moonless dark.
By dawn he was gone.
                We have stood here since,
in our new life.
        We have waited.
                            He does not return.
It is said he made his earth-journey, and lost
what he sought.
        It is said they felled him
and cut up his limbs for firewood.
                            And it is said
his head still sang and was swept out to sea singing.
Perhaps he will not return.
                But what we have lived
comes back to us.
        We see more.
                    We feel, as our rings increase,
something that lifts our branches, that stretches our furthest
                                            leaf-tips
further.
        The wind, the birds,
                    do not sound poorer but clearer,
recalling our agony, and the way we danced.
The music!

Denise Levertov (b.1923)

ANDY POLLAK 465

The Irish Times
28 January 1997

Dear Ralph, Caroline and Gareth,

Thank you very much for the invitation to contribute my two ha'pence worth to your third Lifelines *anthology to raise money for Third World children.*

Ever since I was a young boy growing up in a dull London suburb and spending every summer with my grandparents in County Antrim, Ireland has seemed a magical place to me. Even after nearly 25 years of living here, it retains some of that aura of wildness and wonder. Many of W B Yeats's early poems catch the strange magic of Ireland perfectly. One of my favourites is 'The Host of the Air', which I first heard recited by one of the Clancy Brothers from the stage of London's Albert Hall.

Good luck with your splendid project.
Andy Pollak

The Host of the Air

O'Driscoll drove with a song
The wild duck and the drake
From the tall and the tufted reeds
Of the drear Hart Lake.

And he saw how the reeds grew dark
At the coming of night-tide,
And dreamed of the long dim hair
Of Bridget his bride.

He heard while he sang and dreamed
A piper piping away,
And never was piping so sad,
And never was piping so gay.

And he saw young men and young girls
Who danced on a level place,
And Bridget his bride among them,
With a sad and a gay face.

The dancers crowded about him
And many a sweet thing said,
And a young man brought him red wine
And a young girl white bread.

But Bridget drew him by the sleeve
Away from the merry bands,
To old men playing at cards
With a twinkling of ancient hands.

The bread and the wine had a doom,
For these were the host of the air;
He sat and played in a dream
Of her long dim hair.

He played with the merry old men
And thought not of evil chance,
Until one bore Bridget his bride
Away from the merry dance.

He bore her away in his arms,
The handsomest young man there,
And his neck and his breast and his arms
Were drowned in her long dim hair.

O'Driscoll scattered the cards
And out of his dream awoke:
Old men and young men and young girls
Were gone like a drifting smoke;

But he heard high up in the air
A piper piping away,
And never was piping so sad,
And never was piping so gay.

W B Yeats (1865–1939)

PETER SIRR 466

14 January 1997

Dear Ralph, Caroline and Gareth,

My favourite poem depends on what day of the week, time of the day I'm asked, or on who I happen to be reading at the time. Like anybody interested in trying to write poems, I carry around a constantly shifting anthology of favourites. I've always liked these lines from 'Jubilate Agno' by Christopher Smart, both for their precision of observation (this is a man who knows about his cat) and also for their sheer exaggerated biblical craziness and wonderfully sustained energy. Like all good poems, there's something slightly mad about it: like his cat, the poem is a mixture 'of gravity and waggery' and, like the cat's fur, this is a poem which bristles with electricity.

Good luck with the project.

Kind regards,
Peter Sirr

from *Jubilate Agno*

For I will consider my Cat Jeoffry.
For he is the servant of the Living God duly and daily serving
    him.
For at the first glance of the glory of God in the East he
    worships in his way.

For is this done by wreathing his body seven times round with elegant quickness.
For then he leaps up to catch the musk, which is the blessing of God upon his prayer.
For he rolls upon prank to work it in.
For having done duty and received blessing he begins to consider himself.
For this he performs in ten degrees.
For first he looks upon his fore-paws to see if they are clean.
For secondly he kicks up behind to clear away there.
For thirdly he works it upon stretch with the fore-paws extended.
For fourthly he sharpens his paws by wood.
For fifthly he washes himself.
For Sixthly he rolls upon wash.
For Seventhly he fleas himself, that he may not be interrupted upon the beat.
For Eighthly he rubs himself against a post.
For ninthly he rubs himself against a post.
For tenthly he goes in quest of food.
For having consider'd God and himself he will consider his neighbour.
For if he meets another cat he will kiss her in kindness.
For when he takes his prey he plays with it to give it a chance.
For one mouse in seven escapes by his dallying.
For when his day's work is done his business more properly begins.
For he keeps the Lord's watch in the night against the adversary.
For he counteracts the powers of darkness by his electrical skin & glaring eyes.
For he counteracts the Devil, who is death, by brisking about the life.
For in his morning orisons he loves the sun and the sun loves him.
For he is of the tribe of Tiger.
For the Cherub Cat is a term of the Angel Tiger.
For he has the subtlety and hissing of a serpent, which in goodness he suppresses.
For he will not do destruction if he is well-fed, neither will he spit without provocation.
For he purrs in thankfulness, when God tells him he's a good Cat.
For he is an instrument for the children to learn benevolence upon.
For every house is incompleat without him & a blessing is lacking in the spirit.
For the Lord commanded Moses concerning the cats at the departure of the Children of Israel from Egypt.
For every family had one cat at least in the bag.

For the English Cats are the best in Europe.
For he is the cleanest in the use of his fore-paws of any
  quadrupede.
For the dexterity of his defence is an instance of the love of
  God to him exceedingly.
For he is the quickest to his mark of any creature.
For he is tenacious of his point.
For he is a mixture of gravity and waggery.
For he knows that God is his Saviour.
For there is nothing sweeter than his peace when at rest.
For there is nothing brisker than his life when in motion.
For he is of the Lord's poor and so indeed is he called by
  benevolence perpetually — Poor Jeoffry! poor Jeoffry! the
  rat has bit thy throat.
For I bless the name of the Lord Jesus that Jeoffry is better.
For the divine spirit comes about his body to sustain it in
  compleat cat.
For his tongue is exceeding pure so that it has in purity what it
  wants in musick.
For he is docile and can learn certain things.
For he can set up with gravity which is patience upon
  approbation.
For he can fetch and carry, which is patience in employment.
For he can jump over a stick which is patience upon proof
  positive.
For he can spraggle upon waggle at the word of command.
For he can jump from an eminence into his master's bosom.
For he can catch the cork and toss it again.
For he is hated by the hypocrite and miser.
For the former is afraid of detection.
For the latter refuses the charge.
For he camels his back to bear the first notion of business.
For he is good to think on, if a man would express himself
  neatly.
For he made a great figure in Egypt for his signal services.
For he killed the Icneumon-rat very pernicious by land.
For his ears are so acute that they sting again.
For from this proceeds the passing quickness of his attention.
For by stroking of him I have found out electricity.
For I have perceived God's light about him both wax and fire.
For the Electrical fire is the spiritual substance, which God sends
  from heaven to sustain the bodies both of man and beast.
For God has blessed him in the variety of his movements.
For, tho he cannot fly, he is an excellent clamberer.
For his motions upon the face of the earth are more than any
  other quadrupede.
For he can tread to all the measures upon the musick.
For he can swim for life.
For he can creep.

Christopher Smart (1722–1771)

TREVOR SARGENT

15 Eanáir 1997

Ralph, Caroline agus Gareth, a Chairde,

Being a Green Party/Comhaontas Glas politician is a frustrating experience at the best of times, so when an opportunity to help the victims of the current economic order presents itself, I am delighted to do all I can. Thank you for asking me for my favourite poem.

The poem 'Ní Ceadmhach Neamhshuim' by the late Seán Ó Ríordáin was published in a 1971 collection called Línte Liombó. *The poem is very special to me as I recall reading it to an international conference on Celtic spirituality and ecological wisdom in Killarney some years ago. Having paraphrased in English, the audience, mainly American, listened intently to the thoughts in Irish of a man overwhelmed by the responsibilities he felt to every living life form. He recognised the connectedness of life and celebrated the diversity of it all. After all is said and done, he like us must answer to God for the efforts we have made to understand the world and provide help where it is needed to ease the disease.*

To paraphrase, the title says 'Disinterest is not Permissable' and the poem says:

> There is not a fly, a tree, a bee which God has created,
> There is not a man whose welfare is not our duty
> Whatever things happen whether faraway in South Africa or
> close to home behind the walls of a mental institution
> they are all part of us because there is no place in this world
> in which we were not born.

I enclose the original poem, the sounds of which, when recited slowly, bring tears to my eyes.

Le gach dea-ghuí,
Trevor Sargent

Ní Ceadmhach Neamhshuim

Níl cuil, níl leamhan, níl beach
Dar chruthaigh Dia, níl fear,
Nach dualgas dúinn a leas,
Níl bean; ní ceadmhach neamhshuim
A dhéanamh dá n-imní;
Níl gealt i ngleann na ngealt,
Nár chuí dhúinn suí lena ais,
Á thionlacan an fhaid
A iompraíonn thar ár gceann
Ár dtinneas-ne 'na mheabhair.

Níl áit, níl sruth, níl sceach,
Dá iargúlta iad, níl leac,
Bídís thuaidh, thoir, thiar nó theas,
Nár cheart dúinn machnamh ar a suíomh
Le gean is le báidhíocht;
Dá fhaid uainn Afraic Theas,
Dá airde í gealach,
Is cuid dínn iad ó cheart:
Níl áit ar fuaid na cruinne
Nach ann a saolaíodh sinne.

Seán Ó Ríordáin (1916–1977)

ANDREA CORR   468

Dear Ralph, Caroline and Gareth,

Thanks for your letter — favourite poem, 'The Donkey' by G K Chesterton. Simply powerful and inspiring.

Good luck and best wishes,
Andrea

The Donkey

When fishes flew and forests walked,
    And figs grew upon thorn,
Some moment when the moon was blood
    Then surely I was born;

With monstrous head and sickening cry
    And ears like errant wings,
The devil's walking parody
    On all four-footed things.

The tattered outlaw of the earth,
    Of ancient crooked will;
Starve, scourge, deride me: I am dumb,
    I keep my secret still.

Fools! for I also had my hour;
    One far fierce hour and sweet:
There was a shout about my ears,
    And palms before my feet.

G K Chesterton (1874–1936)

PENELOPE FITZGERALD 469

13 February 1997

Dear Ralph, Caroline and Gareth,

I'm afraid I've taken a long time answering your letter, but you must forgive me, because it unfortunately took a long time to arrive. Your anthology Lifelines *was a wonderful idea, and I very much regret that it must be too late now for me to contribute, but if by any chance it's not, I should like to say that my favourite poem (or one of them, because I care a lot about poetry) is Yeats's* 'The Stare's Nest by My Window'*, and I hardly need to explain why it means so much to me, as there must be many millions all over the world who make the same prayer for honey-bees to come to the empty house. In fact, I daresay it's been suggested to you often already. But meantime, I should like to send you all my best wishes for* Lifelines 3.

Penelope Fitzgerald

The Stare's Nest by My Window

The bees build in the crevices
Of loosening masonry, and there
The mother birds bring grubs and flies.
My wall is loosening; honey-bees,
Come build in the empty house of the stare.

We are closed in, and the key is turned
On our uncertainty; somewhere
A man is killed, or a house burned,
Yet no clear fact to be discerned:
Come build in the empty house of the stare.

A barricade of stone or of wood;
Some fourteen days of civil war;
Last night they trundled down the road
That dead young soldier in his blood:
Come build in the empty house of the stare.

We had fed the heart on fantasies,
The heart's grown brutal from the fare;
More substance in our enmities
Than in our love; O honey-bees,
Come build in the empty house of the stare.

W B Yeats (1865–1939)

AIDAN MATHEWS 470

15 February 1997

Dear Ralph, Caroline and Gareth,

Thanks very much for your January letter. I'm sorry to be late in answering it.

I would like to nominate the 51st psalm as my choice for your anthology, and I leave it to you to select whichever translation you prefer. Like many catholic Christians, I would have grown up with the revised Standard version (for devotional purposes) and with the King James psalter (for literary pleasure), and have gone on more recently to the English edition of the Jerusalem Bible and to the New English Bible, but I have no way of knowing which, if any, is the senior or the sounder likeness to the original work in the Writings. The most influential treatment of this particular psalm is possibly the Vulgate setting by Allegri which Mozart is supposed to have notated on his shirt-cuff during a service in the Sistine Chapel.

I love this poem for the same reasons everybody else does, and that in itself is one of the most refreshing things about biblical and liturgical texts. They allow you to skip the quest for the prestige of an original insight, which is the aim of so much educated reading. The 51st psalm embodies our strange and damaged lives in the heartbreaking loveliness of a language which draws radical theological values from humdrum human states. It cannot be read and overcome, it can only be re-read and undergone; and it therefore frees us from the tedium of having rapid and ready opinions about it such as we're supposed to have in the present age of soundbytes, stop-press amnesia and media blink-think. Instead, it accompanies us in silence through all our stars and disasters as long as we choose to live.

It can do that because its author is neither here nor there, all autograph and no biography. The life of his work continues without him in the work of our lives, and the reader benefits from this impersonality by achieving from time to time the grace of his own anonymity before it. For a moment, he or she is a self and not an ego. In addition, the hodge-podge production of any part of scripture — which is after all creativity by committee, translations from translations, English from Latin from Greek and Hebrew — reminds us that the relationship between a reader and a text is more higgledy-piggledy than any straightline enlightenment model of devour-and-digest, that great work can be done in solidarity and not in solitude, and that the intimacy of print calls into being a community of very different dead and dying readers across many cultures and centuries for whom the verses of the 51st psalm signify not just the familiarity of a mood or the foreignness of a mode, not just impressionism or expressivity, but something pure and imperfect, a presence past all our projections.

Best wishes,

Aidan Mathews

Psalm 51

To the chief Musician, A Psalm of David, when Nathan the prophet came unto him, after he had gone to Bath-sheba.

1 Have mercy upon me, O God, according to thy loving kindness: according unto the multitude of thy tender mercies blot out my transgressions.

2 Wash me thoroughly from mine iniquity, and cleanse me from my sin.

3 For I acknowledge my transgressions: and my sin *is* ever before me.

4 Against thee, thee only, have I sinned, and done *this* evil in thy sight: that thou mightest be justified when thou speakest, and be clear when thou judgest.

5 Behold, I was shapen in iniquity; and in sin did my mother conceive me.

6 Behold, thou desirest truth in the inward parts: and in the hidden part thou shalt make me to know wisdom.

7 Purge me with hyssop, and I shall be clean: wash me, and I shall be whiter than snow.

8 Make me to hear joy and gladness; *that* the bones *which* thou hast broken may rejoice.

9 Hide thy face from my sins, and blot out all mine iniquities.

10 Create in me a clean heart, O God; and renew a right spirit within me.

11 Cast me not away from thy presence; and take not thy holy spirit from me.

12 Restore unto me the joy of thy salvation; and uphold me *with thy* free spirit.

13 *Then* will I teach transgressors thy ways; and sinners shall be converted unto thee.

14 Deliver me from bloodguiltiness, O God, thou God of my salvation: *and* my tongue shall sing aloud of thy righteousness.

15 O Lord, open thou my lips; and my mouth shall shew forth thy praise.

16 For thou desirest not sacrifice; else would I give *it*: thou delightest not in burnt offering.

17 The sacrifices of God *are* a broken spirit: a broken and contrite heart, O God, thou wilt not despise.

18 Do good in thy good pleasure unto Zion: build thou the walls of Jerusalem.

19 Then shalt thou be pleased with the sacrifices of righteousness, with burnt offering and whole burnt offering: then shall they offer bullocks upon thine altar.

Authorised King James version

MARIE FOLEY 471

Dear Ralph, Caroline and Gareth,

Thank you for your letter which arrived while I was in Mali, West Africa. I would love to be part of this wonderful ongoing project. Having just returned from one of the five poorest countries in the world, I am acutely aware of how rich we are and of how important sharing is.

I have a long long list of favourite poems, but Rainer Maria Rilke has been a constant source of inspiration and revelation for me since I crossed paths with his work when I was a fledgling art student. His visionary work opens the closed doors of my mind, generating growth in barren parts. Close to the Great Pulse his words extend my vision and offer me a vehicle into the unknown. Each fresh reading expands this experience. This is the ultimate test of a true artist. Rilke is one of the Greats of this Century. I choose a small poem for inclusion but would encourage Lifelines 3 *readers to seek out more, weightier, illuminating work if you wish to know this wonderful poet.*

With best wishes for your good work,
Marie Foley

Durch den sich Vögel werfen

Durch den sich Vögel werfen, ist nicht der
vertraute Raum, der die Gestalt dir steigert.
(Im Freien, dorten, bist du dir verweigert
und schwindest weiter ohne Wiederkehr.)

Raum greift aus uns und übersetzt die Dinge:
daß dir das Dasein eines Baums gelinge,
wirf Innenraum um ihn, aus jenem Raum,
der in dir west. Umgieb ihn mit Verhaltung.
Er grenzt sich nicht. Erst in der Eingestaltung
in dein Verzichten wird er wirklich Baum.

What birds plunge through

What birds plunge through is not the intimate space
in which you see all forms intensified.
(Out in the Open, you would be denied
your self, would disappear into that vastness.)

Space reaches *from* us and construes the world:
to know a tree, in its true element,
throw inner space around it, from that pure
abundance in you. Surround it with restraint.
It has no limits. Not till it is held
in your renouncing is it truly there.

Rainer Maria Rilke (1875–1926)

ROZ COWMAN 472

25 February 1997

Dear Ralph, Caroline and Gareth,

When I was twelve, we used to rehearse 'The White Birds' by W B Yeats for a verse-speaking class at school. I was enthralled by the rhythm of the spoken words, which had seemed (and still do!) quite flat on the page. This was the first poem to convey to me that poetry has an evocative power which transcends its meaning, and makes it live. Nearly fifty years later, that discovery is still a source of joy.

I wish you every success with the new Lifelines *and thank you so much for including my choice.*

With kind regards,
Roz Cowman

The White Birds

I would that we were, my beloved, white birds on the foam of
　the sea!
We tire of the flame of the meteor, before it can fade and flee;
And the flame of the blue star of twilight, hung low on the rim
　of the sky,
Has awaked in our hearts, my beloved, a sadness that may not
　die.

A weariness comes from those dreamers, dew-dabbled, the lily
　and rose;
Ah, dream not of them, my beloved, the flame of the meteor
　that goes,
Or the flame of the blue star that lingers hung low in the fall of
　the dew:
For I would we were changed to white birds on the wandering
　foam: I and you!

I am haunted by numberless islands, and many a Danaan
　shore,
Where Time would surely forget us, and Sorrow come near us
　no more;
Soon far from the rose and the lily and fret of the flames would
　we be,
Were we only white birds, my beloved, buoyed out on the
　foam of the sea!

W B Yeats (1865–1939)

BRIAN FALLON   473

Arts Section
The Irish Times
15 January 1997

Dear Ralph Croly and others,

Your letter arrived a little late here, so I am only replying now. Is it licit to name a Latin poem — an ode by Horace? If so, you might like to use the first poem enclosed; if not, then use the second, which is much shorter. I have appended a few lines of explication to both.

Yours sincerely,
Brian Fallon
Chief Critic
Irish Times

A E Housman, a truly great Latinist as well as an indispensable English poet, thought this ode the most beautiful poem surviving from the antique world. (Incidentally, his own English version is the only adequate one that I know of — a pity that Louis MacNeice, a good Horation, never tried his hand at translating it also.) Horace was a magnificent verse technician, capable of balancing a relaxed, genial, almost conversational tone with the lapidary compression which is peculiar to Latin. In the third stanza, the yearly round of the seasons is compressed into four haunting lines — a remarkable feat.

Ode VII, Book 4

Diffugere nives, redeunt iam gramina campis
    arboribusque comae;
mutat terra vices et decrescentia ripas
    flumina praetereunt;

Gratia cum Nymphis geminisque sororibus audet
    ducere nuda choros.
immortalia ne speres, monet annus et almum
    quae rapit hora diem.

frigora mitescunt zephyris, ver proterit aestas
    interitura, simul
pomifer autumnus fruges effuderit, et mox
    bruma recurrit iners.

damna tamen celeres reparant caelestia lunae;
    nos ubi decidimus
quo pius Aeneas, quo Tullus dives et Anchus,
    pulvis et umbra sumus.

quis scit an adiciant hodiernae crastina summae
    tempora di superi?
cuncta manus avidos fugient heredis, amico
    quae dederis animo.

cum semel occideris et de te splendida Minos
    fecerit arbitria,
non, Torquate, genus, non te facundia, non te
    restituet pietas;

infernis neque enim tenebris Diana pudicum
    liberat Hippolytum,
nec Lethaea valet Theseus abrumpere caro
    vincula Pirithoo.

Horace (65BC–8BC)

The snows are fled away, leaves on the shaws
    And grasses in the mead renew their birth,
The river to the river-bed withdraws,
    And altered is the fashion of the earth.

The Nymphs and Graces three put off their fear
    And unapparelled in the woodland play.
The swift hour and the brief prime of the year
    Say to the soul, *Thou wast not born for aye.*

Thaw follows frost; hard on the heels of Spring
    Treads Summer sure to die, for hard on hers
Comes Autumn, with his apples scattering;
    Then back to wintertide, when nothing stirs.

But oh, whate'er the sky-led seasons mar,
    Moon upon moon rebuilds it with her beams:
Come *we* where Tullus and where Ancus are,
    And good Aeneas, we are dust and dreams.

Torquatus, if the gods in heaven shall add
    The morrow to the day, what tongue has told?
Feast then thy heart, for what thy heart has had
    The fingers of no heir will ever hold.

When thou decendest once the shades among,
    The stern assize and equal judgment o'er,
Not thy long lineage nor thy golden tongue,
    No, nor thy righteousness, shall friend thee more.

Night holds Hippolytus the pure of stain,
    Diana steads him nothing, he must stay;
And Theseus leaves Pirithöus in the chain
    The love of comrades cannot take away.

Translated by A E Housman (1859–1936)

Landor seems to me the most underrated poet in the English canon, or at any rate the least popular and the least read. No doubt a classical education is an aid to enjoying him either in prose or verse, but his poetry, while lapidary and cameo-like, is usually tuneful, direct and deeply felt. It is also witty — a charge you could never bring against other Romantics such as Wordsworth or Shelley. Landor is unique in combining Romantic intensity with the poise and aristocratic tone of the 18th century. Obviously, this poem has a special appeal to me as an art critic!

His Painters

First bring me Raphael, who alone hath seen
In all her purity Heaven's virgin Queen,
Alone hath felt true beauty; bring me then
Titian, ennobler of the noblest men,
And next the sweet Correggio, nor chastise
His little Cupids for those wicked eyes.
I want not Rubens's pink puffy bloom
Nor Rembrandt's glimmer in a dusty room.
With those, and Poussin's nymph-frequented woods,
His templed heights and long-drawn solitudes,
I am content, yet fain would look abroad
On one warm sunset by Ausonian Claude.

Walter Savage Landor (1775–1864)

JAMES RYAN 474

10 February 1997

Dear Ralph Croly, Caroline Dowling and Gareth McCluskey,

Thank you for your letter outlining the background to the Lifelines *anthology. I would have thought that at this stage it needs little introduction, being something of a national institution and a very worthy one at that. I'm honoured to be included among those asked to name their favourite poem. Making that choice was enjoyable but not at all easy. The short list included Ted Hughes' 'The Horses', Emily Dickinson's 'My Life it stood a Loaded Gun', the opening section of Eliot's 'East Coker', Eavan Boland's 'A Ballad of Home' and finally Wallace Stevens' 'Le Monocle de Mon Oncle'. I have selected Ted Hughes' 'The Horses' from his collection,* The Hawk in the Rain. *It was a poem I read so often in the seventies that I came to know it off by heart. So I no longer actually read it but periodically stumble into it. I particularly enjoy the enormous leap it makes in the final stanza, boldly catapulting itself right out of the static domain of description. It is as if the whole process by which experience becomes memory is captured in that leap.*

Again thank you for the opportunity to contribute to Lifelines. *I wish you every success with the project.*

Sincerely,
James Ryan

The Horses

I climbed through woods in the hour-before-dawn dark.
Evil air, a frost-making stillness,

Not a leaf, not a bird, —
A world cast in frost. I came out above the wood

Where my breath left tortuous statues in the iron light.
But the valleys were draining the darkness

Till the moorline — blackening dregs of the brightening grey —
Halved the sky ahead. And I saw the horses:

Huge in the dense grey — ten together —
Megalith-still. They breathed, making no move,

With draped manes and tilted hind-hooves,
Making no sound.

I passed: not one snorted or jerked its head.
Grey silent fragments

Of a grey silent world.

I listened in emptiness on the moor-ridge.
The curlew's tear turned its edge on the silence.

Slowly detail leafed from the darkness. Then the sun
Orange, red, red erupted.

Silently, and splitting to its core tore and flung cloud,
Shook the gulf open, showed blue,

And the big planets hanging —
I turned

Stumbling in the fever of a dream, down towards
The dark woods, from the kindling tops,

And came to the horses.
                        There, still they stood,
But now steaming and glistening under the flow of light,

Their draped stone manes, their tilted hind-hooves
Stirring under a thaw while all around them

The frost showed its fires. But still they made no sound.
Not one snorted or stamped,

Their hung heads patient as the horizons
High over valleys, in the red levelling rays —

In din of the crowded streets, going among the years, the faces,
May I still meet my memory in so lonely a place

Between the streams and the red clouds, hearing curlews,
Hearing the horizons endure.

Ted Hughes (b.1930)

GARY LINEKER 475

4 February 1997

To you all,

Thank you for your letter. An all-time favourite poem is difficult to identify because so much depends on my mood at any given time. But I think one of my favourites has to be 'Sea Fever' by John Masefield. I need only to hear the first two or three lines to be transported to the coast, to hear the gulls crying and to see those 'tall ships' in my mind's eye. For me it is a very evocative poem and perhaps that is why it endures.

I wish you every success with the latest edition of Lifelines.

Yours sincerely,
Gary Lineker

Sea Fever

I must go down to the seas again, to the lonely sea and the sky,
And all I ask is a tall ship and a star to steer her by,
And the wheel's kick and the wind's song and the white sails
    shaking,
And a grey mist on the sea's face and a grey dawn breaking.

I must go down to the seas again, for the call of the running
    tide
Is a wild call and a clear call that may not be denied;
And all I ask is a windy day with the white clouds flying,
And the flung spray and the blown spume, and the sea-gulls
    crying.

I must go down to the seas again, to the vagrant gipsy life,
To the gull's way and the whale's way where the wind's like a
    whetted knife;
And all I ask is a merry yarn from a laughing fellow-rover,
And quiet sleep and a sweet dream when the long trick's over.

John Masefield (1878–1967)

FRANK RONAN

Dear Editors,

Firstly, continued good luck with Lifelines *and, secondly, thank you for asking me to contribute. I have thought about it quite a bit and come to the conclusion that whatever poem I nominate would have to be qualified as a favourite poem, since different poems become relatively more or less important within a personal canon, depending on our circumstances (and it is all too easy, in times of happiness, to forget the debt we owe to the poetry of despair). In the end, I felt I had to choose one of Shakespeare's sonnets. Within the cycle of that work, almost everything is covered and, from beginning to end, the narrative reads like a novel (though you do have to forgive him for being a bit of a luvvy at times) which, for someone who believes the novel to be a more transcendent form of literature than the poem, has to be a bonus. Anyway, what can I say about this poem? It has seen me through some bad times (for some reason I find it easy to recall and have no need to look it up when I need it — no-one ever says a poem has to be memorable to be good, but maybe that's the case) and helped me count the blessings of better times. The favourite poem is, maybe, the one most likely to be there when you need it.*

I can't remember the number of it, and my copies of Shakespeare are in France and Dublin at the moment, so you'll have to look that up, and maybe check I've got the wording right. Anyway, it's the one that goes:

XXIX

When, in disgrace with Fortune and men's eyes,
I all alone beweep my outcast state,
And trouble deaf heaven with my bootless cries,
And look upon myself, and curse my fate,
Wishing me like to one more rich in hope,
Featured like him, like him with friends possessed,
Desiring this man's art, and that man's scope,
With what I most enjoy contented least;
Yet in these thoughts myself almost despising,
Haply I think on thee, — and then my state
Like to the lark at break of day arising
From sullen earth, sings hymns at Heaven's gate;
    For thy sweet love remember'd such wealth brings,
    That then I scorn to change my state with kings.

William Shakespeare (1564–1616)

Having boasted that I could remember it, the third quatrain now looks a bit dodgy to me, also the punctuation is entirely guesswork and I'm a lousy speller. Do check it carefully. Again, the best of luck to you,

Yours sincerely,
Frank Ronan

FRANK KERMODE

Houston
Texas
22 January 1997

Dear Mr Croly and friends,

Thank you for your letter which has just been sent on to me here.

I seem to have different favourites at different times, and since I have recently been re-reading Yeats with all the old wonder and admiration the poem which resounds most in my mind is 'The Cold Heaven'. *It is memorable not only for its mood — the icy sky, the epiphany of remorse ('riddled with light') — but for its surging rhythms, its controlled metrical freedom. A great poet who has come into his strength, and will do even more extraordinary feats hereafter.*

I hope this will serve your admirable purpose.

Yours sincerely,
Frank Kermode

The Cold Heaven

Suddenly I saw the cold and rook-delighting heaven
That seemed as though ice burned and was but the more ice,
And thereupon imagination and heart were driven
So wild that every casual thought of that and this
Vanished, and left but memories, that should be out of season
With the hot blood of youth, of love crossed long ago;
And I took all the blame out of all sense and reason,
Until I cried and trembled and rocked to and fro,
Riddled with light. Ah! when the ghost begins to quicken,
Confusion of the death-bed over, is it sent
Out naked on the roads, as the books say, and stricken
By the injustice of the skies for punishment?

W B Yeats (1865–1939)

['The Cold Heaven' was also Tom Paulin's choice in *Lifelines 2*.]

BRENDA MADDOX   478

25 January 1997

Dear Editors,

Thank you for your letter. My favourite poem is W B Yeats's 'Circus Animals' Desertion'. I admire the poem's boldness in expressing the realisation that a long life has been spent in self-deception and that the only reality is the human heart.

With best wishes,
Brenda Maddox

The Circus Animals' Desertion

I

I sought a theme and sought for it in vain,
I sought it daily for six weeks or so.
Maybe at last, being but a broken man,
I must be satisfied with my heart, although
Winter and summer till old age began
My circus animals were all on show,
Those stilted boys, that burnished chariot,
Lion and woman and the Lord knows what.

II
What can I but enumerate old themes?
First that sea-rider Oisín led by the nose
Through three enchanted islands, allegorical dreams,
Vain gaiety, vain battle, vain repose,
Themes of the embittered heart, or so it seems,
That might adorn old songs or courtly shows;
But what cared I that set him on to ride,
I, starved for the bosom of his faery bride?

And then a counter-truth filled out its play,
The Countess Cathleen was the name I gave it;
She, pity-crazed, had given her soul away,
But masterful Heaven had intervened to save it.
I thought my dear must her own soul destroy,
So did fanaticism and hate enslave it,
And this brought forth a dream and soon enough
This dream itself had all my thought and love.

And when the Fool and Blind Man stole the bread
Cuchulain fought the ungovernable sea;
Heart-mysteries there, and yet when all is said
It was the dream itself enchanted me:
Character isolated by a deed
To engross the present and dominate memory.
Players and painted stage took all my love,
And not those things that they were emblems of.

III
Those masterful images because complete
Grew in pure mind, but out of what began?
A mound of refuse or the sweepings of a street,
Old kettles, old bottles, and a broken can,
Old iron, old bones, old rags, that raving slut
Who keeps the till. Now that my ladder's gone,
I must lie down where all the ladders start,
In the foul rag-and-bone shop of the heart.

W B Yeats (1865–1939)

RODDY DOYLE

28 February 1997

Dear Mr Croly, Ms Dowling and Mr McCluskey

Here is my poem. I hope it's of use to you. Good luck with the project.

Yours,
Roddy Doyle

Base Details

If I were fierce, and bald, and short of breath,
    I'd live with scarlet Majors at the Base,
And speed glum heroes up the line to death.
    You'd see me with my puffy petulant face,
Guzzling and gulping in the best hotel,
    Reading the Roll of Honour. 'Poor young chap,'
I'd say — 'I used to know his father well;
    Yes, we've lost heavily in this last scrap.'
And when the war is done and youth stone dead,
I'd toddle safely home and die — in bed.

Rouen, 4 March 1917
Siegfried Sassoon (1886–1967)

I first read 'Base Details' in 1974. It was one of the Inter Cert poems, along with 'The Dong with the Luminous Nose' and twenty-odd other poems about Spring and waterfalls and the love of God. I'll never forget the first reading. The teacher read it like he read everything, like he was looking for a dentist's name in the phone book. But the poem hit me between the eyes, almost smashed my glasses. Its anger and sarcasm were mine. The language was fresh and ordinary; there was nothing old-fashioned or dainty about it. Each word seemed to invite dozens of images and meanings. It was honest and brutal, clever and funny. And it was a poem about modern war. There is nothing romantic or heroic about it — except for the heroism of the poet.

ANNE ROBINSON

24 February 1997

Dear Ralph Croly, Caroline Dowling and Gareth McCluskey,

Thank you very much for your letter. The very best of luck with your next anthology. My favourite poem is 'Message to the Editor', *a copy of which is enclosed. It is wonderfully funny. Very cheering and very Irish.*

Yours sincerely,
Anne Robinson
(An Irish Liverpudlian!)

Message to the Editor

Sir —

> The Lord pardon the people of this town
> Because I can't.
> When I dropped dead in the street
> Three weeks ago
> I thought they'd bury me in style.
> A state funeral was the least of it
> With Heads of Government and the Nobility
> In attendance.
> I even looked forward to the funeral oration
> In Irish
> With a few words on my past achievements:
> Our greatest poet, a seat in heaven to the man
> And how I deserved better.

But did I get it?
My corpse lay in Baggot Street
For a fortnight
Before anyone noticed it.
And when I was finally removed
To the mortuary
I was abused by a medical student
Who couldn't open a bag of chips
Let alone the body of your greatest poet.
Then, to add to the indignity
I was pushed into an ice-box
And some clod stuck a label on my foot
Saying: unknown bard — probably foreign.

If it wasn't
For a drunken Corkman
Who thought I was his dead brother
I'd still be lying there unclaimed.
At least
The man had the decency to bury me.
But where am I?
Boxed in some common graveyard
Surrounded by peasants
And people of no background.
When I think of the poems I wrote
And the great prophecies I made
I could choke.

I can't write now
Because the coffin is too narrow
And there's no light.
I'm trying to send this
Through a medium
But you know what they're like —
Table-tapping bastards
Reeking of ectoplasm.
If you manage to receive this
I'd be glad if you'd print it.
There's no point in asking you
To send me a copy —
I don't even know my address.

Patrick Galvin (b.1927)

EUGENE LAMBERT 481

Lambert Puppet Theatre and Museum
Monkstown
26 February 1997

Dear Ralph, Caroline and Gareth,

Many thanks for your letter, inviting me to select a poem for inclusion in your latest edition of Lifelines.

I am honoured to have been invited, and delighted to give you my selection, and the reasons, as follows:

'The Stolen Child' by W B Yeats is the poem I have selected.

When I was a small child, growing up in Sligo, I was surrounded by books and literature of all sorts. My father Jack was the county librarian, and my mother Eileen was one of the founders of the Yeats Summer School, and of Feis Sligigh. So poetry and great writing were a regular part of our lives, and we grew up in an atmosphere where the love of these things was a most natural part of our lives.

The poem 'The Stolen Child', with its haunting invitation to a child to leave behind the everyday cares and go with them to the fairy land, was something I recognised from an early age, and I always felt that the invitation was for me, to enter into a fantasy world, where in some way I would remain a child forever.

And, although I grew up, married, had a family, did all the things that are expected of one, yet I chose the life of puppetry, a life as surely filled with fantasy as any big child could wish for.

Hope this is what you are looking for.

Kindest regards,
Eugene Lambert

The Stolen Child

Where dips the rocky highland
Of Sleuth Wood in the lake,
There lies a leafy island
Where flapping herons wake
The drowsy water-rats;
There we've hid our faery vats,
Full of berries
And of reddest stolen cherries.
Come away, O human child!
To the waters and the wild
With a faery, hand in hand,
For the world's more full of weeping than you can understand.

Where the wave of moonlight glosses
The dim grey sands with light,
Far off by furthest Rosses
We foot it all the night,
Weaving olden dances,
Mingling hands and mingling glances
Till the moon has taken flight;
To and fro we leap
And chase the frothy bubbles,
While the world is full of troubles
And is anxious in its sleep.
Come away, O human child!
To the waters and the wild
With a faery, hand in hand,
For the world's more full of weeping than you can understand.

Where the wandering water gushes
From the hills above Glen-Car,
In pools among the rushes
That scarce could bathe a star,
We seek for slumbering trout
And whispering in their ears
Give them unquiet dreams;
Leaning softly out
From ferns that drop their tears
Over the young streams.
Come away, O human child!
To the waters and the wild
With a faery, hand in hand,
For the world's more full of weeping than you can understand.

Away with us he's going,
The solemn-eyed:
He'll hear no more the lowing
Of the calves on the warm hillside
Or the kettle on the hob
Sing peace into his breast,
Or see the brown mice bob
Round and round the oatmeal-chest.
For he comes, the human child,
To the waters and the wild
With a faery, hand in hand,
From a world more full of weeping than he can understand.

W B Yeats (1865–1939)

['The Stolen Child' was chosen by Gerrit van Gelderen and Mary Mooney in *Lifelines* and by John Shinnors in *Lifelines 2*.]

HARRY SECOMBE 482

3 March 1997

Dear Ralph Croly and Friends,

Thank you for your letter to Sir Harry Secombe requesting a favourite poem.

Sir Harry receives such a huge amount of mail that I'm afraid he isn't always able to respond personally to every letter, although he does take great pleasure in reading them all. I'm enclosing a poem which Sir Harry wrote especially for a recent edition of Songs of Praise *about celebration of old age. We hope that you will like it.*

Yours sincerely,
Yvonne Vaughan-Jones
Correspondence Secretary

On Growing Old

I want the mornings to last longer
    and the twilight to linger.

I want to clutch the present to my bosom
    and never let it go.

I resent the tyranny of the lock in the hall
    nagging me to get on with the day.

I am a time traveller
    but a traveller who would rather walk
    than fly.

And yet:
    there is a lot to be said for growing old.

The major battles in life are over
    though minor skirmishes may still occur.

There is an armistice of the heart,
    a truce with passion.

Compromise becomes preferable to conflict
    and old animosities blur with time.

There is still one last hurdle to cross
    and the joy of your life measures your
    reluctance to approach it.

But if you have lived your life with love
    there will be nothing to fear
    because a warm welcome will await you
    on the other side.

Harry Secombe (b.1921)

FEARGAL QUINN — 483

Superquinn
10 March 1997

'Digging' by Seamus Heaney.

Each of us has a memory of our parents. My memory of my father — like that of Seamus Heaney — is of him at work.

Seamus's memory of his father was of him digging. The tool was a spade.

My memory of my father was of him making his guests welcome. His tool was a smile.

'My God, the old man could handle a spade' — that was Mr Heaney Senior.

My father achieved success in being a good host. A spade or a smile — either will do!

Feargal Quinn

Digging

Between my finger and my thumb
The squat pen rests; snug as a gun.

Under my window, a clean rasping sound
When the spade sinks into gravelly ground:
My father, digging. I look down

Till his straining rump among the flowerbeds
Bends low, comes up twenty years away
Stooping in rhythm through potato drills
Where he was digging.

The coarse boot nestled on the lug, the shaft
Against the inside knee was levered firmly.
He rooted out tall tops, buried the bright edge deep
To scatter new potatoes that we picked,
Loving their cool hardness in our hands.

By God, the old man could handle a spade.
Just like his old man.

My grandfather cut more turf in a day
Than any other man on Toner's bog.
Once I carried him milk in a bottle
Corked sloppily with paper. He straightened up
To drink it, then fell to right away
Nicking and slicing neatly, heaving sods
Over his shoulder, going down and down
For the good turf. Digging.

The cold smell of potato mould, the squelch and slap
Of soggy peat, the curt cuts of an edge
Through living roots awaken in my head.
But I've no spade to follow men like them.

Between my finger and my thumb
The squat pen rests.
I'll dig with it.

Seamus Heaney (b.1939)

['Digging' was also chosen by Marita Conlon-McKenna in Lifelines 2.]

DECLAN McGONAGLE

The Irish Museum of Modern Art
14 February 1997

Dear Ralph Croly, Caroline Dowling and Gareth McCluskey,

Sorry for the delay but I am happy to participate in Lifelines 3. *I hope this is still in time. Congratulations on the success of part 1 and 2 and hope for the same for part 3.*

Thanks,
Declan McGonagle
Director

Stopping by Woods on a Snowy Evening

Whose woods these are I think I know.
His house is in the village, though;
He will not see me stopping here
To watch his woods fill up with snow.

My little horse must think it queer
To stop without a farmhouse near
Between the woods and frozen lake
The darkest evening of the year.

He gives his harness bells a shake
To ask if there is some mistake.
The only other sound's the sweep
Of easy wind and downy flake.

The woods are lovely, dark, and deep,
But I have promises to keep,
And miles to go before I sleep,
And miles to go before I sleep.

Robert Frost (1874–1963)

This is practically a love poem where the poet acknowledges the importance of the relationship between mankind and nature.
That he is able to convey very profound meaning in such direct, understandable language is a measure of the strength of his vision. As I know from my schooldays the poem communicates very clearly and is easily remembered. The rhythm and cadence of the poet's 'voice' is insistent but also lulling as well. The poem is really a description of a moment of stillness when meaning in life is perceptible in a flash of understanding before we move on again towards an inevitable end.

['Stopping by Woods on a Snowy Evening' was also chosen by Laurie Lee in *Lifelines* and by Kate Atkinson in this volume.]

ÁINE NÍ GHLINN

28 January 1997

Dear Ralph, Caroline and Gareth,

Thank you for your invitation to contribute to Lifelines 3.

'The Fairies' by William Allingham was the first poem I ever learned and even still, it never fails to bring back memories of my first days in a small two-teacher primary school in County Tipperary.

I wasn't quite four years old and hadn't yet been officially registered on the school roll book. However, as my father was 'the master', I had been allowed to sit beside my 'big sister' in 'the master's room'.

I can still recall with ease the big open fire at the top of the room and the sing-song of the senior students as they chanted,

>   Up the airy mountain, down the rushy glen,
>   We daren't go a-hunting for fear of little men.

Before I ever made it to Junior Infants I knew it by heart and, to this day, 'The Fairies' is not so much a favourite poem as a poem which sparks off some 'favourite memories'!

Áine Ní Ghlinn

The Fairies

Up the airy mountain,
    Down the rushy glen,
We daren't go a-hunting
    For fear of little men;
Wee folk, good folk,
    Trooping all together;
Green jacket, red cap,
    And white owl's feather!

Down along the rocky shore
    Some make their home,
They live on crispy pancakes
    Of yellow tide-foam;
Some in the reeds
    Of the black mountain lake,
With frogs for their watch-dogs,
    All night awake.

High on the hill-top
    The old King sits;
He is now so old and gray
    He's nigh lost his wits.
With a bridge of white mist
    Columbkill he crosses,
On his stately journeys
    From Slieveleague to Rosses;
Or going up with music
    On cold starry nights
To sup with the Queen
    Of the gay Northern Lights.

They stole little Bridget
    For seven years long;
When she came down again
    Her friends were all gone.
They took her lightly back,
    Between the night and morrow,
They thought that she was fast asleep,
    But she was dead with sorrow.
They have kept her ever since
    Deep within the lake,
On a bed of flag-leaves,
    Watching till she wake.

By the craggy hill-side,
    Through the mosses bare,
They have planted thorn-trees
    For pleasure here and there.

If any man so daring
  As dig them up in spite,
He shall find their sharpest thorns
  In his bed at night.

Up the airy mountain,
  Down the rushy glen,
We daren't go a-hunting
  For fear of little men;
Wee folk, good folk,
  Trooping all together;
Green jacket, red cap,
  And white owl's feather!

William Allingham (1824–1889)

MARY GORDON 486

Columbia University, New York
17 February 1997

Dear Ralph Croly, Caroline Dowling, Gareth McCluskey,

It is of course an impossible task to choose one poem. I was tormented at the thought that in choosing Auden's 'The Shield of Achilles', *I was rejecting Emily Dickinson's* 'There's a certain Slant of light', *Yeats's* 'The Wild Swans at Coole' *and George Herbert's* 'Love', *but finally I chose the Auden because it has these shockingly beautiful lines:*

>   ... they were small
> And could not hope for help and no help came

In these words is contained the history and tragedy of the moral life.

Yours truly,
Mary Gordon

The Shield of Achilles

        She looked over his shoulder
          For vines and olive trees,
        Marble well-governed cities
          And ships upon untamed seas,
        But there on the shining metal
          His hands had put instead
        An artificial wilderness
          And a sky like lead.

A plain without a feature, bare and brown,
　　No blade of grass, no sign of neighbourhood,
Nothing to eat and nowhere to sit down,
　　Yet, congregated on its blankness, stood
　　An unintelligible multitude,
A million eyes, a million boots in line,
Without expression, waiting for a sign.

Out of the air a voice without a face
　　Proved by statistics that some cause was just
In tones as dry and level as the place:
　　No one was cheered and nothing was discussed;
　　Column by column in a cloud of dust
They marched away enduring a belief
Whose logic brought them, somewhere else, to grief.

　　　　She looked over his shoulder
　　　　　　For ritual pieties,
　　　　White flower-garlanded heifers,
　　　　　　Libation and sacrifice,
　　　　But there on the shining metal
　　　　　　Where the altar should have been,
　　　　She saw by his flickering forge-light
　　　　　　Quite another scene.

Barbed wire enclosed an arbitrary spot
　　Where bored officials lounged (one cracked a joke)
And sentries sweated for the day was hot:
　　A crowd of ordinary decent folk
　　Watched from without and neither moved nor spoke
As three pale figures were led forth and bound
To three posts driven upright in the ground.

The mass and majesty of this world, all
　　That carries weight and always weighs the same
Lay in the hands of others; they were small
　　And could not hope for help and no help came:
　　What their foes liked to do was done, their shame
Was all the worst could wish; they lost their pride
And died as men before their bodies died.

　　　　She looked over his shoulder
　　　　　　For athletes at their games,
　　　　Men and women in a dance
　　　　　　Moving their sweet limbs
　　　　Quick, quick, to music,
　　　　　　But there on the shining shield
　　　　His hands had set no dancing-floor
　　　　　　But a weed-choked field.

A ragged urchin, aimless and alone,
　　Loitered about that vacancy, a bird
Flew up to safety from his well-aimed stone:

That girls are raped, that two boys knife a third,
Were axioms to him, who'd never heard
Of any world where promises were kept,
Or one could weep because another wept.

>   The thin-lipped armourer,
>   Hephaestos hobbled away,
>   Thetis of the shining breasts
>   Cried out in dismay
>   At what the god had wrought
>   To please her son, the strong
>   Iron-hearted man-slaying Achilles
>   Who would not live long.

W H Auden (1907–1973)

KATHARINE WHITEHORN 487

The Observer
24 January 1997

Dear Ralph Croly, Caroline Dowling and Gareth McCluskey,

Thank you for your letter. It's very hard to say which is my favourite poem, as over the years this has obviously changed. I think at the moment probably my favourite is the Shakespeare sonnet that begins 'That time of year thou mayst in me behold...' *But previous favourites have included W B Yeats's* 'Second Coming', *Browning's* 'One Word More' *and Henry Reed's* 'A Map of Verona'. *Good luck to the project.*

Yours cordially,
Katharine Whitehorn

LXXIII

That time of year thou mayst in me behold
When yellow leaves, or none, or few, do hang
Upon those boughs which shake against the cold,
Bare ruin'd choirs, where late the sweet birds sang.
In me thou seest the twilight of such day
As after sunset fadeth in the west,
Which by and by black night doth take away,
Death's second self, that seals up all in rest.
In me thou seest the glowing of such fire
That on the ashes of his youth doth lie,
As the death-bed whereon it must expire,
Consum'd with that which it was nourish'd by.
   This thou perceiv'st, which makes thy love more strong,
   To love that well which thou must leave ere long.

William Shakespeare (1564–1616)

RONNIE CORBETT 488

5 February 1997

Dear Ralph, Caroline and Gareth,

Thank you for your letter telling me about the series of Lifelines *poetry books, which have been published to help raise funds for Third World children.*

As requested I am delighted to enclose a copy of a favourite poem of mine by Robert Louis Stevenson, which was written by him in praise of the nannie who nursed him as a sick child, and is one I find particularly poignant.

Hope this is the sort of thing you wanted and best wishes with the new Lifelines *book, which I hope will be even more successful than the others.*

Kind regards,

Yours sincerely,
Ronnie Corbett

Dedication
To Alison Cunningham
From her boy

For the long nights you lay awake
And watched for my unworthy sake:
For your most comfortable hand
That led me through the uneven land:
For all the story-books you read,
For all the pains you comforted,
For all you pitied, all you bore,
In sad and happy days of yore —
My second Mother, my first Wife,
The angel of my infant life —
From the sick child, now well and old,
Take, nurse, the little book you hold!

And grant it, Heaven, that all who read
May find as dear a nurse at need,
And every child who lists my rhyme
In the bright fireside, nursery clime,
May hear it in as kind a voice
As made my childish days rejoice!

Robert Louis Stevenson (1850–1894)

TERRY EAGLETON

I recently overheard a schoolgirl announcing that she had fourteen best friends. It's much the same with poems. But Edward Thomas's 'Old Man' (about a shrub, actually, not an elderly gentleman), has always haunted me with its mixture of memory and desire. Thomas was killed in the first world war, and later his widow Helen went to Flanders to plant a sprig of the bush on his grave.

Terry Eagleton

Old Man

Old Man, or Lad's-love, — in the name there's nothing
To one that knows not Lad's-love, or Old Man,
The hoar-green feathery herb, almost a tree,
Growing with rosemary and lavender.
Even to one that knows it well, the names
Half decorate, half perplex, the thing it is:
At least, what that is clings not to the names
In spite of time. And yet I like the names.

The herb itself I like not, but for certain
I love it, as some day the child will love it
Who plucks a feather from the door-side bush
Whenever she goes in or out of the house.
Often she waits there, snipping the tips and shrivelling
The shreds at last on to the path, perhaps
Thinking, perhaps of nothing, till she sniffs
Her fingers and runs off. The bush is still
But half as tall as she, though it is as old;
So well she clips it. Not a word she says;
And I can only wonder how much hereafter
She will remember, with that bitter scent,
Of garden rows, and ancient damson trees
Topping a hedge, a bent path to a door,
A low thick bush beside the door, and me
Forbidding her to pick.
                     As for myself,
Where first I met the bitter scent is lost.
I, too, often shrivel the grey shreds,
Sniff them and think and sniff again and try
Once more to think what it is I am remembering,
Always in vain. I cannot like the scent,
Yet I would rather give up others more sweet,
With no meaning, than this bitter one.
I have mislaid the key. I sniff the spray
And think of nothing; I see and hear nothing;

Yet seem, too, to be listening, lying in wait
For what I should, yet never can, remember:
No garden appears, no path, no hoar-green bush
Of Lad's-love, or Old Man, no child beside,
Neither father nor mother, nor any playmate;
Only an avenue, dark, nameless, without end.

Edward Thomas (1878–1917)

['Old Man' was also chosen by Edna Longley in *Lifelines 2*.]

BARBARA TRAPIDO 490

24 February 1997

Dear Pupils,

I applaud your achievement and hope I am not too late to contribute to your anthology.

There are, of course, so many poems one could choose — and most of them, doubtless, already chosen. (I had in mind at first, Frost's 'Tree at My Window', but my son heard Seamus Heaney choose it on Radio 4.)

May I choose Robert Frost's 'Fragmentary Blue'? I love this poem because the sound is so perfect, with the rhyming first and fourth lines in each stanza and the two central rhyming couplets. I love its brevity and simplicity, combined with its implications of romantic yearning for the unreachable. It has so many echoes of Hopkins — another poet I love — in the brave rhythms and especially in the phrase, 'heaven presents in sheets the solid hue'.

I hope this meets the case. Good luck with your endeavours.

Yours sincerely,
Barbara Trapido

Fragmentary Blue

Why make so much of fragmentary blue
In here and there a bird, or butterfly,
Or flower, or wearing-stone, or open eye,
When heaven presents in sheets the solid hue?

Since earth is earth, perhaps, not heaven (as yet) —
Though some savants make earth include the sky;
And blue so far above us comes so high,
It only gives our wish for blue a whet.

Robert Frost (1874–1963)

MICHAEL SCHMIDT 491

Carcanet
3 February 1997

Dear Ralph, Caroline and Gareth,

Thank you for your letter dated January 1997. I am delighted that you are continuing with the excellent Lifelines *project.*

The poem I would choose is by Elizabeth Bishop. It is called 'Questions of Travel' and is included in her book of the same title published in this country by Chatto and Windus. I like the poem because it is a meditation full of rich and exotic detail but unlike so many travel poems it does not take liberties with those details: the world to which she has travelled and the worlds through which she travels are not her worlds and there is a continuous sense of difference and exclusion. The conclusion of the poem is wonderful because it recognises that the traveller finds herself only in herself and though the various details that she sees are rich and wonderful, they do not provide stability or happiness. It is a poem that is at once beautiful, amusing and 'altering', because if you come to terms with it you come to terms with a very basic human truth.

Good luck with your project.

Yours sincerely,

Michael Schmidt

Questions of Travel

There are too many waterfalls here; the crowded streams
hurry too rapidly down to the sea,
and the pressure of so many clouds on the mountaintops
makes them spill over the sides in soft slow-motion,
turning to waterfalls under our very eyes.
— For if those streaks, those mile-long, shiny, tearstains,
aren't waterfalls yet,
in a quick age or so, as ages go here,
they probably will be.
But if the streams and clouds keep travelling, travelling,
the mountains look like the hulls of capsized ships,
slime-hung and barnacled.

Think of the long trip home.
Should we have stayed at home and thought of here?
Where should we be today?
Is it right to be watching strangers in a play
in this strangest of theatres?

What childishness is it that while there's a breath of life
in our bodies, we are determined to rush
to see the sun the other way around?
The tiniest green hummingbird in the world?
To stare at some inexplicable old stonework,
inexplicable and impenetrable,
at any view,
instantly seen and always, always delightful?
Oh, must we dream our dreams
and have them, too?
And have we room
for one more folded sunset, still quite warm?

But surely it would have been a pity
not to have seen the trees along this road,
really exaggerated in their beauty,
not to have seen them gesturing
like noble pantomimists, robed in pink.
— Not to have had to stop for gas and heard
the sad, two-noted, wooden tune
of disparate wooden clogs
carelessly clacking over
a grease-stained filling-station floor.
(In another country the clogs would all be tested.
Each pair there would have identical pitch.)
— A pity not to have heard
the other, less primitive music of the fat brown bird
who sings above the broken gasoline pump
in a bamboo church of Jesuit baroque:
three towers, five silver crosses.
— Yes, a pity not to have pondered,
blurr'dly and inconclusively,
on what connection can exist for centuries
between the crudest wooden footwear
and, careful and finicky,
the whittled fantasies of wooden cages.
— Never to have studied history in
the weak calligraphy of songbirds' cages.
— And never to have had to listen to rain
so much like politicians' speeches:
two hours of unrelenting oratory
and then a sudden golden silence
in which the traveller takes a notebook, writes:

'Is it lack of imagination that makes us come
to imagined places, not just stay at home?
Or could Pascal have been not entirely right
about sitting quietly in one's room?

Continent, city, country, society:
the choice is never wide and never free.
And here, or there . . . No. Should we have stayed at home,
wherever that may be?'

Elizabeth Bishop (1911–1979)

ROBERT WELCH 492

Yeats's 'Byzantium' *is a poem in which the scenes and images come alive in the brain: the town, the gong sounding, the ghost moves, there are magic flames on a pavement going down to the sea, there is great turbulence as the dolphins swim ashore, the waves beat on the stone terrace. The poem is about the conflict of opposites, but the whole thing is pure energy and brilliant form and excitement.*

Robert Welch

Byzantium

The unpurged images of day recede;
The Emperor's drunken soldiery are abed;
Night resonance recedes, night-walkers' song
After great cathedral gong;
A starlit or a moonlit dome disdains
All that man is,
All mere complexities,
The fury and the mire of human veins.

Before me floats an image, man or shade,
Shade more than man, more image than a shade;
For Hades' bobbin bound in mummy-cloth
May unwind the winding path;
A mouth that has no moisture and no breath
Breathless mouths may summon;
I hail the superhuman;
I call it death-in-life and life-in-death.

Miracle, bird or golden handiwork.
More miracle than bird or handiwork,
Planted on the star-lit golden bough,
Can like the cocks of Hades crow,
Or, by the moon embittered, scorn aloud
In glory of changeless metal
Common bird or petal
And all complexities of mire or blood.

At midnight on the Emperor's pavement flit
Flames that no faggot feeds, nor steel has lit,
Nor storm disturbs, flames begotten of flame,
Where blood-begotten spirits come
And all complexities of fury leave,
Dying into a dance,
An agony of trance,
An agony of flame that cannot singe a sleeve.

Astraddle on the dolphin's mire and blood,
Spirit after spirit! The smithies break the flood.
The golden smithies of the Emperor!
Marbles of the dancing floor
Break bitter furies of complexity,
Those images that yet
Fresh images beget,
That dolphin-torn, that gong-tormented sea.

W B Yeats (1865–1939)

SELIMA HILL 493

18 February 1997

Dear Ralph, Caroline and Gareth,

Thank you for your letter about Lifelines.

My favourite poem is this anonymous, title-less poem:

Westron wynde when wyll thow blow
the smalle rayne downe can rayne —
Cryst if my love wer in my armys
and I yn my bed agayne!

Anonymous

I love all its reckless 'w's and 'y's; I love the way it seems to fly somewhere beyond spelling, punctuation, grammar, even meteorology; the way it reminds us how beautiful and sad things are. Poets today don't seem to let themselves write like this, and poetry is so good at it. In fact, that's what it's for. I wish I wrote more lyrically myself and I don't know why I don't. It may be old-fashioned, but I like poetry not only to play but to yearn.
Any one of the magical poems in Michael Longley's Gorse Fires *(1991) or* The Ghost Orchid *(1995) would be my contemporary choice.*

Thank you again for inviting me to contribute; I am delighted to be involved and wish the anthology every possible success.

Selima Hill

SOINBHE LALLY 494

18 January 1997

Dear Ralph, Caroline and Gareth,

Thank you for your invitation to choose a favourite poem for Lifelines 3. *I have chosen 'Vulture', by Francis Harvey, from his recent collection,* The Boa Island Janus, *published by The Dedalus Press.*

I find it difficult to say why a poem is a favourite. I am mainly a hit and run reader, shying away from the ingrown consciousness which some writers demand. Sometimes, however, a poem pulls me up short with that sudden shock of recognition which makes a poem worth reading again and again. 'Vulture' is such a piece, macabre but true.

Yours sincerely,
Soinbhe Lally

Vulture

A sheepman in the Mournes observed it first
gorging on the entrails of a still-born
lamb; next it was disturbed plucking the heart
from an aborted human foetus unborn

for better things elsewhere and on the third
day poachers stoned it from the corpse of an
informer they found gagged with a dragon's turd
and testicles. But it grew weary on

such rich fare, scavenging the abattoirs
of hate until, enormous, gross, and fat
with the viscera of the dove and rat,

sated yet home-sick for the heat and flies,
it bore South again, smelling a sweeter war
where God died long ago of tribal lies.

Francis Harvey

CATHERINE BYRNE 495

20 January 1997

Dear Ralph, Caroline and Gareth,

I just loved Lifelines *and* Lifelines 2 *and feel honoured to be asked to contribute to* Lifelines 3. *I have chosen Seamus Heaney's 'At the*

Wellhead' *as it recalls an especially happy theatrical memory for me. In 1995 during rehearsals for Brian Friel's* Molly Sweeney, *many discussions took place concerning the portrayal of the Blind Woman, who is the play's namesake, and the part I was attempting to play.*

At the end of a long day, Brian showed me this wonderful poem, and I was profoundly moved by it. 'What a marvellous description of her eyes,' I said. 'Could we have that tomorrow at 10 a.m.?' smoothly requested the playwright.

I could but try.

Best wishes and much love,
Catherine Byrne

At the Wellhead

Your songs, when you sing them with your two eyes closed
As you always do, are like a local road
We've known every turn of in the past —
That midge-veiled, high-hedged side-road where you stood
Looking and listening until a car
Would come and go and leave you lonelier
Than you had been to begin with. So, sing on,
Dear shut-eyed one, dear far-voiced veteran,

Sing yourself to where the singing comes from,
Ardent and cut off like our blind neighbour
Who played the piano all day in her bedroom.
Her notes came out to us like hoisted water
Ravelling off a bucket at the wellhead
Where next thing we'd be listening, hushed and awkward.

*

That blind-from-birth, sweet-voiced, withdrawn musician
Was like a silver vein in heavy clay.
Night water glittering in the light of day.
But also just our neighbour, Rosie Keenan.
She touched our cheeks. She let us touch her braille
In books like books wallpaper patterns came in.
Her hands were active and her eyes were full
Of open darkness and a watery shine.

She knew us by our voices. She'd say she 'saw'
Whoever or whatever. Being with her
Was intimate and helpful, like a cure
You didn't notice happening. When I read
A poem with Keenan's well in it, she said,
'I can see the sky at the bottom of it now.'

Seamus Heaney (b.1939)

JUSTIN QUINN

24 January 1997

Dear Ralph Croly, Caroline Dowling, Gareth McCluskey,

Thanks for your invitation to contribute to Lifelines. *Every time I read a really good poem it becomes my new favourite poem, so it's hard to choose; but I suppose my ultimate test for poetry is the test of re-reading. One of the poets I come back to again and again and read with tremendous pleasure is the American poet, Wallace Stevens (1879–1955). 'The Plain Sense of Things' is a poem he wrote near the end of his life: the calmness in the poem is like that which follows huge storms — of seasons and emotions. The poet is left looking over his garden — he is old, there is 'sadness without cause' and there is even the mild humour of chimney (as though he says to himself, 'All that trouble and now even the chimney is falling down. Oh, I give up.'). And yet even at this lowest moment, the human imagination, with sudden agility, comes springing back in the last two lines. So, despite the title, there is no plain sense of things: the imagination has to go on imagining right to the end of the poem and the end of life.*

Yours,
Justin Quinn

The Plain Sense of Things

After the leaves have fallen, we return
To a plain sense of things. It is as if
We had come to an end of the imagination,
Inanimate in an inert savoir.

It is difficult even to choose the adjective
For this blank cold, this sadness without cause.
The great structure has become a minor house.
No turban walks across the lessened floors.

The greenhouse never so badly needed paint.
The chimney is fifty years old and slants to one side.
A fantastic effort has failed, a repetition
In a repetitiousness of men and flies.

Yet the absence of the imagination had
Itself to be imagined. The great pond,
The plain sense of it, without reflections, leaves,
Mud, water like dirty glass, expressing silence

Of a sort, silence of a rat come out to see,
The great pond and its waste of the lilies, all this
Had to be imagined as an inevitable knowledge,
Required, as a necessity requires.

Wallace Stevens (1879–1955)

MICHAEL SCOTT 497

27 January 1997

Dear Ralph, Caroline and Gareth,

Thank you for the invitation to nominate my favourite poem for Lifelines 3. *I recall, when I was reading* Lifelines 2, *wondering which poem I would choose as a favourite and finding it almost impossible to come to a decision. And now, faced with the choice, it is equally difficult.*

There are, however, two poems I keep going back to, two poems I can recite by heart, both — I believe — first heard in my childhood. In truth, however, I never remember learning these verses. In each, the sense of magic and mystery, of suggested secrets and hinted wonders appeals to me, and I try to instil that same sense of wonder into my own writing. I do know that, when I started to write, many years ago, I pinned the poem, 'Lyonesse', to the wall above my desk. It is still there.

Wishing you every success with Lifelines 3.

Yours sincerely,
Michael Scott

When I Set out for Lyonesse

When I set out for Lyonesse,
  A hundred miles away,
  The rime was on the spray,
And starlight lit my lonesomeness
When I set out for Lyonesse
  A hundred miles way.

What would bechance at Lyonesse
  While I should sojourn there
  No prophet durst declare,
Nor did the wisest wizard guess
What would bechance at Lyonesse
  While I should sojourn there.

When I came back from Lyonesse
  With magic in my eyes,
  All marked with mute surmise
My radiance rare and fathomless
When I came back from Lyonesse
  With magic in my eyes!

Thomas Hardy (1840–1928)

Ozymandias

I met a traveller from an antique land
Who said: Two vast and trunkless legs of stone
Stand in the desert . . . Near them, on the sand,
Half sunk, a shattered visage lies, whose frown,
And wrinkled lip, and sneer of cold command,
Tell that its sculptor well those passions read
Which yet survive, stamped on these lifeless things,
The hand that mocked them, and the heart that fed:
And on the pedestal these words appear:
'My name is Ozymandias, king of kings:
Look on my works, ye Mighty, and despair!'
Nothing beside remains. Round the decay
Of that colossal wreck, boundless and bare
The lone and level sands stretch far away.

Percy Bysshe Shelley (1792–1822)

['Ozymandias' was also chosen by Lynn Barber in *Lifelines*.]

KERRY HARDIE

15 January 1997

Dear Ralph, Caroline and Gareth,

Thank you for your letter. I am honoured that you should want me to choose a poem for the new Lifelines *anthology. I think it is a wonderful idea and greatly to your credit that you are working so hard to make it happen. Here is the poem I have chosen, followed by a few lines on my choice.*

September Evening
Deer at Big Basin

When they talk about angels in books
I think what they mean is this sudden
arrival: this gift of an alien country
we guessed all along,

and how these deer are moving in the dark,
bound to the silence, finding our scent in their way
and making us strange, making us all that we are
in the fall of the light,

as if we had entered the myth
of one who is risen, and one who is left behind
in the gap that remains,

a story that gives us the questions we wanted to ask,
and our sense of our presence as creatures,
about to be touched.

John Burnside (b.1955)

I have many favourite poems — it isn't easy to select one — but this is a favourite poem from a Scots poet whose work I love because of his sense of the visionary in the ordinary, and because of the intent quietness of his voice.

Good luck in your enterprise,
Kerry Hardie

SIOBHÁN PARKINSON   499

3 January 1997

Dear Ralph, Caroline and Gareth,

Thank you for your invitation to choose a poem for Lifelines 3. *I am extremely flattered to have been asked to be part of this excellent project.*

I have a problem with the word 'favourite', however. I am always astonished that people can have a favourite colour, for example. How can anyone prefer red to blue or green to yellow (or vice versa or vice versa)? Yellow is my favourite colour for walls and for jerseys for people with copper-coloured hair and especially for egg yolks, but I can't think of a colour I would like less for a pair of shoes or a sandwich.

It's the same with poems. I love poems that are funny and make me smile. And I love poems that are sad and make me cry. I love poems that are clear and translucent and sing to me off the page. And I love poems that are dense and thick and have to be mined for meaning. It's not that there aren't poems I prefer. Of course there are. But I don't have a single favourite poem; I have lots of favourites.

Which is all very fine, but where does it leave me with the task in hand? Precisely nowhere. So then I tried to think less about the idea of favourites and a bit more about the function of Lifelines — *the poetic function, that is, rather than the fund-raising one — and it struck me that one of the great things about this project is the way it brings readers and poems together, sometimes in unexpected ways. So in the end I decided to choose a new poem — this one's new to me at any rate and, since it's from a recent collection, it may be new to other people too — and one that people would be sure to be touched by, whoever they are and whatever their preoccupations; and so I chose this lovely springtime poem by Kerry Hardie.*

May
for Marian

The blessèd stretch and ease of it —
heart's ease. The hills blue. All the flowering weeds
bursting open. Balm in the air. The birdsong
bouncing back out of the sky. The cattle
lain down in the meadow, forgetting to feed.
The horses swishing their tails.
The yellow flare of furze on the near hill.
And the first cream splatters of blossom
high on the thorns where the day rests longest.

All hardship, hunger, treachery of winter forgotten.
This unfounded conviction: forgiveness, hope.

Kerry Hardie (b.1951)

Isn't that just . . . well, isn't it just*! What more can I say?*

Beir beannacht,
Siobhán Parkinson

GERARD BEIRNE

Dear Ralph, Caroline, and Gareth,

Thank you for your letter. My favourite poem? Always a tough question and always a multitude of answers. There are many poems I return to time and time again, but the following poem by David Wagoner, 'The Poets Agree to Be Quiet by the Swamp', recently reared its head once more. I read it both for enjoyment and in a frail attempt to keep me on the straight and narrow.

Sincerely,
Gerard Beirne

The Poets Agree to Be Quiet by the Swamp

They hold their hands over their mouths
And stare at the stretch of water.
What can be said has been said before:
Strokes of light like herons' legs in the cattails,
Mud underneath, frogs lying even deeper.
Therefore the poets may keep quiet.
But the corners of their mouths grin past their hands.
They stick their elbows out into the evening,
Stoop, and begin the ancient croaking.

David Wagoner (b.1926)

IGGY McGOVERN 501

Department of Physics
Trinity College, Dublin
10 January 1997

Dear Ralph, Caroline and Gareth,

Thank you for asking me to contribute to Lifelines 3. *I am delighted to have the opportunity to support this very worthy project.*

A poet I much admire is Miroslav Holub. Probably this is because he is a scientist as well as a poet. I also like his sense of humour and the way he incorporates stories into his poems; I try to use these elements in my own poetry. The poem I have selected is called 'Brief Reflection on Accuracy'; here Holub pokes a little fun at 'scientific research', with the smallest of hints about more serious matters in the last line.

Yours sincerely,
Iggy McGovern
Associate Professor of Physics

Brief Reflection on Accuracy

Fish
    always accurately know where to move and when,
    and likewise
    birds have an accurate built-in time sense
    and orientation.

Humanity, however,
    lacking such instincts resorts to scientific
    research. Its nature is illustrated by the following
    occurrence.

A certain soldier
    had to fire a cannon at six o'clock sharp every evening.
    Being a soldier he did so. When his accuracy was
    investigated he explained:

I go by
    the absolutely accurate chronometer in the window
    of the clockmaker down in the city. Every day at seventeen
    forty-five I set my watch by it and
    climb the hill where my cannon stands ready.
    At seventeen fifty-nine precisely I step up to the cannon
    and at eighteen hours sharp I fire.

And it was clear
    that this method of firing was absolutely accurate.
    All that was left was to check that chronometer. So
    the clockmaker down in the city was questioned about
    his instrument's accuracy.

Oh, said the clockmaker,
    this is one of the most accurate instruments ever. Just
        imagine,
    for many years now a cannon has been fired at six o'clock
        sharp.
    And every day I look at this chronometer
    and always it shows exactly six.

So much for accuracy.
    And fish move in the water, and from the skies
    comes a rushing of wings while

Chronometers tick and cannon boom.

Miroslav Holub (b.1923)
Translated by Ewald Osers

ORLA MELLING

13 January 1997

Dear Ralph, Caroline and Gareth,

Thanks for the honour of asking me to participate in Lifelines 3.

1. 'Pure Praise' by Nina Malinovski. When recently in Copenhagen, I came across the work of this poet. She writes chiefly in Danish, which I am learning, but this is a poem she wrote in English. It is perhaps obvious why it appeals to me. It's about love and I am a romantic.

Pure Praise

By the name of all the living stubborn
    beating hearts
and between them yours
black and silky
reaching out . . .

By every language without words
    and all hidden strength
living in infirmity . . .

By the sparkling sound of silence
in a hall of stems
just before the forest goes to sleep . . .

And in the name of pleasure
nature's untold tastes colours scents
and of course among them ours:
honey for the hungry bees
sweet and bitter supply . . .

By the light of a morning
bursting into a cool cave
of oblivion . . .

By the endless road
in front of us
wanting our soles . . .

By all that's living
even without us
and yet so honoured
by our common eyes
I love you . . .

Nina Malinovski

Nina Malinovski has published five books of poetry with Forlaget Vindrose, Denmark — Fri Tid *(1981),* Under Dansens Haele *(1983),* Fartens Fortaellinger *(1985),* Det Er Sa Enkelt *(1990) and* Forandringer *(1994).*

2. 'Storm Bird' by Padraic Fiacc. Padraic Fiacc has long been one of my favourite poets. This poem in particular I cherish for its line 'I am the blackbird / Of the ruined nest who sings.' Despite the overall bleakness of tone, this is a note of triumph, I think, for all who sing despite their pain . . . or perhaps, even, because of it.

Storm Bird

My comings and goings
Are the comings and goings of wind.

I am the word the wind mutters.
Pay me no mind.

Though I serve beauty and not mankind
The voice is the bird of a word
Wind gives wings to.

I am the blackbird
Of the ruined nest who sings

'All is beauty to the blind.'
Padraic Fiacc (b.1924)

Best of luck with your new edition. Let me know when it's coming out!

Yours,
Orla / 'GV'

RODNEY RICE 503

Radio One
Radio Telefís Éireann

Dear Ralph, Caroline and Gareth,

Here's my poem offered for your collection. It is by John Hewitt and is called 'The Scar.'

The Scar
for Padraic Fiacc

There's not a chance now that I might recover
one syllable of what that sick man said,
tapping upon my great-grandmother's shutter,
and begging, I was told, a piece of bread;
for on his tainted breath there hung infection
rank from the cabins of the stricken west,
the spores from black potato-stalks, the spittle
mottled with poison in his rattling chest;
but she who, by her nature, quickly answered,
accepted in return the famine-fever;
and that chance meeting, that brief confrontation,
conscribed me of the Irishry forever.

Though much I cherish lies outside their vision,
and much they prize I have no claim to share,
yet in that woman's death I found my nation;
the old wound aches and shews its fellow-scar.

John Hewitt (1907–1987)

As a political journalist concerned with the state of both parts of this island, and as the maker of a number of radio programmes on the subject of identity and nationality, I have always found John Hewitt's work thought-provoking and quotable.

He once described his own hierarchy of values thus: 'I'm an Ulsterman of Planter stock. I was born on the island of Ireland, so secondly I'm an Irishman. I was born in the British archipelago, and English is my native tongue, so I am British. The British archipelago are offshore islands to the continent of Europe, so I'm European.'

Confronted with the blind certainties of Ireland's rival tribes, the hatred born of religious sectarianism which smoulders ceaselessly between periodic eruptions, John Hewitt's is a voice we could listen to more often. As most Northern political leaders race madly to be furthest behind the slowest of their followers and Southern leaders relax in the unquestioning comfort of a traditional mono-culturism and homogeneity, it could assist us all to take a wider perspective; to question ourselves as Hewitt did; and to slip into a broader, more inclusive cloth of self-definition.

I also admire the tightness of Hewitt's language as seen in this poem, where not a word is wasted yet clear pictures of poverty, sickness and human generosity emerge, with questions of religion and politics tantalisingly posed. A lesson for both journalists and politicians.
So that's the poem and those are the few lines about why I like it.

Best wishes with Lifelines 3.

Yours,
Rodney Rice

LIA MILLS 504

18 January 1997

Dear Ralph, Caroline and Gareth,

Thank you for your letter asking me to nominate a poem for Lifelines 3. *You've given me days of anguish because I find it very difficult to choose one 'favourite'. There are many poems that I love and return to, at different times and for different reasons. However, I've finally settled on* 'The Pomegranate', *by Eavan Boland.*

Good luck with compiling the anthology. It's a brilliant idea, and I'm very glad to be included in it.

The legend of Demeter (Ceres) and Persephone has always been a favourite of mine, because it can see us through almost anything. The levels of meaning in the myth are both general and personal, and will probably never be exhausted. 'The Pomegranate' *is a recognition of that, and is a reminder of the sustaining and imaginative power of literature, its continuing relevance. I love this poem because its language and imagery make it live and because, while it recognises loss, it also believes in renewal. It is a moving, powerful expression of creativity and of maternal love.*

All the best,
Lia Mills

The Pomegranate

The only legend I have ever loved is
the story of a daughter lost in hell.
And found and rescued there.
Love and blackmail are the gist of it.
Ceres and Persephone the names.
And the best thing about the legend is
I can enter it anywhere. And have.
As a child in exile in
a city of fogs and strange consonants,
I read it first and at first I was
an exiled child in the crackling dusk of
the underworld, the stars blighted. Later
I walked out in a summer twilight
searching for my daughter at bed-time.
When she came running I was ready
to make any bargain to keep her.
I carried her back past whitebeams
and wasps and honey-scented buddleias.
But I was Ceres then and I knew
winter was in store for every leaf
on every tree on that road.
Was inescapable for each one we passed.
And for me.
        It is winter
and the stars are hidden.
I climb the stairs and stand where I can see
my child asleep beside her teen magazines,
her can of Coke, her plate of uncut fruit.
The pomegranate! How did I forget it?
She could have come home and been safe
and ended the story and all
our heart-broken searching but she reached
out a hand and plucked a pomegranate.

She put out her hand and pulled down
the French sound for apple and
the noise of stone and the proof
that even in the place of death,
at the heart of legend, in the midst
of rocks full of unshed tears
ready to be diamonds by the time
the story was told, a child can be
hungry. I could warn her. There is still a chance.
The rain is cold. The road is flint-coloured.
The suburb has cars and cable television.
The veiled stars are above ground.
It is another world. But what else
can a mother give her daughter but such
beautiful rifts in time?
If I defer the grief I will diminish the gift.
The legend will be hers as well as mine.
She will enter it. As I have.
She will wake up. She will hold
the papery flushed skin in her hand.
And to her lips. I will say nothing.

Eavan Boland (b.1944)

['The Pomegranate' was also chosen by Catherine Phil MacCarthy in *Lifelines 2*.]

ITA QUILLIGAN 505

22 January 1997

Dear Poetry Lovers!

I first heard the poem 'For a Father' in the 1960s listening to a reading by Anthony Cronin at the Emmet Gallery. I sought a collection of his work for years. At the launch of the limited edition of Collected Poems *in 1973, I landed the very first copy, signed by the author himself. I then mislaid it but heard it again in 1992 — this time read by my daughter at her father's graveside. I hope you like it.*

With kind regards,
Ita Quilligan

For a Father

With the exact length and pace of his father's stride
The son walks,
Echoes and intonations of his father's speech
Are heard when he talks.

Once when the table was tall,
And the chair a wood,
He absorbed his father's smile and carefully copied
The way that he stood.

He grew into exile slowly,
With pride and remorse,
In some ways better than his begetters,
In others worse.

And now having chosen, with strangers,
Half glad of his choice,
He smiles with his father's hesitant smile
And speaks with his voice.

Anthony Cronin (b.1928)

PATRICK CHAPMAN 506

13 February 1997

Dear Ralph Croly, Caroline Dowling, Gareth McCluskey,

Thanks for your invitation to participate in Lifelines 3. *I wish you every success for this project.*

Best wishes,
Patrick Chapman

The Things You Never See

The marmalade cat, sitting by your patio door,
Watching, as you make breakfast.

A July sunrise, framed in the window behind you
As a vapour trail cuts the sky in half.

A spider labouring on a silken thread above your head
While you read William Trevor.

*

Yourself, laughing with your head thrown back
Across the room at a boring party.

The way you scamper across the cold, tiled floor
After a winter's morning shower.

Me, kissing your eyelids goodnight as you sleep.

David Croft (b.1964)

Apparently ordinary things can have strange properties. In this poem, David Croft reveals the power of intimacy through what at first appears to be the usual detachment of the poet, but what reveals itself as a moving expression of closeness.

Apart from that, it's also a beautiful love poem from a new talent whose first collection, when it arrives, is bound to mark him out as a serious and enduring voice.

SEBASTIAN FAULKS

Dear Lifelines,

My favourite poem is 'For the Union Dead' by Robert Lowell. I like the way it understands the immanence of history in the present; I like its controlled anger; and I like its sinuous, intelligent style.

Best wishes,
Sebastian Faulks

For the Union Dead
'Relinquunt Omnia Servare Rem Publicam.'

The old South Boston Aquarium stands
in a Sahara of snow now. Its broken windows are boarded.
The bronze weathervane cod has lost half its scales.
The airy tanks are dry.

Once my nose crawled like a snail on the glass;
my hand tingled
to burst the bubbles
drifting from the noses of the cowed, compliant fish.

My hand draws back. I often sigh still
for the dark downward and vegetating kingdom
of the fish and reptile. One morning last March,
I pressed against the new barbed and galvanized

fence on the Boston Common. Behind their cage,
yellow dinosaur steamshovels were grunting
as they cropped up tons of mush and grass
to gouge their underworld garage.

Parking spaces luxuriate like civic
sandpiles in the heart of Boston.
A girdle of orange, Puritan-pumpkin colored girders
braces the tingling Statehouse,

shaking over the excavations, as it faces Colonel Shaw
and his bell-cheeked Negro infantry
on St Gaudens' shaking Civil War relief,
propped by a plank splint against the garage's earthquake.

Two months after marching through Boston,
half the regiment was dead;
at the dedication,
William James could almost hear the bronze Negroes breathe.

Their monument sticks like a fishbone
in the city's throat.
Its Colonel is as lean
as a compass-needle.

He has an angry wrenlike vigilance,
a greyhound's gentle tautness;
he seems to wince at pleasure,
and suffocate for privacy.

He is out of bounds now. He rejoices in man's lovely,
peculiar power to choose life and die —
when he leads his black soldiers to death,
he cannot bend his back.

On a thousand small town New England greens,
the old white churches hold their air
of sparse, sincere rebellion; frayed flags
quilt the graveyards of the Grand Army of the Republic.

The stone statues of the abstract Union Soldier
grow slimmer and younger each year —
wasp-waisted, they doze over muskets
and muse through their sideburns . . .

Shaw's father wanted no monument
except the ditch,
where his son's body was thrown
and lost with his 'niggers'.

The ditch is nearer.
There are no statues for the last war here;
on Boylston Street, a commercial photograph
shows Hiroshima boiling

over a Mosler Safe, the 'Rock of Ages'
that survived the blast. Space is nearer.
When I crouch to my television set,
the drained faces of Negro school-children rise like balloons.

Colonel Shaw
is riding on his bubble,
he waits
for the blessèd break.

The Aquarium is gone. Everywhere,
giant finned cars nose forward like fish;
a savage servility
slides by on grease.

Robert Lowell (1917–1977)

AISLING FOSTER

12 March 1997

Dear Caroline, Ralph and Gareth,

The poem that really turns me on these days is 'Valediction'. Louis MacNeice wrote it in 1934, but it still expresses the emigrant's feelings about a country which has let him go, his furious mixture of love and resentment towards a mother who continues her feckless, freewheeling life without a backward glance or care in the world.

With best wishes,
Aisling Foster

Valediction

Their verdure dare not show ... their verdure dare not show ...
Cant and randy — the seals' heads bobbing in the tide-flow
Between the islands, sleek and black and irrelevant
They cannot depose logically what they want:
Died by gunshot under borrowed pennons,
Sniped from the wet gorse and taken by the limp fins
And slung like a dead seal in a boghole, beaten up
By peasants with long lips and the whisky-drinker's cough.
Park your car in the city of Dublin, see Sackville Street
Without the sandbags in the old photos, meet
The statues of the patriots, history never dies,
At any rate in Ireland, arson and murder are legacies
Like old rings hollow-eyed without their stones
Dumb talismans.
See Belfast, devout and profane and hard,
Built on reclaimed mud, hammers playing in the shipyard,
Time punched with holes like a steel sheet, time
Hardening the faces, veneering with a grey and speckled rime
The faces under the shawls and caps:
This was my mother-city, these my paps.

Country of callous lava cooled to stone,
Of minute sodden haycocks, of ship-sirens' moan,
Of falling intonations — I would call you to book
I would say to you, Look;
I would say, This is what you have given me
Indifference and sentimentality
A metallic giggle, a fumbling hand,
A heart that leaps to a fife band:
Set these against your water-shafted air
Of amethyst and moonstone, the horses' feet like bells of hair
Shambling beneath the orange cart, the beer-brown spring
Guzzling between the heather, the green gush of Irish spring.
Cursèd be he that curses his mother. I cannot be
Anyone else than what this land engendered me:
In the back of my mind are snips of white, the sails
Of the Lough's fishing-boats, the bellropes lash their tails
When I would peal my thoughts, the bells pull free —
Memory in apostasy.
I would tot up my factors
But who can stand in the way of his soul's steam-tractors?
I can say Ireland is hooey, Ireland is
A gallery of fake tapestries,
But I cannot deny my past to which my self is wed,
The woven figure cannot undo its thread.
On a cardboard lid I saw when I was four
Was the trade-mark of a hound and a round tower,
And that was Irish glamour, and in the cemetery
Sham Celtic crosses claimed our individuality,
And my father talked about the West where years back
He played hurley on the sands with a stick of wrack.
Park your car in Killarney, buy a souvenir
Of green marble or black bog-oak, run up to Clare,
Climb the cliff in the postcard, visit Galway city,
Romanticise on our Spanish blood, leave ten per cent of pity
Under your plate for the emigrant,
Take credit for our sanctity, our heroism and our sterile want
Columba Kevin and briny Brandan the accepted names,
Wolfe Tone and Grattan and Michael Collins the accepted
   names,
Admire the suavity with which the architect
Is rebuilding the burnt mansion, recollect
The palmy days of the Horse Show, swank your fill,
But take the Holyhead boat before you pay the bill;
Before you face the consequence
Of inbred soul and climatic maleficence
And pay for the trick beauty of a prism
In drug-dull fatalism.
I will exorcise my blood
And not to have my baby-clothes my shroud

I will acquire an attitude not yours
And become as one of your holiday visitors,
And however often I may come
Farewell, my country, and in perpetuum;
Whatever desire I catch when your wind scours my face
I will take home and put in a glass case
And merely look on
At each new fantasy of badge and gun.
Frost will not touch the hedge of fuchsias,
The land will remain as it was,
But no abiding content can grow out of these minds
Fuddled with blood, always caught by blinds;
The eels go up the Shannon over the great dam;
You cannot change a response by giving it a new name.
Fountain of green and blue curling in the wind
I must go east and stay, not looking behind,
Not knowing on which day the mist is blanket-thick
Nor when sun quilts the valley and quick
Winging shadows of white clouds pass
Over the long hills like a fiddle's phrase.
If I were a dog of sunlight I would bound
From Phoenix Park to Achill Sound,
Picking up the scent of a hundred fugitives
That have broken the mesh of ordinary lives,
But being ordinary too I must in course discuss
What we mean to Ireland or Ireland to us;
I have to observe milestone and curio
The beaten buried gold of an old king's bravado,
Falsetto antiquities, I have to gesture,
Take part in, or renounce, each imposture;
Therefore I resign, good-bye the chequered and the quiet hills
The gaudily-striped Atlantic, the linen-mills
That swallow the shawled file, the black moor where half
A turf-stack stands like a ruined cenotaph;
Good-bye your hens running in and out of the white house
Your absent-minded goats along the road, your black cows
Your greyhounds and your hunters beautifully bred
Your drums and your dolled-up Virgins and your ignorant
   dead.

Louis MacNeice (1907–1963)

HAROLD PINTER 509

10 March 1997

Dear Ralph Croly, Caroline Dowling and Gareth McCluskey,

This is certainly my favourite love poem. It is the most tender of poems and its voice is like no other.

Yours sincerely,
Harold Pinter

I Leave This at Your Ear
for Nessie Dunsmuir

I leave this at your ear for when you wake,
A creature in its abstract cage asleep.
Your dreams blindfold you by the light they make.

The owl called from the naked-woman tree
As I came down by the Kyle farm to hear
Your house silent by the speaking sea.

I have come late but I have come before
Later with slaked steps from stone to stone
To hope to find you listening for the door.

I stand in the ticking room. My dear, I take
A moth kiss from your breath. The shore gulls cry.
I leave this at your ear for when you wake.

W S Graham (1918–1986)

MIRIAM O'CALLAGHAN 510

RTÉ
4 February 1997

Dear Ralph, Caroline and Gareth,

I am delighted to be involved in Lifelines 3. *My choice of poem is 'A Woman Untouched' by the playwright and poet Frank McGuinness. It was a poem he wrote in 1995 for my sister Anne O'Callaghan, and it was published in a limited edition of 300.*

It is a beautiful and moving tribute to my sister Anne, who died at a tragically young age from cancer in 1995. Everyone loved Anne and everyone who met her felt they knew her quite well. But as Frank McGuinness brilliantly captures in his poem, Anne was complex and multi-layered and, ultimately, she was a very private and dignified young woman.

This poem is special and, most importantly of all, Anne would have loved it. Thank you Frank McGuinness.

Yours faithfully,
Miriam O'Callaghan

A Woman Untouched
An elegy for Anne O'Callaghan

I
I am flying to California on Virgin Airlines
When the death of Helen is announced in Ireland.

Let the sky turn metallic and weep buckets.
Let my hands be raised in supplication.

It cannot be so. Most beautiful Helen.
I am not prepared for her eternity.

She the loveliest, the most gentle of women,
She the funniest, the best of all times,

Helen is dead. Let the heavens rip open
The veil of the temple of the sweet Atlantic.

Is that her soul ascending? Helen,
There is laughter in the whole happiness

Of your friendship. For your thirty-three years,
You have graced this earth. Grace the air I fly.

Give me strength through grace to say savage words.
Helen is dead. Helen of Troy is dead.

II
She moved through life like a woman untouched.
Her radiant face concealed its secrets.
When she chose to speak, there was wisdom stirring.
She kept her counsel, she believed in fate.

Believing in wisdom, she faced it squarely.
Poor fate didn't know what it had taken on.
All fights, my friend, are fights to the bitter end.
As soon stop the sun shining as the end be sweet.

III
You say I was beautiful — and I was.
Yet beauty is a mask of beaten gold.
I might approve of this appellation,
This Helen of Troy, were it ever true.
But it's not. So, call me by my own name.
Say it, even if it breaks your heart.
Do you not think my heart is broken?
Do you think mythology eases my pained heart?
One day I looked at myself in a mirror;
The loveliest woman in Ireland looked out at me.
I told her where to get off that instant.
I'm a working woman, I've a job to do.
That woman in the mirror then laughed like myself.
My strength is that I can see through myself.

IV
The spring is coming to California:
In Booterstown Avenue a palm tree grows.

Exotic growth, no place to be here,
Like yourself, Anne O'Callaghan.

No chance now it will be ever uprooted
From shading my house. Dance on its leaves and

Let your soul ascend as a tree ascends.
I phone Kaye Fanning from California.

She said, she's dead, our loved girl is dead.
I cried for an hour in a motel room.

Early morning there, late night at home.
I went out and taught Anton Chekhov. *Three Sisters*.

I call on the sister of the spring that comes
To California, of the palm tree that grows

In Booterstown Avenue, flying on Virgin Airlines,
The sky turned metallic and weeping buckets.

She the loveliest, the most gentle of women,
She the funniest, the best of all times,

Helen is dead. Let the heavens rip open
The veil of the temple of the sweet Atlantic.

Frank McGuinness (b.1953)

JOHN HUGHES   511

5 March 1997

Dear Ralph Croly, Caroline Dowling, Gareth McCluskey,

One of my favourite poems is 'Mortification' by George Herbert.

This is a poem to be read at 3 a.m., when death is closer than we imagine.

Yours sincerely,
John Hughes

Mortification

How soon doth man decay!
When clothes are taken from a chest of sweets
To swaddle infants, whose young breath
Scarce knows the way:
Those clouts are little winding sheets,
Which do consign and send them unto death.

When boys go first to bed,
They step into their voluntary graves,
Sleep binds them fast; only their breath
Makes them not dead:
Successive nights, like rolling waves,
Convey them quickly, who are bound for death.

When youth is frank and free,
And calls for music, while his veins do swell,
All day exchanging mirth and breath
In company:
That music summons to the knell,
Which shall befriend him at the hour of death.

When man grows staid and wise,
Getting a house and home, where he may move
Within the circle of his breath,
Schooling his eyes:
That dumb enclosure maketh love
Unto the coffin, that attends his death.

When age grows low and weak,
Marking his grave, and thawing ev'ry year,
Till all do melt, and drown his breath
When he would speak:
A chair or litter shows the bier,
Which shall convey him to the house of death.

> Man, ere he is aware,
> Hath put together a solemnity,
> And dress'd his hearse, while he has breath
>   As yet to spare:
> Yet Lord, instruct us so to die,
> That all these dyings may be life in death.

George Herbert (1593–1633)

TERRY PRONE

9 January 1997

Dear Ralph, Caroline and Gareth,

The earlier editions of Lifelines *have been a great pleasure and — in some cases — surprise to me, so it's an honour to be invited to contribute to* Lifelines 3.

My favourite is one of Auden's. Favourite because it underlines the tension between what is heroic, what is tragic, what is unique, and what is routine, what is driven by the imperative of the 'little round of deeds and days'. It's usually an unregistered and unacknowledged tension — with today's trivia triumphant . . . I love it, too, because once you know the poem, you know the painting in a quite different way.

Yours sincerely,
Terry Prone

Musée des Beaux Arts

About suffering they were never wrong,
The Old Masters: how well they understood
Its human position; how it takes place
While someone else is eating or opening a window or just
    walking dully along;
How, when the aged are reverently, passionately waiting
For the miraculous birth, there always must be
Children who did not specially want it to happen, skating
On a pond at the edge of the wood:
They never forgot
That even the dreadful martyrdom must run its course
Anyhow in a corner, some untidy spot
Where the dogs go on with their doggy life and the torturer's
    horse
Scratches its innocent behind on a tree.

In Brueghel's *Icarus*, for instance: how everything turns away
Quite leisurely from the disaster; the ploughman may
Have heard the splash, the forsaken cry,
But for him it was not an important failure; the sun shone
As it had to on the white legs disappearing into the green
Water; and the expensive delicate ship that must have seen
Something amazing, a boy falling out of the sky,
Had somewhere to get to and sailed calmly on.

W H Auden (1907–1973)

MARIE HEANEY 513

Dear Editors,

First of all, congratulations on carrying on the marvellous work of your predecessors in helping to alleviate famine in the Third World.

I haven't got just one *favourite poem; I have a nucleus of poems that I love and that I turn to at different times and for different reasons.*

The one I'm nominating for Lifelines 3 *is* 'Musée des Beaux Arts' *by W H Auden. This poem contemplates beauty, suffering and human indifference in a clear-eyed way. By being a beautiful thing itself, it assuages pain to some degree. It* does *make something happen.*

Every success with Lifelines 3.

Sincerely,
Marie Heaney

DESMOND O'GRADY 514

13 January 1997

To Ralph Croly, Caroline Dowling and Gareth McCluskey,

A thirty-three year old — the age of Christ on the cross — converted Catholic, Hopkins was ordained a priest the year he wrote this 'Italian' sonnet, in 1877. When I first read the poem, in an Irish Cistercian boarding school, I was sixteen and had never heard of Hopkins. His startling language baffled me. What it all meant eluded me. Was this 'modern' poetry? Hearing the poem read by my teacher Mr Cole I was captivated, pleasured by its musically swingy, jumpy rhythms and accents — conducted with Tom Cole's palms, elbows, head, shoulders, legs and feet — by its alliteration, assonance, dissonance, its eccentric juxtaposition of simple and strange words. It was like reading aloud the numbers in mathematical formulae that spell the meaning of the equation, which I was then beginning to see as a kind of poetry, painting, silent music. The sounds, rhythms and emphases of Hopkins's poem harmonised with old Gaelic poems I knew by heart, without understanding them fully either, for the same reasons. But, moved by them, their meaning didn't matter. Their music stirred my soul. This was dramatic lyric, the highest form of poetry, of art, of human expression.

With study, Hopkins's challenging craft clarified. This gave me the added enjoyment of his word jamming and line enjambment. It evoked Anglo-Saxon and Gaelic poetry and the English of Dylan Thomas's poems. What Hopkins called 'inscape', Dedalus–Joyce called the whatness or thingness of things. Like him, Hopkins's method was implosive, to effect an explosive revelation or meaning. This connected for me with Joyce's concept and method of verbal epiphany and situation epiphany, the whatness of words and state of things. Also, Hopkins's, still jumpy to me, 'sprung-rhythm' and pauses or stops evoked associations with classical music, bell ringing, jazz, while his 'inscape' connected with the Cubism of Picasso — all of which I was discovering, adolescently becoming aware of joyfully together with my secret, spiritual selfness. In class Mr Thomas Cole asked: 'Which is more important in a poem: what the poet says or how he says it?' What was said often sounded mundane or incomprehensible to me. How it was said often expanded my awareness of things and situations. How Hopkins had made 'The Windhover' hit me between the eyes as new, daring, modern, exciting. Yet its basic form was the sonnet, its techniques classical. For me 'The Windhover' was Hopkins's epiphany of himself as person, priest, poet momentarily aware of God's divine nature, of his own human nature, of his spiritual, aesthetic and creative self who, like the hawk momentarily hovering before he whistles down the wind, may pounce on his prey of chosen words that will give expression to that self-awareness in a poem which is his prayer for strength to 'rebuff the big wind' of life's gusts of doubt and despair. This 'happening', 'inscape', 'epiphany' reveals God to Hopkins in all creation, from the poised, wingspread kestrel, symbol of the God of peace, to Hopkins himself as priest wingspread between hope and despair, by way of God–Man–Lord Christ between life and death, vocation and revelation, on the cross and back to the mundane reality of the hawk that is the inscape of the priest and poet's epiphany. The poem is Hopkins's exalting prayer to his lord-God in celebration of life and the joyous living of it. Similar experiences had come to my adolescent self on long cross-country walks and religious retreats at boarding school.

As a teenager, this was my start at enjoying poetry. It refocused the world around me forever. It stimulated my own first verses. Today, Hopkins was sixteen years dead at my age now and I haven't grown wings strong enough for flight yet, never mind windhovering.

Desmond O'Grady

The Windhover

To Christ our Lord

I caught this morning morning's minion, kingdom of daylight's
    dauphin, dapple-dawn-drawn Falcon, in his riding
  Of the rolling level underneath him steady air, and striding
High there, how he rung upon the rein of a wimpling wing
In his ecstasy! then off, off forth on swing,
    As a skate's heel sweeps smooth on a bow-bend: the hurl
      and gliding
  Rebuffed the big wind. My heart in hiding
Stirred for a bird, — the achieve of, the mastery of the thing!

Brute beauty and valour and act, oh, air, pride, plume, here
    Buckle! AND the fire that breaks from thee then, a billion
Times told lovelier, more dangerous, O my chevalier!

    No wonder of it: shéer plód makes plough down sillion
Shine, and blue-bleak embers, ah my dear,
    Fall, gall themselves, and gash gold-vermilion.

Gerard Manley Hopkins (1844–1889)

['The Windhover' was chosen by Joe Duffy in *Lifelines 2*.]

One of my own favourite poems is 'Professor Kelleher and the Charles River'. *It was written during the winter of 1963–64 while I was studying Celtic and Irish literature at Harvard University. It is a simple poem at first reading. On the naturalistic level a professor and a student are walking and talking on the banks of the Charles River in Cambridge, New England. It is springtime's beginning. The professor talks of the past. The student listens and is reminded of childhood walks on the Shannon river in Ireland with an uncle who told him stories of the past. This touches the poet in the student who subconsciously becomes aware of the, like the river, flowing past of time, of the seasons changing, now out of winter into spring. This is all written in six six-line stanzas with a flexible five beat rhythm and a fixed rhyme scheme — except in the last stanza where one rhyme is broken.*

On the social level we have an Irish-American professor of Harvard and an Irish-European student of his who is also a poet. In age they span two generations of Irish in America from the labouring Irish emigrants that produced the professor to the new Irish academic emigrants that the student–poet represents and both at the most prestigious university in America. With names like Kelleher and O'Grady they are Irish Catholic. They pass the graveyard of Protestant New Englanders. The poet is reminded of his father rowing on the Shannon river and he thinks of the ploughman brother across the Atlantic common to both poet and professor.

On the historic level both professor and student–poet embody the history of Irish Catholic emigration and the history of Irish culture in Europe and America.

On the symbolic level the two rivers generally and the Charles in particular evoke the passing of time and life; the spring brings new life and flow; the Atlantic receives both rivers and continues to erode the coasts of both continents. At this point we reach the mythic level, where the young poet–student, with this poem forming in his mind, and the ageing professor with the past in his, begin their ageless struggle of dying and bearing. Here too the struggle between the Classic and the Romantic, the Apollonian and Dionysian begins like some ancient dance. Out of this emerges the deliberate echo of Yeats's lines as he must, with the professor, give ground to the new academic and poetic generation being born this spring in this poem. Mythically, behind all this emerges the foundation of the poem which is the underlying theme of the Oresteia of Greek myth and Aeschylus's tragic trilogy. The poet student acknowledges the past and Yeats but is looking up-river to the birth of a new life and order in the future generations who will be the lights of a new awareness and order. This is the pyramidal base of the poem in western cultural history from where the reader looks up through the peak of the pyramid which is the epiphanic moment of a teacher and student walking and talking.

Writing this poem helped me to manage more matter than I had in previous poems. Without this step I would never have begun The Dying Gaul *that autumn in Rome.*

Professor Kelleher and the Charles River

The Charles river reaps here like a sickle. April
Light sweeps flat as ice on the inner curve
Of the living water. Overhead, far from the wave, a dove
White gull heads inland. The spring air, still
Lean from winter, thaws. Walking, John
Kelleher and I talk on the civic lawn.

West, to our left, past some trees, over the ivy walls,
The clock towers, pinnacles, the pillared university yard,
The Protestant past of Cambridge New England
    selfconsciously dead
In the thawing clay of the Old Burying Ground. Miles
East, over the godless Atlantic, our common brother,
Ploughing his myth-muddy fields, embodies our order.

But here, while the students row by eights and fours on the
    river —
As my father used to row on the Shannon when, still a child,
I'd cross Thomond Bridge every Sunday, my back to the walled
And turreted castle, listening to that uncle Mykie deliver
His version of history — I listen now to John Kelleher
Unravel the past a short generation later.

Down at the green bank's nerve ends, its roots half in the river,
A leafing tree gathers refuse. The secret force
Of the water worries away the live earth's under-surface.
But his words, for the moment, hold back time's being's destroyer
While the falling wave on both thighs of the ocean
Erodes the coast, at its dying conceptual motion.

Two men, one young, one old, stand stopped acrobats in the blue
Day, their bitch river to heel. Beyond,
Some scraper, tower or ancestral house's gable end.
Then, helplessly, as in some ancient dance, the two
Begin their ageless struggle, while the tree's shadow
With all its arms, crawls on the offal-strewn meadow.

Locked in their mute struggle there by the blood-loosed tide
The two abjure all innocence, tear down past order —
The one calm, dispassionate, clearsighted, the other
Wild with ecstasy, intoxicated, world mad.
Surely some new order is at hand;
Some new form emerging where they stand.

Dusk. The great dim tide of shadows from the past
Gathers for the end — the living and the dead.
All force is fruitful. All opposing powers combine.
Aristocratic privilege, divine sanction, anarchy at last
Yield the new order. The saffron sun sets.
All shadows procession in an acropolis of lights.

Desmond O'Grady (b.1935)

A N WILSON

Dear Ralph Croly, Caroline Dowling, Gareth McCluskey,

It would not be possible to select one favourite poem from the many which have been read and committed to memory and become part of the inner life. Thomas Hardy's 'God's Funeral' confronts the strange phenomenon of nineteenth-century unbelief. God's absence and death were key 'events' in the development of the human consciousness. Many, as in Hardy's poem, do not believe they happened — 'still he lives for us!' Hardy writes from the point of view of one who sympathized with these believers, having been one himself. In spite of its provocative title, it is a stately, dream-like (almost cinematic) poem which is more visionary than polemic. It encapsulates a particular moment in the collective consciousness; and the date at the end — 1908–10 — is a crucial part of it.

A N Wilson

God's Funeral

I
I saw a slowly-stepping train —
Lined on the brows, scoop-eyed and bent and hoar —
Following in files across a twilit plain
A strange and mystic form the foremost bore.

II
And by contagious throbs of thought
Or latent knowledge that within me lay
And had already stirred me, I was wrought
To consciousness of sorrow even as they.

III
The fore-borne shape, to my blurred eyes,
At first seemed man-like, and anon to change
To an amorphous cloud of marvellous size,
At times endowed with wings of glorious range

IV
And this phantasmal variousness
Ever possessed it as they drew along:
Yet throughout all it symboled none the less
Potency vast and loving-kindness strong.

V
Almost before I knew I bent
Towards the moving columns without a word;
They, growing in bulk and numbers as they went,
Struck out sick thoughts that could be overheard: —

VI
'O man-projected Figure, of late
Imaged as we, thy knell who shall survive?
Whence came it we were tempted to create
One whom we can no longer keep alive?

VII
'Framing him jealous, fierce, at first,
We gave him justice as the ages rolled,
Will to bless those by circumstance accurst,
And longsuffering, and mercies manifold.

VIII
'And, tricked by our own early dream
And need of solace, we grew self-deceived,
Our making soon our maker did we deem,
And what we had imagined we believed.

IX

'Till, in Time's stayless stealthy swing,
Uncompromising rude reality
Mangled the Monarch of our fashioning,
Who quavered, sank; and now has ceased to be.

X

'So, toward our myth's oblivion,
Darkling, and languid-lipped, we creep and grope
Sadlier than those who wept in Babylon,
Whose Zion was a still abiding hope.

XI

'How sweet it was in years far hied
To start the wheels of day with trustful prayer,
To lie down liegely at the eventide
And feel a blest assurance he was there!

XII

'And who or what shall fill his place?
Whither will wanderers turn distracted eyes
For some fixed star to stimulate their pace
Towards the goal of their enterprise?' . . .

XIII

Some in the background then I saw,
Sweet women, youths, men, all incredulous,
Who chimed: 'This is a counterfeit of straw,
This requiem mockery! Still he lives to us!'

XIV

I could not buoy their faith: and yet
Many I had known: with all I sympathized;
And though struck speechless, I did not forget
That what was mourned for, I, too, long had prized.

XV

Still, how to bear such loss I deemed
The insistent question for each animate mind,
And gazing, to my growing sight there seemed
A pale yet positive gleam low down behind,

XVI

Whereof, to lift the general night,
A certain few who stood aloof had said,
'See you upon the horizon that small light —
Swelling somewhat?' Each mourner shook his head.

XVII
And they composed a crowd of whom
Some were right good, and many nigh the best . . .
Thus dazed and puzzled 'twixt the gleam and gloom
Mechanically I followed with the rest.

1908–10
Thomas Hardy (1840–1928)

PAT BORAN 516

10 January 1997

Dear Caroline, Ralph and Gareth,

Many thanks for your invitation to nominate a poem for inclusion in Lifelines 3. The previous anthologies have done a great deal for the Third World through the raising of much-needed funds and, perhaps as importantly, awareness. They have also, of course, done much for poetry.

The task of deciding on a single *favourite poem I found almost impossible, though it seemed important that it should be something from our own century, if only to prove that poetry is not something that happened only in the distant past, something made exclusively by men with cardigans, butterfly nets and generous patrons. Still, how to choose from among Robert Frost's 'Birches', Wislawa Szymborska's 'Lot's Wife', Yehuda Amichai's 'A Song of Lies on Sabbath Eve', Charles Simic's 'Bestiary for the Fingers of My Right Hand' . . . ? In the end, however, I suppose I knew it had to be 'The Seventh' by the Hungarian poet Attila József, a poem which over the last year or so I have found myself reading almost every night in bed and consulting in my inside breast pocket up mountains, on trains, in Social Welfare queues. It's only a few poems I have ever felt the need to carry with me, the way some people carry watches, rosary beads or lipstick. This is the one at the moment, so I suppose that makes it my favourite.*

I hope your many readers enjoy it as much as I continue to do, and I wish you the very best with the anthology.

Sincerely,
Pat Boran

The Seventh

If you set out in this world,
better be born seven times.
Once, in a house on fire,
once, in a freezing flood,
once, in a wild madhouse,
once, in a field of ripe wheat,
once, in an empty cloister,
and once among pigs in a sty.
Six babes crying, not enough:
you yourself must be the seventh.

When you must fight to survive,
let your enemy see seven.
One, away from work on Sunday,
one, starting his work on Monday,
one, who teaches without payment,
one, who learned to swim by drowning,
one, who is the seed of a forest,
and one, whom wild forefathers protect,
but all their tricks are not enough:
you yourself must be the seventh.

If you want to find a woman,
let seven men go for her.
One, who gives his heart for words,
one, who takes care of himself,
one, who claims to be a dreamer,
one, who through her skirt can feel her,
one, who knows the hooks and snaps,
one, who steps upon her scarf:
let them buzz like flies around her.
You yourself must be the seventh.

If you write and can afford it,
let seven men write your poem.
One, who builds a marble village,
one, who was born in his sleep,
one, who charts the sky and knows it,
one, whom words call by his name,
one, who perfected his soul,
one, who dissects living rats.
Two are brave and four are wise;
you yourself must be the seventh.

And if all went as was written,
you will die for seven men.
One, who is rocked and suckled,
one, who grabs a hard young breast,
one, who throws down empty dishes,
one, who helps the poor to win,
one, who works till he goes to pieces,
one, who just stares at the moon.
The world will be your tombstone:
you yourself must be the seventh.

Attila József (1905–1937)
Translated by John Batki

MICHAEL MORTELL

President's Office
University College Cork
4 February 1997

Thank you for your invitation to submit a 'favourite' poem. Please find enclosed a poem by John Hewitt.

Best wishes for the forthcoming publication,
Michael P Mortell

After the Fire

After a night when sky was lit with fire,
we wandered down familiar Agnes Street,
and at each side street corner we would meet
the frequent public houses, each a pyre
of smoking rafters, charred, the floors a mass
of smouldering debris, sideboard, table, bed,
smashed counters, empty bottles, shards of glass,
the Catholic landlord and his family fled.

I walked that day with Willie Morrisey;
while I still feared all priests he was my friend.
Though clearly in the wrong, I would defend
his right to his own dark mythology.
You must give freedom if you would be free,
for only friendship matters in the end.

John Hewitt (1907–1987)

TIM ROBINSON 518

7 February 1997

Dear Ralph, Caroline and Gareth,

Here's a suggestion for Lifelines 3; *I hope you haven't had this one already, though it wouldn't surprise me if you had.*

A Ship, an Isle, a Sickle Moon

A ship, an isle, a sickle moon —
With few but with how splendid stars
The mirrors of the sea are strewn
Between their silver bars!

An isle beside an isle she lay,
The pale ship anchored in the bay,
While in the young moon's port of gold
A star-ship — as the mirrors told —
Put forth its great and lonely light
To the unreflecting Ocean, Night.
And still, a ship upon her seas,
The isle and the island cypresses
Went sailing on without the gale:
And still there moved the moon so pale,
A crescent ship without a sail!

James Elroy Flecker (1884–1915)

My earliest poetic excitement, lastingly imprinting the spell of islands, voyaging, night skies and mirrors. Perhaps though, when I discovered it in my teens, I did not note its unsettling insinuation, that islands and therefore all ground, the moon and therefore the earth, poetry and therefore life itself, are adrift on an 'unreflecting' ocean.

With best wishes for your excellent project,
Tim Robinson

PAULINE McLYNN 519

Dear All,

Enclosed is a poem for inclusion in Lifelines 3, *and a little piece as to why. If it has been done before (it hasn't has it?), please let me know and I'll find another.*

Good luck with the venture,
Pauline McLynn

A lot of my favourite poems have already been covered in the previous two volumes in this series. But here's one from Michael Gorman that I love. Like me, he was born in Sligo and has lived in Galway (I grew up there). And I had the pleasure of hearing him read this aloud in 1984 at the launch of his book, Waiting for the Sky to Fall. *To me it describes an Ireland that we're leaving behind as we approach the 21st century, and that we are leaving it is no harm, I think. And it reminds me in a bitter-sweet way of my childhood and especially summers spent in Sligo.*

The People I Grew Up With Were Afraid

The people I grew up with were afraid.
They were alone too long in waiting-rooms,
in dispensaries and in offices whose functions
they did not understand.

To buck themselves up, they thought
of lost causes, of 'Nature-boy'
O'Dea who tried to fly
from his bedroom window;
of the hunch-backed, little typist
who went roller-skating at Strandhill.
Or, they re-lived the last afternoon
of Benny Kirwin, pale, bald,
Protestant shop-assistant in Lyons' drapery.
One Wednesday, the town's half-day,
he hanged himself from a tree
on the shore at Lough Gill.

And what were they afraid of? Rent
collectors, rate collectors, insurance men.
Things to do with money. But,
especially of their vengeful God.
On her death-bed, Ena Phelan prayed
that her son would cut his hair.

Sometimes, they return to me,
Summer lunchtimes, colcannon
for the boys, back-doors
of all the houses open, the
news blaring on the radios.
Our mother's factory pay-packet
is sitting in the kitchen press
and our father, without
humour or relief, is
waiting for the sky to fall.

Michael Gorman (b.1952)

MARY ROSE BINCHY — 520

27 January 1997

Dear Ralph, Caroline and Gareth,

Thank you so much for your letter. How on earth do I choose a favourite poem? I don't think that I have ever thought of any one poem as being my absolute favourite but I do feel that certain poems meet particular needs at different times.

Louise Glück is a poet who takes my breath away and never more so than in her poem 'The White Lilies' (from The Wild Iris, *The Ecco Press, 1992), which is at once exquisitely and painfully beautiful.*

I do not know how to put into my words why this poem has such poignant meaning for me except to say that I find its imagery intensely powerful and that I am overwhelmed by its ultimate sense of peace and healing.

I hope that you and your readers will enjoy it too.

With every good wish for Lifelines 3 — *I am honoured to be a contributor.*

Mary Rose Binchy

The White Lilies

As a man and woman make
a garden between them like
a bed of stars, here
they linger in the summer evening
and the evening turns
cold with their terror: it
could all end, it is capable
of devastation. All, all
can be lost, through scented air
the narrow columns
uselessly rising, and beyond,
a churning sea of poppies —

Hush, beloved. It doesn't matter to me
How many summers I live to return:
this one summer we have entered eternity.
I felt your two hands
bury me to release its splendor.

Louise Glück (b.1943)

MELANIE RAE THON 521

Dear Ralph Croly, Caroline Dowling and Gareth McCluskey,

I am delighted to support your project and hope that this edition of Lifelines *is even more successful than previous editions. I have no single favorite poem — there are so many I love and admire. But I offer this one because it is both simple and eloquent.*

Poem

The only response
to a child's grave is
to lie down before it and play dead

Saint Geraud (b.1940)
[Bill Knott]

I love this poem because I believe there are times when words fail us, when the only way to show our grief and compassion is through a single gesture. We would play with a living child, but we can only play dead with a dead child. All our words of futile explanation, all our prayers, all our rituals might seem cluttered and incomprehensible to a child, but the simplicity of this act — lying down before the grave — will be perfectly understood. In the physical grace of the gesture we may find spiritual comfort.

Thank you for thinking of me. I send my good wishes.

Melanie Rae Thon

MICHAEL SMURFIT 522

10 February 1997

In my view, 'The Ballad of Reading Gaol' is Oscar Wilde's finest poetic piece. It captures perfectly the intense sadness of man facing certain death, the loneliness of a condemned prisoner, and the pitiful self interest of fellow inmates — yet their profound heartfelt sympathy for him.

It is a sad and deeply moving poem which I always enjoy returning to. It helps put a perspective on those things in life which we feel are so important but are not really so.

Michael W J Smurfit

from *The Ballad of Reading Gaol*

IV

There is no chapel on the day
   On which they hang a man:
The Chaplain's heart is far too sick,
   Or his face is far too wan,
Or there is that written in his eyes
   Which none should look upon.

So they kept us close till nigh on noon,
   And then they rang the bell,
And the warders with their jingling keys
   Opened each listening cell,
And down the iron stair we tramped,
   Each from his separate Hell.

Out into God's sweet air we went,
   But not in wonted way,
For this man's face was white with fear,
   And this man's face was grey,
And I never saw sad men who looked
   So wistfully at the day.

I never saw sad men who looked
   With such a wistful eye
Upon the little tent of blue
   We prisoners called the sky,
And at every happy cloud that passed
   In such strange freedom by.

But there were those amongst us all
   Who walked with downcast head,
And knew that, had each got his due,
   They should have died instead:
He had but killed a thing that lived,
   Whilst they had killed the dead.

For he who sins a second time
   Wakes a dead soul to pain,
And draws it from its spotted shroud,
   And makes it bleed again,
And makes it bleed great gouts of blood,
   And makes it bleed in vain!

            *

Like ape or clown, in monstrous garb
   With crooked arrows starred,
Silently we went round and round,
   The slippery asphalt yard;
Silently we went round and round,
   And no man spoke a word.

Silently we went round and round,
    And through each hollow mind
The Memory of dreadful things
    Rushed like a dreadful wind,
And Horror stalked before each man,
    And Terror crept behind.

        *

The warders strutted up and down,
    And watched their herd of brutes,
Their uniforms were spick and span,
    And they wore their Sunday suits,
But we knew the work they had been at
    By the quicklime on their boots.

For where a grave had opened wide,
    There was no grave at all:
Only a stretch of mud and sand
    By the hideous prison-wall,
And a little heap of burning lime,
    That the man should have his pall.

For he has a pall, this wretched man,
    Such as few men can claim:
Deep down below a prison-yard,
    Naked for greater shame,
He lies, with fetters on each foot,
    Wrapt in a sheet of flame!

And all the while the burning lime
    Eats flesh and bone away,
It eats the brittle bone by night,
    And the soft flesh by day,
It eats the flesh and bone by turns,
    But it eats the heart alway.

        *

For three long years they will not sow
    Or root or seedling there:
For three long years the unblessed spot
    Will sterile be and bare,
And look upon the wondering sky
    With unreproachful stare.

They think a murderer's heart would taint
    Each simple seed they sow.
It is not true! God's kindly earth
    Is kindlier than men know,
And the red rose would not blow more red,
    The white rose whiter blow.

Out of his mouth a red, red rose!
   Out of his heart a white!
For who can say by what strange way,
   Christ brings His will to light,
Since the barren staff the pilgrim bore
   Bloomed in the great Pope's sight?

But neither milk-white rose nor red
   May bloom in prison-air;
The shard, the pebble, and the flint,
   Are what they give us there:
For flowers have been known to heal
   A common man's despair.

So never will wine-red rose or white,
   Petal by petal, fall
On that stretch of mud and sand that lies
   By the hideous prison wall,
To tell the men who tramp the yard
   That God's Son died for all.

*

Yet though the hideous prison-wall
   Still hems him round and round,
And a spirit may not walk by night
   That is with fetters bound,
And a spirit may but weep that lies
   In such unholy ground.

He is at peace — this wretched man —
   At peace, or will be soon:
There is no thing to make him mad,
   Nor does Terror walk at noon,
For the lampless Earth in which he lies
   Has neither Sun nor Moon.

They hanged him as a beast is hanged:
   They did not even toll
A requiem that might have brought
   Rest to his startled soul,
But hurriedly they took him out,
   And hid him in a hole.

They warders stripped him of his clothes,
   And gave him to the flies:
They mocked the swollen purple throat,
   And the stark and staring eyes:
And with laughter loud they heaped the shroud
   In which the convict lies.

The Chaplain would not kneel to pray
   By his dishonoured grave:
Nor mark it with that blessed Cross
   That Christ for sinners gave,
Because the man was one of those
   Whom Christ came down to save.

Yet all is well; he has but passed
   To Life's appointed bourne:
And alien tears will fill for him
   Pity's long-broken urn,
For his mourners will be outcast men,
   And outcasts always mourn.

Oscar Wilde (1854–1900)

['The Ballad of Reading Gaol' was Michele Souter's choice in *Lifelines*.]

SUSAN WICKS   523

27 January 1997

Dear Ralph, Caroline and Gareth,

Many thanks for asking me to contribute my favourite poem to Lifelines 3. I feel privileged to be involved in such a worthwhile project — one I'm familiar with, as I was given the first Lifelines *as a present some time ago. Apologies for the delay, but your request came at a very busy time for me, and I have since had flu.*

It seems to me we can all love many poems in many different ways. My first enthusiasms were all for poems written in French, but after those, I think I have to go for 'Candlelight' by Sylvia Plath. I first read Plath properly about eight years ago, when I was running a small educational guidance office and the Faber Collected somehow, incongruously, found itself on my shelves among the prospectuses and directories. Sometimes, during a lonely three-hour night session, Plath's was the only voice to ask me a question I felt I might begin to try to answer . . .

I love many things about this poem — its control and formal complexity, its unsentimental presentation of the intimate connection between mother and child — but, above all, that odd mixture of lyricism and irony that still carries an echo of something unresolved and unresolvable. When I left that office, I was tempted to steal the book. I didn't. I put it back neatly among the files of information. But some of those poems stayed with me anyway as I walked home in the dark.

With best wishes,
Susan Wicks

By Candlelight

This is winter, this is night, small love —
A sort of black horsehair,
A rough, dumb country stuff
Steeled with the sheen
Of what green stars can make it to our gate.
I hold you on my arm.
It is very late.
The dull bells tongue the hour.
The mirror floats us at one candle power.

This is the fluid in which we meet each other,
This haloey radiance that seems to breathe
And lets our shadows wither
Only to blow
Them huge again, violent giants on the wall.
One match scratch makes you real.
At first the candle will not bloom at all —
It snuffs its bud
To almost nothing, to a dull blue dud.

I hold my breath until you creak to life,
Balled hedgehog,
Small and cross. The yellow knife
Grows tall. You clutch your bars.
My singing makes you roar.
I rock you like a boat
Across the Indian carpet, the cold floor,
While the brass man
Kneels, back bent, as best he can

Hefting his white pillar with the light
That keeps the sky at bay,
The sack of black! It is everywhere, tight, tight!
He is yours, the little brassy Atlas —
Poor heirloom, all you have,
At his heels a pile of five brass cannonballs,
No child, no wife.
Five balls! Five bright brass balls!
To juggle with, my love, when the sky falls.

Sylvia Plath (1932–1963)

WILL SELF 524

21 January 1997

Please find attached my favourite poem, by Theodore Roethke. Best of luck with your project,

Will Self

I Knew a Woman

I knew a woman, lovely in her bones,
When small birds sighed, she would sigh back at them;
Ah, when she moved, she moved more ways than one:
The shapes a bright container can contain!
Of her choice virtues only gods should speak,
Or English poets who grew up on Greek
(I'd have them sing in chorus, cheek to cheek).

How well her wishes went! She stroked my chin,
She taught me Turn, and Counter-turn, and Stand;
She taught me Touch, that undulant white skin;
I nibbled meekly from her proffered hand;
She was the sickle; I, poor I, the rake,
Coming behind her for her pretty sake
(But what prodigious mowing we did make).

Love likes a gander, and adores a goose:
Her full lips pursed, the errant note to seize;
She played it quick, she played it light and loose;
My eyes, they dazzled at her flowing knees;
Her several parts could keep a pure repose,
Or one hip quiver with a mobile nose
(She moved in circles, and those circles moved).

Let seed be grass, and grass turn into hay:
I'm martyr to a motion not my own;
What's freedom for? To know eternity.
I swear she cast a shadow white as stone.
But who would count eternity in days?
These old bones live to learn her wanton ways:
(I measure time by how a body sways).

Theodore Roethke (1908–1963)

MARY RYAN   525

3 February 1997

Dear Ralph, Caroline and Gareth,

Thank you for writing to me.

I love so many poems that it is difficult to nominate a favourite. However, one poem which has haunted me since my teens is 'The Rubáiyát of Omar Khayyám' (as rendered into English by Edward FitzGerald).

I love it for its power and its music, and because Khayyám, the twelfth-century Persian poet, astronomer and mathematician, defied dogma.

As it is a very long poem the verses given here are only a portion of the whole.

Good luck with your endeavour. I very much enjoyed the earlier Lifelines *and the gems therein.*

Mary Ryan

from *The Rubáiyát of Omar Khayyám*

I must abjure the Balm of Life, I must,
Scared by some After-reckoning, ta'en on trust,
Or lured with Hope of some Diviner Drink,
To fill the Cup — when crumbled into Dust!

Oh threats of Hell and Hopes of Paradise!
One thing at least is certain — *This* Life flies;
One thing is certain and the rest is Lies;
The Flower that once has blown forever dies.

Strange, is it not? that of the myriads who
Before us pass'd the door of Darkness through,
Not one returns to tell us of the Road,
Which to discover we must travel too.

The Revelations of Devout and Learn'd
Who rose before us and as Prophets burn'd,
Are all but Stories, which, awoke from Sleep
They told their comrades and to Sleep return'd.

I sent my Soul through the Invisible,
Some letter of that After-life to spell;
And by and by my Soul return'd to me,
And answered 'I Myself am Heav'n and Hell':

Heav'n but the vision of fulfilled Desire,
And Hell the Shadow from a Soul on fire,
Cast on the Darkness into which Ourselves,
So late emerged from, shall so soon expire.

We are no other than a moving row
Of Magic Shadow-shapes that come and go
Round with the Sun-illumined Lantern held
In Midnight by the Master of the Show;

But helpless Pieces of the Game He plays
Upon this Chequer-board of Nights and Days;
Hither and thither moves, and checks, and slays,
And one by one back in the Closet lays.

Omar Khayyám (?1048–1122)
Translated by Edward FitzGerald (1809–1883)

AENGUS FINUCANE 526

Concern
Dublin 2
26 February 1997

Dear Ralph, Caroline and Gareth,

I am delighted that you are continuing the Wesley Lifelines *tradition and that you again do so with a caring eye on the needs of the Third World.*

I am pleased to be invited to name my favourite poem. I love poetry. Much of that I attribute to the headmaster of the Model School in Limerick who taught me when I was ten years old. He was a gentle giant who could be quite severe. My favourite poem is Goldsmith's 'The Village Schoolmaster'.

Because 'The Village Schoolmaster' featured in an earlier Lifelines, *I was tempted to name another of my 'favourites'. But 'The Village Schoolmaster' prevailed. The choice was copper-fastened by the recent death of a friend, who for forty years was schoolmaster in Knockea, a village in County Limerick. I recited this poem as a tribute to him when he was in his eighties.*

My preference is for people centred poems. My schoolmasters live in Goldsmith's lines. This poem says so much, so beautifully.

Best wishes,
Sincerely,
Aengus Finucane
Chief Executive

from *The Deserted Village*

Beside yon straggling fence that skirts the way,
With blossomed furze unprofitably gay,
There, in his noisy mansion, skill'd to rule,
The village master taught his little school;
A man severe he was, and stern to view,
I knew him well, and every truant knew;
Well had the boding tremblers learned to trace
The day's disasters in his morning face;
Full well they laugh'd, with counterfeited glee,
At all his jokes, for many a joke had he;
Full well the busy whisper circling round,
Conveyed the dismal tidings when he frowned;
Yet he was kind, or if severe in aught,
The love he bore to learning was in fault;
The village all declared how much he knew;
'Twas certain he could write and cypher too;
Lands he could measure, terms and tides presage,
And even the story ran that he could gauge.
In arguing too, the parson owned his skill,
For e'en tho' vanquished, he could argue still;
While words of learned length and thundering sound,
Amazed the gazing rustics ranged around,
And still they gazed, and still the wonder grew,
That one small head could carry all he knew.

But past is all his fame. The very spot
Where many a time he triumphed, is forgot.

Oliver Goldsmith (?1730–1774)

[This excerpt from 'The Deserted Village' was chosen by Jimmy Magee in *Lifelines*.]

MARTIN DRURY

The Ark, A Cultural Centre for Children,
Temple Bar
28 January 1997

Dear Ralph, Caroline and Gareth,

Thank you for your letter inviting me to contribute to Lifelines 3. *I am delighted to be asked as I have enjoyed the previous books immensely and consider it a wonderful project.*

The problem now of course is that the previous books contain many dozens of 'my favourite poems'. However, that fact liberates me to propose a poem I like a great deal: 'Though There Are Torturers' *by Michael Coady.*

This is one of those poems that has lodged for years in the recesses of my mind, surfacing occasionally and with such a quiet insistence that I have realised it matters to me. Apart from its craft, I choose it for its values: I think that the dark side of humanity is so evident in contemporary life that we need to remember that our nature is also distinguished by capacities and dispositions which are joyful and graceful.

With renewed thanks and best wishes for another successful Lifelines,

Yours sincerely,
Martin Drury
Director

Though There Are Torturers

Though there are torturers in the world
There are also musicians.

Though, at this moment, men
Are screaming in prisons
There are jazzmen raising storms
Of sensuous celebration
And orchestras releasing
Glories of the spirit.

Though the image of God
Is everywhere defiled
A man in West Clare
Is playing the concertina,
The Sistine Choir is levitating
Under the dome of St Peter's
And a drunk man on the road
Is singing for no reason.

Michael Coady (b.1939)

ROBERT AYLING

British Airways
Heathrow Airport
3 March 1997

Dear Ralph, Caroline and Gareth,

Many thanks for your letter. I am not sure that I could tell you which of the many poems I have enjoyed is my favourite. When I was young it used to be Gray's 'Elegy in a Country Churchyard'*, but I think I have moved on a bit since that. I recently very much enjoyed Seamus*

Heaney's 'The Flight Path'. Why? Because it is a poem which contains allusions to flying, which conjures up such marvellous mental images and which is so clever with the association of one idea with another.

Yours sincerely,
Robert Ayling
Chief Executive

The Flight Path

1
The first fold first, then more foldovers drawn
Tighter and neater every time until
The whole of the paper got itself reduced
To a pleated square he'd take up by two corners,
Then hold like a promise he had the power to break
But never did.
           A dove rose in my breast
Every time my father's hands came clean
With a paper boat between them, ark in air,
The lines of it as taut as a pegged tent:
High-sterned, splay-bottomed, the little pyramid
At the centre every bit as hollow
As a part of me that sank because it knew
The whole thing would go soggy once you launched it.

2
Equal and opposite, the part that lifts
Into those *full-starred heavens that winter sees*
When I stand in Wicklow under the flight path
Of a late jet out of Dublin, its risen light
Winking ahead of what it hauls away:
Heavy engine noise and its abatement
Widening far back down, a wake through starlight.

The sycamore speaks in sycamore from darkness,
The light behind my shoulder's cottage lamplight.
I'm in the doorway early in the night,
Standing-in in myself for all of those
The stance perpetuates: the stay-at-homes
Who leant against the jamb and watched and waited,
The ones we learned to love by waving back at
Or coming towards again in different clothes
They were slightly shy of.
                    Who never once forgot
A name or a face, nor looked down suddenly
As the plane was reaching cruising altitude
To realise that the house they'd just passed over —
Too far back now to see — was the same house
They'd left an hour before, still kissing, kissing,
As the taxi driver loaded up the cases.

3
Up and away. The buzz from duty free.
Black Velvet. Bourbon. Love letters on high.
The spacewalk of Manhattan. The re-entry.

Then California. Laid-back Tiburon.
Burgers at Sam's, deck-tables and champagne,
Plus a wall-eyed, hard-baked seagull looking on.

Again re-entry. Vows revowed. And off —
Reculer pour sauter, within one year of
Coming back, less long goodbye than stand-off.

So to Glanmore. Glanmore. Glanmore. Glanmore.
At bay, at one, at work, at risk and sure.
Covert and pad. Oak, bay and sycamore.

Jet-sitting next. Across and across and across.
Westering, eastering, the jumbo a school bus,
'The Yard' a cross between the farm and campus,

A holding pattern and a tautening purchase —
Sweeney astray in home truths out of Horace:
Skies change, not cares, for those who cross the seas.

4
The following for the record, in the light
Of everything before and since:
One bright May morning, nineteen-seventy-nine,
Just off the red-eye special from New York,
I'm on the train for Belfast. Plain, simple
Exhilaration at being back: the sea
At Skerries, the nuptial hawthorn bloom,
The trip north taking sweet hold like a chain
On every bodily sprocket.
                       Enter then —
As if he were some *film noir* border guard —
Enter this one I'd last met in a dream,
More grimfaced now than in the dream itself
When he'd flagged me down at the side of a mountain road,
Come up and leant his elbow on the roof
And explained through the open window of the car
That all I'd have to do was drive a van
Carefully in to the next customs post
At Pettigo, switch off, get out as if
I were on my way with dockets to the office —
But then instead I'd walk ten yards more down
Towards the main street and get in with — here
Another schoolfriend's name, a wink and smile,
I'd know him all right, he'd be in a Ford
And I'd be home in three hours' time, as safe
As houses . . .

So he enters and sits down
Opposite and goes for me head on.
'When, for fuck's sake, are you going to write
Something for us?' 'If I do write something,
Whatever it is, I'll be writing for myself.'
And that was that. Or words to that effect.

The gaol walls all those months were smeared with shite.
Out of Long Kesh after his dirty protest
The red eyes were the eyes of Ciaran Nugent
Like something out of Dante's scurfy hell,
Drilling their way through the rhymes and images
Where I too walked behind the righteous Virgil,
As safe as houses and translating freely:
When he had said all this, his eyes rolled
And his teeth, like a dog's teeth clamping round a bone,
Bit into the skull and again took hold.

5
When I answered that I came from 'far away',
The policeman at the roadblock snapped, 'Where's that?'
He'd only half-heard what I said and thought
It was the name of some place up the country.

And now it is — both where I have been living
And where I left — a distance still to go
Like starlight that is light years on the go
From far away and takes light years arriving.

6
Out of the blue then, the sheer exaltation
Of remembering climbing zig-zag up warm steps
To the hermit's eyrie above Rocamadour.
Crows sailing high and close, a lizard pulsing
On gravel at my feet, its front legs set
Like the jointed front struts of a moon vehicle.
And bigly, softly as the breath of life
In a breath of air, a lime-green butterfly
Crossing the pilgrims' sunstruck *via crucis*.

Eleven in the morning. I made a note:
'Rock-lover, loner, sky-sentry, all hail!'
And somewhere the dove rose. And kept on rising.

Seamus Heaney (b.1939)

TOM STOPPARD 529

A 'favourite poem' is an elusive idea — one likes different poems for different reasons at different times in different moods. But I'll nominate Larkin's 'Whitsun Weddings', which would be remarkable as descriptive prose if it were in prose, and is miraculous in its organisation as poetry; and mainly for the last two lines, most of all for the final three words which always give me a kick, after hundreds of readings (and which Kingsley Amis somewhere says are meaningless).

Tom Stoppard

The Whitsun Weddings

That Whitsun, I was late getting away:
    Not till about
One-twenty on the sunlit Saturday
Did my three-quarters-empty train pull out,
All windows down, all cushions hot, all sense
Of being in a hurry gone. We ran
Behind the backs of houses, crossed a street
Of blinding windscreens, smelt the fish-dock; thence
The river's level drifting breadth began,
Where sky and Lincolnshire and water meet.

All afternoon, through the tall heat that slept
    For miles inland,
A slow and stopping curve southwards we kept.
Wide farms went by, short-shadowed cattle, and
Canals with floatings of industrial froth;
A hothouse flashed uniquely: hedges dipped
And rose: and now and then a smell of grass
Displaced the reek of buttoned carriage-cloth
Until the next town, new and nondescript,
Approached with acres of dismantled cars.

At first, I didn't notice what a noise
    The weddings made
Each station that we stopped at: sun destroys
The interest of what's happening in the shade,
And down the long cool platforms whoops and skirls
I took for porters larking with the mails,
And went on reading. Once we started, though,
We passed them, grinning and pomaded, girls
In parodies of fashion, heels and veils,
All posed irresolutely, watching us go,

As if out on the end of an event
    Waving goodbye
To something that survived it. Struck, I leant
More promptly out next time, more curiously,
And saw it all again in different terms:
The fathers with broad belts under their suits
And seamy foreheads; mothers loud and fat;
An uncle shouting smut; and then the perms,
The nylon gloves and jewellery-substitutes,
The lemons, mauves, and olive-ochres that

Marked off the girls unreally from the rest.
    Yes, from cafés
And banquet-halls up yards, and bunting-dressed
Coach-party annexes, the wedding-days
Were coming to an end. All down the line
Fresh couples climbed aboard: the rest stood round;
The last confetti and advice were thrown,
And, as we moved, each face seemed to define
Just what it saw departing: children frowned
At something dull; fathers had never known

Success so huge and wholly farcical;
    The women shared
The secret like a happy funeral;
While girls, gripping their handbags tighter, stared
At a religious wounding. Free at last,
And loaded with the sum of all they saw,
We hurried towards London, shuffling gouts of steam.
Now fields were building-plots, and poplars cast
Long shadows over major roads, and for
Some fifty minutes, that in time would seem

Just long enough to settle hats and say
    I nearly died,
A dozen marriages got under way.
They watched the landscape, sitting side by side
— An Odeon went past, a cooling tower,
And someone running up to bowl — and none
Thought of the others they would never meet
Or how their lives would all contain this hour.
I thought of London spread out in the sun,
Its postal districts packed like squares of wheat:

There we were aimed. And as we raced across
    Bright knots of rail
Past standing Pullmans, walls of blackened moss
Came close, and it was nearly done, this frail

Travelling coincidence; and what it held
Stood ready to be loosed with all the power
That being changed can give. We slowed again,
And as the tightened brakes took hold, there swelled
A sense of falling, like an arrow-shower
Sent out of sight, somewhere becoming rain.

Philip Larkin (1922–1985)

KATY HAYES

1 February 1997

Dear Ralph, Caroline and Gareth,

Thank you for your invitation. The poem I have chosen, enclosed here in Irish and with an English translation, is 'Gan do Chuid Éadaigh' *by Nuala Ní Dhomhnaill. Poems about male beauty are so rare that, when one comes across such a delightful one as this, it has the same arresting power as beauty itself.*

Good luck with your anthology. I've read and thoroughly enjoyed the previous ones!

Yours sincerely,
Katy Hayes

P.S. The version of the poem's translation I have enclosed is by the poet herself, and I prefer it.

Gan Do Chuid Éadaigh

Is fearr liom tú
gan do chuid éadaigh ort —
do léine shíoda,
is do charabhat,
do scáth fearthainne faoi t'ascaill
is do chulaith
trí phíosa faiseanta
le barr feabhais táilliúrachta,

do bhróga ar a mbíonn
i gcónaí snas,
do láimhinní craiceann eilite
ar do bhois,
do hata crombie
feirchte ar fhaobhar na cluaise —
ní chuireann siad aon ruainne
le do thuairisc.

Mar thíos fúthu,
i ngan fhios don slua
tá corp gan mhaisle, mháchaill
ná míbhua,
lúfaireacht ainmhí allta,
cat mór a bhíonn amuigh
san oíche
is a fhágann sceimhle ina mharbhshruth.

Do ghuailne leathan fairsing
is do thaobh
chomh slím le sneachta séidte
ar an sliabh;
do dhrom, do bhásta singil
is i do ghabhal
an rúta
go bhfuil barr pléisiúrtha ann.

Do chraiceann atá chomh dorcha
is slím
le síoda go mbeadh tiumhas bheilbhite
ina shníomh
is é ar chumhracht airgid luachra
nó meadhg na habhann
go ndeirtear faoi
go bhfuil suathadh fear is ban ann.

Mar sin is dá bhrí sin
is tú ag rince liom anocht,
cé go mb'fhearr liom tú
gan do chuid éadaigh ort,
b'fhéidir nárbh aon díobháil duit
gléasadh anois ar an dtoirt
in ionad leath ban Éireann
a mhillead is a lot.

Without Your Clothes

Though I much prefer you
minus your clothes —
your silk shirt
and your tie
your umbrella tucked under the oxter
and your three-piece suit
tailored in sartorial elegance,

your shoes which always sport
a high shine
your doe-skin gloves
on your hands

your crombie hat
tipped elegantly over the ear —
none of them add
a single whit to your presence.

For underneath them
unbeknownst to all
is a peerless body
without blemish or fault
the litheness of a wild animal
a great nocturnal cat
prowling and leaving destruction
in its wake.

Your broad strong shoulders
and your skin
as smooth as windblown snow
on the mountainside
your back, your slender waist
and in your crotch
that growing root
that is pleasure's very source.

Your complexion so dark
and soft
as silk with the pile of velvet
in its weave
and smelling very much of meadowsweet
or watermead, as it is called
that they say has power
to lead men and women astray.

Therefore, and for that reason
when you go dancing with me tonight
though I would prefer you stark naked
by my side
I suppose you had better
put your clothes on
rather than have half the women of Ireland
totally undone.

Poem and translation by Nuala Ní Dhomhnaill (b.1952)

['Gan Do Chuid Éadaigh' was chosen by Katie Donovan in *Lifelines 2*.]

BRENDAN O'CARROLL 531

22 January 1997

A Chara,

Please find enclosed an original work for your anthology Lifelines 3. *I hope it is of some help to you, in what I regard as a very noble project.*

I wish you the best of success with your new project and if you think of it please send me a copy.

Yours sincerely,
Brendan O'Carroll

In Praise of Women

She utters the screech at the birth of my life,
She purrs at my infant contentment,
She sheds tears of celebration at my first steps, my first
　　achievement,
She pains for my disappointments, and,
She bears up my heart when it is too heavy for a mere man,
She is cunning enough to allow me to see her follow, as she
　　leads me,
She is selfless enough to applaud me for her strength,
She is thoughtful enough to remember every monument in my
　　life, without reference to the foundation she laid,
She is a coalminer's daughter,
She is a doctor's sister,
She is a criminal's mother,
She is a plumber's wife,
She is an admiral's mistress,
She is a journalist's niece,
She is a friend,
She is every woman I have ever known,
The most important collection of cells on this planet.

Brendan O'Carroll

TONY ROCHE 532

Department of English
University College Dublin
1 February 1997

Dear Ralph, Caroline and Gareth,

Thank you for your invitation to contribute to Lifelines 3. *I think it's an important and worthwhile project and I wish you continued success with it. I've very much enjoyed the earlier volumes, both to come upon the unknown fine poems and to see how the poetic sweepstakes (Yeats, Kavanagh, Heaney, etc.) are going.*

My favourite poet is W B Yeats. Yeats is not a directly confessional poet. The circumstances of his life which may have given rise to the poem are transformed by the act of imagination; there is always, as he says, a phantasmagoria. But Yeats carries the original emotion with him and embodies it in the poem in ways that others can share. There are many of his poems that have meant a great deal to me at various times in my life. I have chosen 'When You Are Old' for two related reasons: it was read by Anna Hayes on the occasion of my marriage to her daughter, Katy, and the seventh line speaks to what I love about my wife.

Thank you for asking me to contribute to Lifelines.

Yours sincerely,
Tony Roche
Dr Anthony Roche

When You Are Old

When you are old and grey and full of sleep,
And nodding by the fire, take down this book,
And slowly read, and dream of the soft look
Your eyes had once, and of their shadows deep;

How many loved your moments of glad grace,
And loved your beauty with love false or true,
But one man loved the pilgrim soul in you,
And loved the sorrows of your changing face;

And bending down beside the glowing bars,
Murmur, a little sadly, how Love fled
And paced upon the mountains overhead
And hid his face amid a crowd of stars.

W B Yeats (1865–1939)

FIONNUALA NÍ CHIOSÁIN 533

20 January 1997

Dear Ralph, Caroline and Gareth,

In response to your letter I send you this very short Japanese poem. I don't have a favourite poem but I suppose I could say that over the past five or six years or so my favourite type of poetry is Japanese, including traditional forms as well as contemporary work. I collect poetry volumes and keep them in the studio, referring to them often. I think the book I've looked at most since I bought it is Kenneth Rexroth's One

Hundred Poems from the Japanese, *which contains the poem I have selected, written by the poetess Ono No Kamachi (who lived from 834 to 880, and is translated here by Rexroth, the American poet). I like Japanese poetry because of its purity, intensity and concentration.*

In these compressed and controlled poems one finds a remarkable timelessness and universality.

All the best,
Fionnuala Ní Chiosáin

As certain as color
Passes from the petal,
Irrevocable as flesh,
The gazing eye falls through the world.

> *Hana no iro wa*
> *Utsuri ni keri na*
> *Itazura ni*
> *Waga mi yo ni furu*
> *Nagame seshi ma ni*

Ono No Komachi (834–880)

PAULINE STAINER 534

14 January 1997
Dear Ralph, Caroline and Gareth,

Thank you for your letter asking me about a favourite poem for Lifelines 3. I enclose a copy of a fifteenth-century lyric which I love.

I have chosen this poem for its bright mystery, its incantatory quality and its simplicity.

I wish you luck with your project,

Best wishes,
Pauline Stainer

The Maidens Came

The maidens came
When I was in my mother's bower
I had all that I would.
The baily beareth the bell away
The lily, the rose, the rose I lay,
The silver is white, red is the gold;
The robes they lay in fold;

The baily beareth the bell away
The lily, the rose, the rose I lay;
And through the glass window
Shines the sun.
How should I love and I so young?
The baily beareth the bell away,
The lily, the rose, the rose I lay.

Anonymous (English, 15th century)

JOYCE CAROL OATES   535

Princeton
New Jersey
USA
30 January 1997

Dear Ralph Croly,

Thanks for your recent letter. My favorite poem is Robert Frost's 'After Apple-Picking'. It's beautifully nuanced, haunting, and profound in its suggestion of a life so passionately lived, or a career so energetically mined, that it has utterly satiated its original appetite. But what mystery in Frost's rhythms and words! It's just a perfect poem.

Joyce Carol Oates

After Apple-Picking

My long two-pointed ladder's sticking through a tree
Toward heaven still,
And there's a barrel that I didn't fill
Beside it, and there may be two or three
Apples I didn't pick upon some bough.
But I am done with apple-picking now.
Essence of winter sleep is on the night,
The scent of apples: I am drowsing off.
I cannot rub the strangeness from my sight
I got from looking through a pane of glass
I skimmed this morning from the drinking trough
And held against the world of hoary grass.
It melted, and I let it fall and break.
But I was well
Upon my way to sleep before it fell,
And I could tell
What form my dreaming was about to take.
Magnified apples appear and disappear,
Stem end and blossom end,
And every fleck of russet showing clear.

My instep arch not only keeps the ache,
It keeps the pressure of a ladder-round.
I feel the ladder sway as the boughs bend.
And I keep hearing from the cellar bin
The rumbling sound
Of load on load of apples coming in.
For I have had too much
Of apple-picking: I am overtired
Of the great harvest I myself desired.
There were ten thousand thousand fruit to touch,
Cherish in hand, lift down, and not let fall.
For all
That struck the earth,
No matter if not bruised or spiked with stubble,
Went surely to the cider-apple heap
As of no worth.
One can see what will trouble
This sleep of mine, whatever sleep it is.
Were he not gone,
The woodchuck could say whether it's like his
Long sleep, as I describe its coming on,
Or just some human sleep.

Robert Frost (1874–1963)

['After Apple-Picking' was also chosen by Ciaran Carson in *Lifelines 2*.]

ANDREW HAMILTON   536

Worcester College
Oxford
13 May 1997

Dear Caroline, Ralph and Gareth,

Thank you for asking me to contribute to Lifelines 3. *I am very honoured.*

I have decided to choose the sonnet 'It is a beauteous Evening' by William Wordsworth. I first heard this poem when I was twelve, during one of Niall MacMonagle's English classes. We all lay on the floor with our eyes closed and listened to a recording of it spoken by the actor Alan Bates. From that moment I was captivated by the sounds of the words; memorising it was easy and it is still one of the only poems I can recite by heart.

I love this poem firstly for its aural beauty and secondly for the way Wordsworth controls his own deep personal emotions.

I set this piece to music when I was sixteen but now I think that nothing can be added to it; that it should exist on its own.

All the best with the book,
Yours,
Andrew Hamilton

It is a beauteous Evening, calm and free

It is a beauteous Evening, calm and free;
The holy time is quiet as a Nun
Breathless with adoration; the broad sun
Is sinking down in its tranquillity;
The gentleness of heaven broods o'er the Sea:
Listen! the mighty Being is awake,
And doth with his eternal motion make
A sound like thunder — everlastingly.
Dear Child! dear Girl! that walkest with me here,
If thou appear untouched by solemn thought,
Thy nature is not therefore less divine:
Thou liest in Abraham's bosom all the year;
And worship'st at the Temple's inner shrine,
God being with thee when we know it not.

William Wordsworth (1770–1850)

ANNE HAVERTY 537

April 1997

Dear Ralph, Caroline and Gareth,

I hope the enclosed poem will be in time for your edition of Lifelines.

I like it for its poignant opening stanzas and because it expresses with a circumstantial precision the awful fact of our mortality. This is often a subject in poems; but Housman addresses it with the indignation it deserves, along with a sense of pathos and irony and the bitter kind of acceptance that we now regard as Beckettian.

Yours sincerely,
Anne Haverty

from *Last Poems*

IX
The chestnut casts his flambeaux, and the flowers
    Stream from the hawthorn on the wind away,
The doors clap to, the pane is blind with showers.
    Pass me the can, lad; there's an end of May.

There's one spoilt spring to scant our mortal lot,
    One season ruined of our little store.
May will be fine next year as like as not:
    Oh ay, but then we shall be twenty-four.

We for a certainty are not the first
    Have sat in taverns while the tempest hurled
Their hopeful plans to emptiness, and cursed
    Whatever brute and blackguard made the world.

It is in truth iniquity on high
    To cheat our sentenced souls of aught they crave,
And mar the merriment as you and I
    Fare on our long fool's-errand to the grave.

Iniquity it is; but pass the can.
    My lad, no pair of kings our mothers bore;
Our only portion is the estate of man:
    We want the moon, but we shall get no more.

If here to-day the cloud of thunder lours
    To-morrow it will hie on far behests;
The flesh will grieve on other bones than ours
    Soon, and the soul will mourn in other breasts.

The troubles of our proud and angry dust
    Are from eternity, and shall not fail.
Bear them we can, and if we can we must.
    Shoulder the sky, my lad, and drink your ale.

A E Housman (1859–1936)

TOM COURTENAY   538

Putney
21 March 1997

Dear Three,

My favourite poem is Shakespeare's fifty-sixth sonnet: 'Sweet love, renew thy force'.

There's nothing better. It uses reason to show the power, the specialness of 'love'. The argument is carried through to the last two lines:

    Or call it winter, which, being full of care,
    Makes summer's welcome thrice more wished, more rare.

Or you could say the argument is carried through to the last two words — 'more rare'.

Or the last word: 'rare'. Meaning precious. Such is love.

Sincerely,
Tom Courtenay

Sonnet LVI

Sweet love, renew thy force; be it not said,
Thy edge should blunter be than appetite,
Which but today by feeding is allayed,
Tomorrow sharpened in his former might:
So, love, be thou; although today thou fill
Thy hungry eyes, even till they wink with fulness,
Tomorrow see again, and do not kill
The spirit of love with a perpetual dullness.
Let this sad interim like the ocean be
Which parts the shore, where two contracted-new
Come daily to the banks, then, when they see
Return of love, more blest may be the view;
   Or call it winter, which, being full of care,
   Makes summer's welcome, thrice more wished, more rare.

William Shakespeare (1564–1616)

JOHN KELLY

Dear Ralph, Caroline and Gareth,

Thank you very much for the invitation to contribute to Lifelines*. I have long admired the project. My favourite poem at time of writing is 'Star' by Paddy Kavanagh.*

Kavanagh, the great Ulster poet, has always been a favourite — for his affection, his crankiness, his genuine mysticism, his vulnerability and his wisdom. This short poem is simple, obviously beautiful and yet quite extraordinary — it gets me in the heart, the head, the gut — and somewhere else that only the likes of Kavanagh has any proper sense of. It seems to connect with some other part of me that is often no more than a woolly and potential thing. Kavanagh almost always (for me anyway) puts some shape on things and helps me to know what I don't quite know and this, I feel, is the true poetic achievement. I'm also a sucker for pure melancholic beauty — read it and weep.

Good luck with the project.

Regards,
John Kelly

A Star

Beauty was that
Far vanished flame,
Call it a star
Wanting better name.

And gaze and gaze
Vaguely until
Nothing is left
Save a grey ghost-hill.

Here wait I
On the world's rim
Stretching out hands
To Seraphim.

Patrick Kavanagh (1904–1967)

EAMON DELANEY 540

2 April 1997

Dear Compilers,

Thank you for asking me. My poem for inclusion in Lifelines 3 *is a short one — 'Roundelay' by Samuel Beckett.*

Roundelay

on all that strand
at end of day
steps sole sound
long sole sound
until unbidden stay
then no sound
on all that strand
long no sound
until unbidden go
steps sole sound
long sole sound
on all that strand
at end of day

Samuel Beckett (1906–1989)

Some years ago I was living in New York and had come home to Ireland for Christmas, a time of topsy-turvy emotions for the returned emigrant, but particularly so on this occasion. Some friends of mine had twins and another friend asked me to be best man at his wedding. Most poignant of all, however, was that the father of the girl I was going out with was dying and she had come home from America to be near him. It seemed like the whole world was moving on, and our College days were well behind.

On New Year's Day, I got off the Dart at Blackrock and walked down onto the strand, thinking about all this — the Shakespearean 'round of life'. The strand is an extraordinarily resonant place at such times, with its ribbed lines of sand and its arbitrary pools. You think of the line from 'Ozymandias' — 'The lone and level sands stretch far away'. Later, when I met Oonagh, I told her about this walk and a few days afterwards she gave me this poem. It was just after her father's funeral.

The poem brings back that time immediately and the atmosphere of the strand and the thought of life passing away. It has a jerky and repetitive movement which is like a mantra but which is also haunting, like some kind of spectral ghost has appeared and is doing a dance. And then vanishes.

Good luck in your efforts,
Eamon Delaney

BARRY CASTLE

I am not attracted to gloom, but Stevie Smith's seeming artlessness beguiles me into following her down her paths of deprivation and loneliness.

Barry Castle

Every Lovely Limb's a Desolation

I feel a mortal isolation
Wrap each lovely limb in desolation,
Sight, hearing, all
Suffer a fall.

I see the pretty fields and streams, I hear
Beasts calling and birds singing, oh not clear
But as a prisoner
Who in a train doth pass
And through the glass
Peer;
Ah me, so far away is joy, so near.

Break, break the glass, you say?
These thoughts are but a mood
Blow them away, go free?
They are my whole soul's food.

Ghost's food! Sepulchral aliment!
Thou sleekst in me Death's tegument
And so art bent
To do, and this I know.

Yet there are days, oh brief,
When thought's caught half-asleep
(Most merrily) and drowsing
Set in a meadow browsing.

Ah then, like summer breeze in lovely trees
That comes in little pants unequally,
Or like the little waves of summer seas
That push and fuss
In heaven knows what sort of busyness,
Idly, idly, my thoughts bring me to sleep,
On sunny summer day, to sleep. In sun
I fall asleep.

But I must wake and wake again in pain
Crying — to see where sun was once all dust and stain
As on a window pane —

All, all is isolation
And every lovely limb's a desolation.

Come, Death (II)

I feel ill. What can the matter be?
I'd ask God to have pity on me,
But I turn to the one I know, and say:
Come, Death, and carry me away.

Ah me, sweet Death, you are the only god
Who comes as a servant when he is called, you know,
Listen then to this sound I make, it is sharp,
Come, Death. Do not be slow.

Stevie Smith (1902–1971)

BARBARA WINDSOR 542

17 March 1997

Dear Ralph, Caroline and Gareth,

Barbara Windsor has asked me to write and thank you for your letter and I apologise for the delay in replying.

Barbara does not have any specific favourite poem but thinks the one below, written by John Greenleaf Whittier, has a strong relevance today.

Kind Words

A little word in kindness spoken
    A motion or a tear,
May heal a spirit broken,
    And make a friend sincere.

A word, or look, has crushed to earth
    Oft many a budding flower,
Which, had a smile but owned its birth,
    Would have blest life's latest hour.

Then deem it not an idle thing
    A kindly word to speak;
The face you wear, the smile you bring,
    May soothe a heart or break.

John Greenleaf Whittier (?1807–1892)

Barbara sends her warmest regards to you all and wishes you every success with this project.

Best wishes,
Yvonne I'Anson
P.A. to Barbara Windsor

TOM Mac INTYRE   543

31 Eanair 1997

Dhá mbeadh file níos fearr ná Biddy Jenkinson ag scríobh in Éirinn, níor chuala mé an scéal fós. Sa dán seo, mar is iondúil léi, tá an ceol líomhtha, contúirteach, greannmhar. Go háirithe, tá an mháistríocht aice maidir le macnas is macnas na colainne . . .

    Shnámh iasc dubh
    idir chroí is anam.

Taispeáin na línte sin dod leannán luí. Anocht.

Go n-éirí go geal libh,
Tom Mac Intyre

Gealltúint

'Geall dom gean síoraí'
a dúirt sé go híorónta
ar bharr na haille lá
is faoileáin ag allagar.

'Inis dom nach dteipfidh
choíche ar ár gcumann
Inis dom gur buan
toil, rún, focal.

Geall dom nach n-éagfaidh tú
Móidigh nach n-éagfaidh mise
Maígh nach mbeidh trá,
teip, támhaíl, tuireamh.'

Tháinig creathán aeir
aníos de dhroim na mara.
Shnámh iasc dubh
idir chroí is anam.

D'fhosaigh an ghrian.
Stop an ghaoth dá racán.
Bhí gach fuiseog i dtaobh
lena ndéarfaí sna sceacha.

Faoi dheireadh d'éalaigh leoithne
chucu tríd an aitinn.
Réab amach ina cuilithe
lán póg agus pailin.

Biddy Jenkinson (b.1949)

MELVYN BRAGG   544

LWT
7 April 1997

Dear Ralph, Caroline and Gareth,

Further to your letter, the delay for which I apologise profusely. If I am not too late, please find below my contribution towards Lifelines 3, 'I Wandered Lonely as a Cloud' *by William Wordsworth.*

For me, what gives the poem its deep tap root into our minds is Wordsworth's description of the process which he calls 'the inward eye', on which images 'flash' (influence of his studies in electricity at the time) to bring back or provoke a remembering.

With best wishes,
Yours sincerely,
Melvyn Bragg

I Wandered Lonely as a Cloud

I wandered lonely as a cloud
That floats on high o'er vales and hills,
When all at once I saw a crowd,
A host, of golden daffodils;
Beside the lake, beneath the trees,
Fluttering and dancing in the breeze.

Continuous as the stars that shine
And twinkle on the milky way,
They stretched in never-ending line
Along the margin of a bay:
Ten thousand saw I at a glance,
Tossing their heads in sprightly dance.

The waves beside them danced, but they
Out-did the sparkling waves in glee:
A poet could not but be gay,
In such a jocund company:
I gazed — and gazed — but little thought
What wealth the show to me had brought:

For oft, when on my couch I lie
In vacant or in pensive mood,
They flash upon that inward eye
Which is the bliss of solitude;
And then my heart with pleasure fills,
And dances with the daffodils.

William Wordsworth (1770–1850)

['I Wandered Lonely as a Cloud' was also chosen by Ollie Campbell in *Lifelines*.]

MIKE McCORMACK

Dear Ralph, Caroline & Gareth,

Sorry about the delay in getting back to you on this — it's a difficult question when it pops up out of the blue like that.

I think my favourite poem is one I did in Leaving Cert and which has lived in my imagination ever since. It's the opening book of Paradise Lost. *I love its ambition and processional grandeur and its deeply visual qualities. In Satan it contains one of the most charismatic figures in literature. Wretched and vanquished, he is still towering for all that. In one of his first speeches he looks at hell and in spite of its horrors he more or less resolves to make the best of it. It's a rousing speech and each time I read it I feel like cheering for him, punching the air and shouting, 'way to go, Satan'.*

'Is this the region, this the soil . . .
Regained in Heaven, or what more lost in Hell?'

Best wishes with the book,
Mike McCormack

from *Paradise Lost*
Book I, lines 242–270

    'Is this the region, this the soil, the clime,'
Said then the lost Archangel, 'this the seat
That we must change for Heaven, this mournful gloom
For that celestial light? Be it so, since he
Who now is sovran can dispose and bid
What shall be right: farthest from him is best,
Whom reason hath equalled, force hath made supreme
Above his equals. Farewell, happy fields,
Where joy for ever dwells! Hail, horrors, hail,
Infernal world, and thou, profoundest Hell,
Receive thy new possessor — one who brings
A mind not to be changed by place or time.
The mind is its own place, and in itself
Can make a Heaven of Hell, a Hell of Heaven.
What matter where, if I be still the same,
And what I should be, all but less than he
Whom thunder hath made greater? Here at least
We shall be free; the Almighty hath not built
Here for his envy, will not drive us hence:
Here we may reign secure, and, in my choice,
To reign is worth ambition, though in Hell:
Better to reign in Hell than serve in Heaven.
But wherefore let we then our faithful friends,
The associates and co-partners of our loss,
Lie thus astonished on the oblivious pool,
And call them not to share with us their part
In this unhappy mansion, or once more
With rallied arms to try what may be yet
Regained in Heaven, or what more lost in Hell?'

John Milton (1608–1674)

MYRTLE ALLEN — 546

Ballymaloe House
31 January 1997

Dear Ralph,

Thank you for your letter about Lifelines.

I have been chef in my restaurant since 1964, only recently retiring to take up an equally onerous occupation. Chefs running restaurants get very, very little free time to read anything, even their post, so, sadly, poetry has not come into my life.

All I can say is that, when I go to pick my produce from the garden, the orchards, the glasshouses or, formerly, from beds of watercress by streams, on one of those lovely mellow, golden days in September, I always say to myself, 'Season of mists and mellow fruitfulness'!

Yours sincerely,
Myrtle Allen

To Autumn

I
Season of mists and mellow fruitfulness,
   Close bosom friend of the maturing sun,
Conspiring with him how to load and bless
   With fruit the vines that round the thatch-eves run:
To bend with apples the mossed cottage-trees,
   And fill all fruit with ripeness to the core;
      To swell the gourd, and plump the hazel shells
With a sweet kernel; to set budding more,
   And still more, later flowers for the bees,
   Until they think warm days will never cease,
      For summer has o'er-brimmed their clammy cells.

II
Who hath not seen thee oft amid thy store?
   Sometimes whoever seeks abroad may find
Thee sitting careless on a granary floor,
   Thy hair soft-lifted by the winnowing wind;
Or on a half-reaped furrow sound asleep,
   Drowsed with the fume of poppies, while thy hook
      Spares the next swath and all its twinèd flowers;
And sometimes like a gleaner thou dost keep
   Steady thy laden head across a brook;
   Or by a cyder-press, with patient look,
      Thou watchest the last oozings hours by hours.

III
Where are the songs of spring? Aye, where are they?
　Think not of them, thou hast thy music too —
While barrèd clouds bloom the soft-dying day,
　And touch the stubble-plains with rosy hue.
Then in a wailful choir the small gnats mourn
　Among the river sallows, borne aloft
　　Or sinking as the light wind lives or dies;
And full-grown lambs loud bleat from hilly bourn;
　Hedge-crickets sing; and now with treble soft
　The red-breast whistles from a garden-croft;
　　And gathering swallows twitter in the skies.

John Keats (1795–1821)

['To Autumn' was also chosen by Neil Rudenstine in *Lifelines* and by Seán Lysaght and John Carey in *Lifelines 2*. It was Matthew Dempsey's choice in this volume.]

MICHAEL HARTNETT 547

Dear Caroline,

I enclose a small poem for Lifelines 3. *I only got your letter today. I hope I'm not too late!*

All the best,
Michael Hartnett

The Night Before Patricia's Funeral

the night before Patricia's funeral in 1951,
I stayed up late talking to my father.

how goes the night, boy?
　　the moon is down:
　　dark is the town
　　in this nightfall.
how goes the night, boy?
　　soon is her funeral,
　　her small white burial.
she was my threeyears child,
her honey hair, her eyes
small ovals of thrush-eggs.
how goes the night, boy?
　　it is late: lace
　　at the window
　　blows back in the wind.
how goes the night, boy?
　　— Oh, my poor white fawn!
how goes the night, boy?
　　it is dawn.

Michael Hartnett (b.1941)

CATHERINE COOKSON 548

18 March 1997

Dear Mr Croly, Ms Dowling and Mr McCluskey,

Dame Catherine has been very unwell for some years and is mostly confined to bed. Unfortunately, now in her ninety-first year, she has lost most of her sight, so I help with the mail.

She is in a very low state at the moment as her inherited blood condition has worsened and she has to have a blood transfusion, given at home, every two to three weeks to keep her going. She is in hospital just now having had an operation to stop the bleeding from her stomach.

She asks me to tell you there are two poems that are her particular favourites. One is 'The Children's Hour' by Longfellow and the other, which is the last poem in her book Let Me Make Myself Plain, *is called 'This Is My Prayer' by Minnie Aumonier. People thought Aumonier was a man but she was a gentle lady who wrote lovely poems. Dame Catherine always liked the poem 'The Children's Hour' but remembers the word 'dungeon' in it frightened her as a child.*

She wishes your book every success,

Yours sincerely,
Ann Marshall

The Children's Hour

Between the dark and the daylight,
    When the night is beginning to lower,
Comes a pause in the day's occupations,
    That is known as the Children's Hour.

I hear in the chamber above me
    The patter of little feet,
The sound of a door that is opened,
    And voices soft and sweet.

From my study I see in the lamplight,
    Descending the broad hall stair
Grave Alice, and laughing Allegra,
    And Edith with golden hair.

A whisper, and then a silence:
    Yet I know by their merry eyes
They are plotting and planning together
    To take me by surprise.

A sudden rush from the stairway,
   A sudden raid from the hall!
By three doors left unguarded
   They enter my castle wall!

They climb up into my turret
   O'er the arms and back of my chair;
If I try to escape, they surround me;
   They seem to be everywhere.

They almost devour me with kisses,
   Their arms about me entwine,
Till I think of the Bishop of Bingen
   In his Mouse-Tower on the Rhine!

Do you think, O blue-eyed banditti,
   Because you have scaled the wall,
Such an old moustache as I am
   Is not a match for you all!

I have you fast in my fortress,
   And will not let you depart,
But put you down into the dungeon
   In the round-tower of my heart.

And there will I keep you for ever,
   Yes, for ever and a day,
Till the walls shall crumble to ruin,
   And moulder in dust away!

Henry Wadsworth Longfellow (1807–1882)

This Is My Prayer

   I will seek Beauty all my days

Within the dark chaos of a troubled world I will
   seek and find some Beauteous Thing.

From eyes grown dim with weeping will shine a Light
   to guide me, and in Sorrow's Hour
   I shall behold a great High Courage.

I shall find the wonder of an infinite Patience,
   and a quiet Faith in coming Joy and Peace.

And Love will I seek in the midst of Discord, and
   find swift eager hands out-stretched in welcome.

I will seek Beauty all my days, and in my quest
  I shall not be dismayed.

  I SHALL FIND GOD.

Minnie Aumonier

MICHAEL GORMAN   549

28 April 1997

Dear Ralph, Caroline and Gareth,

I have always liked Robert Hayden's poem, 'Those Winter Sundays', very much. These days a lot of writing seems to be about selling everyone close to you down the river, so Robert Hayden's fidelity is striking and a bit humbling. Another great American poet, James Wright, said the strongest word in the poem for him was the last one, 'offices', from the French office, *meaning a religious service after dark. Anyway, I know I took my own parents for granted, too. Maybe we all do a little.*

Best wishes,
Michael Gorman

Those Winter Sundays

Sundays too my father got up early
and put his clothes on in the blueblack cold,
then with cracked hands that ached
from labor in the weekday weather made
banked fires blaze. No one ever thanked him.

I'd wake and hear the cold splintering, breaking.
When the rooms were warm, he'd call,
and slowly I would rise and dress,
fearing the chronic angers of that house,

Speaking indifferently to him,
who had driven out the cold
and polished my good shoes as well.
What did I know, what did I know
of love's austere and lonely offices?

Robert Hayden (1913–1980)

FERGAL KEANE — 550

BBC
Hong Kong
30 April 1997

Dear Ralph and colleagues,

Sorry for the long delay in replying — I have been travelling extensively.

Raymond Carver is one of my favourite writers and I think his poetry is every bit as good as the short fiction for which he is better known. The poem I have chosen, 'Hummingbird', is taken from his last collection, A New Path to the Waterfall. *It was written when he was dying from cancer. Raymond Carver was a recovered alcoholic — his work is full of compassion, tenderness, regret and love. This particular poem appeals because of its simplicity — it is short but manages to say a great deal. There is a hint of sadness — we know that time is slipping away and perhaps the poet's words gather force because we know this.*

I think Lifelines *is a wonderful project. You should be proud, because you care about your world and are willing to try and change it.*

My best wishes,
Fergal

Hummingbird
For Tess

Suppose I say *summer*,
write the word 'hummingbird',
put it in an envelope,
take it down the hill
to the box. When you open
my letter you will recall
those days and how much,
just how much, I love you.

Raymond Carver (1938–1988)

RICHARD DAWKINS 551

3 February 1997

Dear Mr Croly, Miss Dowling and Mr McCluskey,

Thank you for your letter.

This poem from A Shropshire Lad *has been in my head ever since 1977 when the great evolutionary scientist W D Hamilton quoted it in his long, thoughtful — and poetic — review of my first book. Like many Housman poems it is about life's transience but, in a Darwinian mind, it also evokes life's continuation as an endless cycle of recombination and permutation — not just of atoms (as Housman would have realised) but of coded information (as he presumably did not).*

Yours sincerely,
Richard Dawkins

from *A Shropshire Lad*

XXXII
From far, from eve and morning
   And yon twelve-winded sky,
The stuff of life to knit me
   Blew hither: here am I.

Now — for a breath I tarry
   Nor yet disperse apart —
Take my hand quick and tell me,
   What have you in your heart.

Speak now, and I will answer;
   How shall I help you, say;
Ere to the wind's twelve quarters
   I take my endless way.

A E Housman (1859–1936)

KATE ATKINSON 552

27 March 1997

Dear Pupils,

Kate Atkinson has asked me to send you her favourite poem for your anthology, Lifelines 3. *It is 'Stopping by Woods on a Snowy Evening' by Robert Frost.*

She says: Like all really good poems it defies absolute interpretation, so that although I think that I partly understand it I know it contains something inaccessible that will always defy interpretation. Also — another trait of a good poem for me — it is, on the surface, very simple, the language Frost uses is plain and monosyllabic, almost childlike in places — 'Whose woods these are I think I know' and also familiar and domestic — 'My little horse must think it queer'. There is a constant use of assonance and all those lovely long open vowel sounds — 'The only other sound's the sweep / Of easy wind and downy flake' — that build up into an overall effect that's strangely hallucinatory and incantational, especially in that wonderful final stanza. It's a poem that reveals the numinous and the mystical at the heart of the ordinary.

She wishes you even more success with this new volume of poetry.

Yours sincerely,
Judith Murdoch
Literary agent

['Stopping by Woods on a Snowy Evening' was also chosen by Laurie Lee in *Lifelines* and by Declan McGonagle in this volume. The poem can be found on page 98.]

TONY KUSHNER 553

New York City
15 February 1997

Dear Mr Croly, Ms Dowling and Mr McCluskey,

Thank you so much for writing to me. What a glorious project! I'd love to buy copies of the previous editions; how can I do that?

It's completely impossible, of course, to choose a favorite poem — there are so many I love, and different occasions of joy or exigency will make one or another absolutely essential. If I were forced to choose a single poem, I couldn't do it entirely on the basis of merit, because how could one choose, for instance, between the Psalms, Shakespeare, Donne, Wordsworth, Whitman, Auden, Brecht, H D, Pound, Milosz or Heaney? Impossible! But there is a single poem which has haunted me perhaps more than any other, and I reveal an embarrassment of information about myself by selecting it. The poem is 'My Mother Would Be a Falconress' by the American poet Robert Duncan.

I love the poem's harshness, its bloodiness, its chilly, pseudo-medieval rhythms and the archaic, even invented words, like 'falconress'. I love the odd disjunctive use of prepositions, as in the first stanza's 'Where I dream in my little hood . . .', which makes the poem feel fragmentary, ancient, broken. For all its savagery, its S & M imagery (hoods and tethers and bleeding birds and wrists), it is ultimately intimate and gentle, quietly feminist — one of the few poems I know to treat of this theme of mothers struggling with their children without engaging in misogyny. Duncan's empathy is for the falcon and the falconress as well; the engagement and struggle are terribly costly to both. In the end, the falcon/son fares better, breaks free, escapes to flights and heights and distant lands and love; but all this is gained through terrible loss, and the poem is finally a eulogy, an elegy. Any Freudian can make a meal of this — my analyst and I talk about it all the time. My mother, who died seven years ago, was a talented, proud woman, a brilliant musician, afraid of her own ambitions, afraid of the burden these largely unrealized ambitions placed upon her children — especially me, I think. She was far less fearsome, more loving than the falconress, but the first time I encountered Duncan's poem I felt as if I'd known of it, known it and had been reading it all my life — as if it actually were the old traditional song of lamentation it seems to be pretending to be. Duncan writes about its masterful first line in another poem, 'A Lammas Tiding', as having come to him in a dream. I think perhaps what I love most in the poem is that it balances itself so perfectly between the political (in that it is a description of a kind of gendered, constructed, social and hence possibly preventable tragedy) and the mythic (as a perfect and frightening metaphor of the selfishness and selflessness of love). I do not believe this to be a perfect poem, though it is a great one. Duncan is unafraid of inelegance and strangeness; Berryman called him 'unpityingly pretentious'. All these flaws become virtues in his art; I've learned and continue to learn much from him.

Thanks again for asking. I hope this is what you wanted.

All best,
Tony Kushner

My Mother Would Be a Falconress

My mother would be a falconress,
And I, her gay falcon treading her wrist,
would fly to bring back
from the blue of the sky to her, bleeding, a prize,
where I dream in my little hood with many bells
jangling when I'd turn my head.

My mother would be a falconress,
and she sends me as far as her will goes.
She lets me ride to the end of her curb
where I fall back in anguish.
I dread that she will cast me away,
for I fall, I mis-take, I fail in her mission.

She would bring down the little birds.
And I would bring down the little birds.
When will she let me bring down the little birds,
pierced from their flight with their necks broken,
their heads like flowers limp from the stem?

I tread my mother's wrist and would draw blood.
Behind the little hood my eyes are hooded.
I have gone back into my hooded silence,
talking to myself and dropping off to sleep.

For she has muffled my dreams in the hood she has made me,
sewn round with bells, jangling when I move.
She rides with her little falcon upon her wrist.
She uses a barb that brings me to cower.
She sends me abroad to try my wings
and I come back to her.   I would bring down
the little birds to her
I may not tear into, I must bring back perfectly.

I tear at her wrist with my beak to draw blood,
and her eye holds me, anguisht, terrifying.
She draws a limit to my flight.
Never beyond my sight, she says.
She trains me to fetch and to limit myself in fetching.
She rewards me with meat for my dinner.
But I must never eat what she sends me to bring her.

Yet it would have been beautiful, if she would have carried me,
always, in a little hood with the bells ringing,
at her wrist, and her riding
to the great falcon hunt, and me
flying up to the curb of my heart from her heart
to bring down the skylark from the blue to her feet,
straining, and then released for the flight.

My mother would be a falconress,
and I her gerfalcon, raised at her will,
from her wrist sent flying, as if I were her own
pride, as if her pride
knew no limits, as if her mind
sought in me flight beyond the horizon.

Ah, but high, high in the air I flew.
And far, far beyond the curb of her will,
were the blue hills where the falcons nest.
And then I saw west to the dying sun —
it seemd my human soul went down in flames.

I tore at her wrist, at the hold she had for me,
until the blood ran hot and I heard her cry out,
far, far beyond the curb of her will   •

to horizons of stars beyond the ringing hills of the world
    where the falcons nest
I saw, and I tore at her wrist with my savage beak.
I flew, as if sight flew from the anguish in her eye beyond her
    sight,
sent from my striking loose, from the cruel strike at her wrist,
striking out from the blood to be free of her.

My mother would be a falconress,
and even now, years after this,
when the wounds I left her had surely heald,
and the woman is dead,
her fierce eyes closed, and if her heart
were broken, it is stilld   •

I would be a falcon and go free.
I tread her wrist and wear the hood,
talking to myself, and would draw blood.

Robert Duncan (1919–1988)

MOLLY McCLOSKEY 554

26 February 1997

Dear Ralph, Caroline and Gareth,

Thanks for your invitation to pick a poem for the upcoming book. Sorry I couldn't reply sooner, but I was away for a spell and am just catching up. Hope it's not too late.

I don't know that 'favourite' is the word I would use but it's one that's stayed with me since I read it last year — 'Late Fragment' by Raymond Carver. Unadorned, and yet quite powerful, like so much of his writing. In light of the circumstances of his life, and written when he knew that he was dying, it's full — in those few lines — of reconciliation, acceptance and gratitude. So, though it reads like an epitaph, it feels strangely inclusive.

Thanks again for your letter and good luck with the book. I'll look forward to it.

Yours,
Molly McCloskey

Late Fragment

And did you get what
you wanted from this life, even so?
I did.
And what did you want?
To call myself beloved, to feel myself
beloved on the earth.

Raymond Carver (1939–1988)

['Late Fragment' was also chosen by Madeleine Keane, Jo Slade and John MacKenna in *Lifelines 2*.]

ROLF HARRIS

Dear Ralph, Caroline and Gareth,

Sorry to be so long — I've just got your letter. My favourite poem was from a classic children's book from Australia in the late 1920s — the book was The Magic Pudding *and the poem was* 'The Pudding Thief'.

It was a wonderfully irreverent book and the poem was great fun. It was a very lurid tale of what happened to a pudding thief. (A very moral tale really.)

It had wonderful illustrations, as the author was one of Australia's great artists — Norman Lindsay.

Yours,
Rolf Harris

The Tale of a Despicable Puddin' Thief

A puddin'-thief, as I've heard tell,
   Quite lost to noble feeling,
Spent all his days, and nights as well,
   In constant puddin'-stealing.

He stole them here, he stole them there,
   He knew no moderation;
He stole the coarse, he stole the rare,
   He stole without cessation.

He stole the steak-and-kidney stew
   That housewives in a rage hid;
He stole the infants' Puddin' too,
   The Puddin' of the aged.

He lived that Puddin's he might lure,
   Into his clutches stealthy;
He stole the Puddin' of the poor,
   The Puddin' of the wealthy.

The evil wight went forth one night
   Intent on puddin'-stealing,
When he beheld a hidden light
   A secret room revealing.

Within he saw a fearful man,
   With eyes like coals a-glowing,
Whose frightful whiskers over-ran
   His face, like weeds a-blowing;

And there this fearful, frightful man,
   A sight to set you quaking,
With pot and pan and curse and ban,
   Began a puddin' making.

'Twas made of buns and boiling oil,
   A carrot and some nails-O!
A lobster's claws, the knobs off doors,
   An onion and some snails-O!

A pound of fat, an old man rat,
   A pint of kerosene-O!
A box of tacks, some cobbler's wax,
   Some gum and glycerine-O!

Gunpowder too, a hob-nailed shoe
   He stirred into his pottage;
Some Irish stew, a pound of glue,
   A high explosive sausage.

The deed was done, that frightful one
   With glare of vulture famished
Blew out the light, and in the night
   Gave several howls, and vanished.

Our thieving lout, ensconced without,
   Came through the window slinking
He grabbed the pot and on the spot
   Began to eat like winking.

He ate the lot, this guzzling sot —
  Such appetite amazes —
Until those high explosives wrought
  Within his tum a loud report,
  And blew him all to blazes.

For him who steals ill-gotten meals
  Our moral is a good un.
We hope he feels that it reveals
  The danger he is stood in
Who steals a high explosive bomb,
  Mistaking it for Puddin'.

Norman Lindsay (1879–1969)

DECLAN HUGHES

24 March 1997

Dear Ralph, Caroline and Gareth,

Thanks for asking me to contribute to Lifelines 3. *My favourite poem is* 'Long Distance II' *by poet/playwright Tony Harrison.*

Long Distance II

Though my mother was already two years dead
Dad kept her slippers warming by the gas,
put hot water bottles her side of the bed
and still went to renew her transport pass.

You couldn't just drop in. You had to phone.
He'd put you off an hour to give him time
to clear away her things and look alone
as though his still raw love were such a crime.

He couldn't risk my blight of disbelief
though sure that very soon he'd hear her key
scrape in the rusted lock and end his grief.
He *knew* she'd just popped out to get the tea.

I believe life ends with death, and that is all.
You haven't both gone shopping; just the same,
in my new black leather phone book there's your name
and the disconnected number I still call.

Tony Harrison (b.1937)

The father's 'still raw love' lies at the heart of this extraordinarily moving poem, opposed by the rational poet's 'blight of disbelief' at such grief-stricken self-delusion. The opposition between reason and emotion collapses at the end with the haunted sceptic persistently dialling a discontinued phone number: a perfectly alienated, late-century metaphor for the confusion and pain of bereavement. A masterpiece.

All the best with the anthology,
Declan Hughes

MATTHEW DEMPSEY 557

Farmers Journal
16 January 1997

Dear Mr Croly,

Many thanks for your request for my favourite poem. I have a few.

If the autumn is fine and the harvest good, then, as a farmer, it has to be Keats's 'To Autumn':

Season of mists and mellow fruitfulness,
Close bosom friend of the maturing sun . . .

Wishing you every success with your project.

Yours sincerely,
Matthew Dempsey
Editor and Chief Executive

['To Autumn' was also Myrtle Allen's choice. The poem can be found on page 183.]

MILDRED FOX 558

Dáil Éireann,
Baile Átha Cliath 2
12 February 1997

I knew that this poem was the right one to submit. As soon as I read it, it struck a chord. I have on a couple of occasions been made feel inadequate, due to lack of material possessions, especially when I was much younger. For that reason, I detest when people judge others, without making an attempt to get to know them. We are probably all guilty and need to be reminded that we are all vulnerable.

Kind regards,
Mildred Fox, TD

On the Elevator Going Down

A Caucasian gets on at
    the 17th floor.
He is old, fat and expensively
    dressed

I say hello / I'm friendly.
    He says, 'Hi'.

Then he looks very carefully at
    my clothes.

I'm not very expensively dressed.
I think his left shoe costs more
than everything I am wearing.

He doesn't want to talk to me
    any more.

I think that he is not totally aware
that we are really going down
and there are no clothes after you have
been dead for a few thousand years.

He thinks as we silently travel
down and get off at the bottom
    floor
that we are going separate
    ways.

Richard Brautigan (1933–1984)

MICHAEL CURTIN

2 February 1997

Dear Ralph, Caroline and Gareth,

Thank you for your letter. My favourite poem is 'Oft in the Stilly Night' *by Thomas Moore.*

I come from a city that proudly wallows in song and I have heard this poem sung many times particularly by elderly people and I am always moved to tears when they lament:

    Sad memory brings the light
    Of other days around me.

Good luck with your venture,
Michael Curtin

Oft, in the stilly night

Oft, in the stilly night,
   Ere Slumber's chain has bound me,
Fond Memory brings the light
   Of other days around me;
     The smiles, the tears,
     Of boyhood's years,
   The words of love then spoken;
     The eyes that shone,
     Now dimm'd and gone,
   The cheerful hearts now broken!
Thus, in the stilly night,
   Ere Slumber's chain hath bound me,
Sad Memory brings the light
   Of other days around me.

When I remember all
   The friends, so link'd together,
I've seen around me fall,
   Like leaves in wintry weather;
     I feel like one,
     Who treads alone
   Some banquet-hall deserted,
     Whose lights are fled,
     Whose garlands dead,
   And all but he departed!
Thus, in the stilly night,
   Ere Slumber's chain has bound me,
Sad Memory brings the light
   Of other days around me.

Thomas Moore (1779–1852)

HAYDEN CARRUTH 560

8 January 1997

Dear Mr Croly, Ms Dowling and Mr McCluskey,

My favorite poem is the dirge from Act IV, Scene ii, of Cymbeline. As a poet vastly interested in what I hear, I cannot help responding, again and again, to the prosodic genius of this song: not only the momentous metrical change from the first to the second part of it, but the rhyming and syntax throughout. As for the substance, it's an elegy. All western poetry, whatever its putative topic, is elegy; and for all I know so is all eastern and southern poetry as well.

Yours sincerely,
Hayden Carruth

Fear no more the heat o' the sun

Fear no more the heat o' the sun,
   Nor the furious winter's rages;
Thou thy worldly task hast done,
   Home art gone and ta'en thy wages;
Golden lads and girls all must
   As chimney-sweepers, come to dust.

Fear no more the frown o' the great,
   Thou art past the tyrant's stroke:
Care no more to clothe and eat;
   To thee the reed is as the oak;
The sceptre, learning, physic, must
   All follow this, and come to dust.

Fear no more the lightning-flash,
   Nor the all-dreaded thunder-stone;
Fear not slander, censure rash;
   Thou hast finish'd joy and moan:
All lovers young, all lovers must
   Consign to thee, and come to dust.

No exorcizer harm thee!
   Nor no witchcraft charm thee!
Ghost unlaid forbear thee!
   Nothing ill come near thee!
Quiet consummation have;
   And renowned be thy grave!

William Shakespeare (1564–1616)

[This was also Kenneth Branagh's choice in *Lifelines*.]

CHARLES HANDY

12 February 1997

Dear Ralph, Caroline and Gareth,

Here is my favourite poem. It is by the Nobel prizewinning poet Derek Walcott. I like it because it reminds me to try and be true to myself, so that I will be comfortable with my life at the end.

I think it's a great project.

Yours,
Charles Handy

Love after Love

The time will come
when, with elation,
you will greet yourself arriving
at your own door, in your own mirror,
and each will smile at the other's welcome,

and say, sit here. Eat.
You will love again the stranger who was your self.
Give wine. Give bread. Give back your heart
to itself, to the stranger who has loved you

all your life, whom you ignored
for another, who knows you by heart.
Take down the love letters from the bookshelf,

the photographs, the desperate notes,
peel your own image from the mirror.
Sit. Feast on your life.

Derek Walcott (b.1930)

BERNARD O'DONOGHUE

Wadham College
Oxford
12 January 1997

Dear Ralph, Caroline and Gareth,

Thank you very much for writing to me about Lifelines; *I am full of admiration for the project and very honoured to be asked to contribute to it.*

My favourite poem (most of the time, anyway) is Austin Clarke's 'The Planter's Daughter'. The first thing I admire about it is the way that it keeps a loose rein on emotion (as in the closing exclamation 'And O she was the Sunday / In every week') by a light but firmly held form, drawn distantly from Old Irish. Even more though I suppose I admire its mystery: its distant and understated politics and universality. The fact that the planter's house is recognised by the trees means his daughter is entitled to be proud: we see that, though it is said with great lightness. This order of things is as universal as the fact that a fire draws a crowd in on a bad night; it's a social fact. And it is a rather conformist fact which, just this once, doesn't matter.

Congratulations on the enterprise and good luck with the book.

With very best wishes,
Bernard O'Donoghue

The Planter's Daughter

When night stirred at sea
And the fire brought a crowd in,
They say that her beauty
Was music in mouth
And few in the candlelight
Thought her too proud,
For the house of the planter
Is known by the trees.

Men that had seen her
Drank deep and were silent,
The women were speaking
Wherever she went —
As a bell that is rung
Or a wonder told shyly
And O she was the Sunday
In every week.

Austin Clarke (1896–1974)

['The Planter's Daughter' was chosen by Mary McEvoy in *Lifelines*.]

BRIAN ASHTON

7 February 1997

Dear Ralph, Caroline and Gareth,

Thank you for your letter re Lifelines. *An extremely worthy cause and one that I am delighted to support.*

I have chosen John Milton's 'Paradise Lost' *as my favourite poem.*

The immensity of the poem: the innumerable biblical and classical references; the dramatic impact of the language; the sheer belief the detail of the participants infers all attract me to this. But above all is the description of the Underworld and its inhabitants that have constantly stayed in my mind since I first was encouraged to read the poem at the age of sixteen for 'A' Level English Literature at the Royal Grammar School, Lancaster.

Consequently I have selected from Book II lines 704–722.

Good luck with your project,
Brian Ashton

from *Paradise Lost*
Book II, lines 704–722

    So spake the grisly Terror, and in shape,
So speaking and so threatening, grew tenfold
More dreadful and deform. On the other side,
Incensed with indignation Satan stood
Unterrified, and like a comet burned,
That fires the length of Ophiuchus huge
In the arctic sky, and from his horrid hair
Shakes pestilence and war. Each at the head
Levelled his deadly aim; their fatal hands
No second stroke intend; and such a frown
Each cast at the other, as when two black clouds
With Heaven's artillery fraught, come rattling on
Over the Caspian, then stand front to front
Hovering a space, till winds the signal blow
To join their dark encounter in mid-air:
So frowned the mighty combatants, that Hell
Grew darker at their frown, so matched they stood;
For never but once more was either like
To meet so great a foe.

John Milton (1608–1674)

EIMEAR QUINN   564

Dear Ralph, Caroline and Gareth,

The poem I have chosen is 'Alicante' *by Jacques Prévert.*

I chose it not only for personal reasons but also because of how striking the imagery is, and how full of emotion the poem is, in spite of the sparseness of the language.

Regards,
Eimear Quinn

Alicante

Une orange sur la table
Ta robe sur le tapis
Et toi dans mon lit
Deux présent du présent
Fraicheur de la nuit
Chaleur de ma vie

Jacques Prévert (1900–1977)

TONY BLAIR 565

House of Commons
London
21 March 1997

Dear Ralph, Caroline and Gareth,

Thank you for your letter to the Rt Hon Tony Blair MP, on whose behalf I have been asked to reply.

Mr Blair's favourite poem is 'The Soldier' by Rupert Brooke.

Best wishes,
Yours sincerely,
Ms S Gibson
Assistant to the Rt Hon Tony Blair MP

The Soldier

If I should die, think only this of me:
    That there's some corner of a foreign field
That is for ever England. There shall be
    In that rich earth a richer dust concealed;
A dust whom England bore, shaped, made aware,
    Gave, once, her flowers to love, her ways to roam,
A body of England's, breathing English air,
    Washed by the rivers, blest by suns of home.

And think, this heart, all evil shed away,
    A pulse in the eternal mind, no less
        Gives somewhere back the thoughts by England given;
Her sights and sounds; dreams happy as her day;
    And laughter, learnt of friends; and gentleness,
        In hearts at peace, under an English heaven.

Rupert Brooke (1887–1915)

ELAINE CROWLEY 566

14 February 1997

Dear Ralph Croly, Caroline Dowling and Gareth McCluskey,

Thank you for inviting me to send a favourite poem for your next edition of Lifelines. *I was very pleased that you did and have great admiration for what you have achieved so far.*

I have six children and seventeen grandchildren. I'm fortunate to be closely involved with them. And family resemblances have always thrilled and fascinated me. Mine and my husband's immortality. So what else could I choose but Hardy's **'Heredity'**.

Yours sincerely,
Elaine Crowley

Heredity

I am the family face;
Flesh perishes, I live on,
Projecting trait and trace
Through time to times anon,
And leaping from place to place
Over oblivion.

The years-heired feature that can
In curve and voice and eye
Despise the human span
Of durance — that is I;
The eternal thing in man,
That heeds no call to die.

Thomas Hardy (1840–1928)

CONOR McPHERSON 567

Dear Ralph, Caroline and Gareth,

Please forgive my late reply. Enclosed is a copy of a poem I like: Milton's sonnet 'Methought I saw my late espousèd saint'.

Sonnet XXIII

Methought I saw my late espousèd saint
    Brought to me like Alcestis from the grave,
    Whom Jove's great son to her glad husband gave,
    Rescued from death by force, though pale and faint.
Mine, as whom washed from spot of child-bed taint
    Purification in the Old Law did save,
    And such as yet once more I trust to have
    Full sight of her in Heaven without restraint,
Came vested all in white, pure as her mind.
    Her face was veiled, yet to my fancied sight
    Love, sweetness, goodness, in her person shined
So clear as in no face with more delight.
    But O, as to embrace me she inclined,
    I waked, she fled, and day brought back my night.

John Milton (1608–1674)

I find this poem very moving. Milton wrote it about his second wife, Katherine Woodcock, whom he married in 1656. It is generally accepted that Milton was totally blind at this stage and so never actually saw what she looked like. They had a daughter together in 1657, but both mother and child died in 1658.

What I find so touching about the poem is that even though Milton meets his dead wife in a dream, her face is covered with a veil, and so he still doesn't see how she looked. And to me that's a shocking and unsettling detail.

Considering that Milton is famous for epic works about religion and politics, this is a rare and intriguing glimpse of his personal feelings. And it's interesting to note that he is thought to have begun work on his most well-known poem, Paradise Lost, *that same tragic year.*

The best of luck with Lifelines 3.

Yours,
Conor McPherson

PETER READING 568

14 January 1997

Dear Ralph Croly, Caroline Dowling and Gareth McCluskey,

I have today received your letter and I identify my choice for your Lifelines 3, *together with a few words of apologia, below.*

Yrs. &e.,
Peter Reading

No worst, there is none

No worst, there is none. Pitched past pitch of grief,
More pangs will, schooled at forepangs, wilder wring.
Comforter, where, where is your comforting?
Mary, mother of us, where is your relief?
My cries heave, herds-long; huddle in a main, a chief
Woe, wórld-sorrow; on an áge-old anvil wince and sing —
Then lull, then leave off. Fury had shrieked 'No ling–
ering! Let me be fell: force I must be brief'.

   O the mind, mind has mountains; cliffs of fall
Frightful, sheer, no-man-fathomed. Hold them cheap
May who ne'er hung there. Nor does long our small
Durance deal with that steep or deep. Here! creep,
Wretch, under a comfort serves in a whirlwind: all
Life death does end and each day dies with sleep.

Gerard Manley Hopkins (1844–1889)

This 'sonnet of desolation' (like the one beginning 'I wake and feel the fell of dark, not day') plumbs the depths of despair and the agonising tension between faith and doubt. There is, however, an implicit stoical resilience in the elaborate and original construction of Hopkins's Petrarchan fourteen-liner, and a Beckett-like grimness in confronting life's onslaughts: 'No worst, there is none'; 'Here! creep, / Wretch, under a comfort serves in a whirlwind: all / Life death does end and each day dies with sleep.'

SUSAN McKENNA-LAWLOR

Space Technology (Ireland) Ltd
Spais Teicneolaioct Éire Teoranta
17 April 1997

Dear Ralph, Caroline and Gareth,

Thank you for your kind invitation to contribute a few lines from a favourite poem to Lifelines 3. *I propose that you include the following five lines from a poem by William Butler Yeats's* 'To a Wealthy Man'.

> Look up in the sun's eye and give
> What the exultant heart calls good
> That some new day may breed the best
> Because you gave, not what they would,
> But the right twigs for an eagle's nest!

This encapsulates for me the argument that one should endeavour, during one's lifetime, to provide a noble gift for the generations that are to come, even though it is not recognised by contemporaries that the gift is valuable.

I wish you great success in your endeavour to help the stricken children of the Third World.

Sincerely yours,
Susan McKenna-Lawlor

To a Wealthy Man Who Promised a Second Subscription to the Dublin Municipal Gallery if it Were Proved the People Wanted Pictures

> You gave, but will not give again
> Until enough of Paudeen's pence
> By Biddy's halfpennies have lain
> To be 'some sort of evidence',
> Before you'll put your guineas down,
> That things it were a pride to give
> Are what the blind and ignorant town
> Imagines best to make it thrive.

What cared Duke Ercole, that bid
His mummers to the market-place,
What th' onion-sellers thought or did
So that his Plautus set the pace
For the Italian comedies?
And Guidobaldo, when he made
That grammar school of courtesies
Where wit and beauty learned their trade
Upon Urbino's windy hill,
Had sent no runners to and fro
That he might learn the shepherds' will.
And when they drove out Cosimo,
Indifferent how the rancour ran,
He gave the hours they had set free
To Michelozzo's latest plan
For the San Marco Library,
Whence turbulent Italy should draw
Delight in Art whose end is peace,
In logic and in natural law
By sucking at the dugs of Greece.

Your open hand but shows our loss,
For he knew better how to live.
Let Paudeens play at pitch and toss,
Look up in the sun's eye and give
What the exultant heart calls good
That some new day may breed the best
Because you gave, not what they would,
But the right twigs for an eagle's nest!

W B Yeats (1865–1939)

EAMONN LAWLOR

Dear Ralph Croly, Caroline Dowling and Gareth McCluskey,

Thank you for asking me to contribute — and please forgive me for having brooded so long over my answer.

My poem is 'The Trout', by John Montague. I heard John Montague read this in Cork nearly 30 years ago, and remember it as my first 'grown up' experience of poetry. At school I had fallen under the sensual spell of Wordsworth and Yeats, as young people readily do.

This poem, and Montague's reading of it, taught me that words have an even stronger magic: the power to reach where neither sense nor mind alone will serve us, and tickle great truth.

The Trout
for Barrie Cooke

Flat on the bank I parted
Rushes to ease my hands
In the water without a ripple
And tilt them slowly downstream
To where he lay, tendril-light,
In his fluid sensual dream.

Bodiless lord of creation,
I hung briefly above him
Savouring my own absence,
Senses expanding in the slow
Motion, the photographic calm
That grows before action.

As the curve of my hands
Swung under his body
He surged, with visible pleasure.
I was so preternaturally close
I could count every stipple
But still cast no shadow, until

The two palms crossed in a cage
Under the lightly pulsing gills.
Then (entering my own enlarged
Shape, which rode on the water)
I gripped. To this day I can
Taste his terror on my hands.

John Montague (b.1929)

JOHN HARRIS   571

Wesley College
28 May 1997

Dear Ralph, Caroline and Gareth,

I appreciate very much your kind invitation to contribute to Lifelines 3. *I find it very difficult to choose a* favourite *poem, as my feelings about particular poems or styles of poetry can vary according to my mood at the time. However, I have decided to choose 'Concert-Interpretation' by Siegfried Sassoon on this occasion.*

The poem appeals to me because it captures so accurately how difficult it can be for any new creative form to gain acceptance initially — as clearly was the case with the initial exposure to the works of

Stravinsky, the subject of the poem. The second reason it appeals to me so much is because of the way in which the poet makes this an orchestral work in words. To listen to it read aloud evokes so strikingly the sound of Stravinsky's music.

I congratulate you most warmly for your initiative in compiling Lifelines 3 and for your support for such a worthy cause.

Yours sincerely,
John W Harris
Dr John W Harris
Principal

Concert-Interpretation
(Le Sacré du Printemps)

The audience pricks an intellectual Ear . . .
Stravinsky . . . Quite the Concert of the Year!

Forgetting now that none-so-distant date
When they (or folk facsimilar in state
Of mind) first heard with hisses — hoots — guffaws —
This abstract Symphony (they booed because
Stravinsky jumped their Wagner palisade
With modes that seemed cacophonous and queer),
Forgetting now the hullabaloo they made,
The Audience pricks an intellectual ear.

Bassoons begin . . . Sonority envelops
Our auditory innocence; and brings
To Me, I must admit, some drift of things
Omnific, seminal, and adolescent.
Polyphony through dissonance develops
A serpent-conscious Eden, crude but pleasant;
While vibro-atmospheric copulations
With mezzo-forte mysteries of noise
Prelude Stravinsky's statement of the joys
That unify the monkeydom of nations.

This matter is most indelicate indeed!
Yet one perceives no symptom of stampede.
The Stalls remain unruffled: craniums gleam:
Swept by a storm of pizzicato chords,
Elaborate ladies re-assure their lords
With lifting brows that signify 'Supreme!'
While orchestrated gallantry of goats
Impugns the astigmatic programme-notes.

In the Grand Circle one observes no sign
Of riot: peace prevails along the line.
And in the Gallery, cargoed to capacity,
No tremor bodes eruptions and alarms.
They are listening to this not-quite-new audacity
As though it were by someone dead, — like Brahms.

But savagery pervades Me; I am frantic
With corybantic rupturing of laws.
Come, dance, and seize this clamorous chance to function
Creatively, — abandoning compunction
In anti-social rhapsodic applause!
Lynch the conductor! Jugulate the drums!
Butcher the brass! Ensanguinate the strings!
Throttle the flutes! . . . Stravinsky's April comes
With pitiless pomp and pain of sacred springs . . .
Incendiarize the Hall with resinous fires
Of sacrificial fiddles scorched and snapping! . . .

Meanwhile the music blazes and expires;
And the delighted Audience is clapping.

Siegfried Sassoon (1886–1967)

ROBERT DUNBAR 572

The Church of Ireland College of Education
Coláiste Oideachais Eaglais na hÉireann
8 January 1997

Dear Ralph, Caroline and Gareth,

Thank you very much for your invitation to contribute to Lifelines 3: *I have been a great admirer of the previous volumes and I wish this one every possible success.*

As for my 'favourite poem' . . . I have to say that I do not honestly have one favourite poem. Rather, there are hundreds of poems which appeal to me in more or less equal measure and if I were forced to single out any one of them my choice would probably depend to some extent on the mood I was in, the day of the week, the time of day, what I had been doing, reading or thinking about over the previous few hours. I very much like poems which speak to me directly, moving me by the intensity of the experience which they describe. In contemporary Irish poetry I am particularly fond of the work of Paula Meehan and one of her poems which I find especially touching is 'Buying Winkles'. *It is a poem about love, about warmth, about the intimacy of mother and daughter, abstractions all given wonderful concrete expression in the details of the setting, characterisation and dialogue. The note of pride in the closing line — 'like torches' — is a triumphant conclusion to this beautifully observed and brilliantly reported anecdote.*

With every good wish.
Yours sincerely,
Robert Dunbar

Buying Winkles

My mother would spare me sixpence and say,
'Hurry up now and don't be talking to strange
men on the way.' I'd dash from the ghosts
on the stairs where the bulb had blown
out into Gardiner Street, all relief.
A bonus if the moon was in the strip of sky
between the tall houses, or stars out,
but even in rain I was happy — the winkles
would be wet and glisten blue like little
night skies themselves. I'd hold the tanner tight
and jump every crack in the pavement,
I'd wave up to women at sills or those
lingering in doorways and weave a glad path through
men heading out for the night.

She'd be sitting outside the Rosebowl Bar
on an orange-crate, a pram loaded
with pails of winkles before her.
When the bar doors swung open they'd leak
the smell of men together with drink
and I'd see light in golden mirrors.
I envied each soul in the hot interior.

I'd ask her again to show me the right way
to do *it*. She'd take a pin from her shawl —
'Open the eyelid. So. Stick it in
till you feel a grip, then slither him out.
Gently, mind.' The sweetest extra winkle
that brought the sea to me.
'Tell yer Ma I picked them fresh this morning.'

I'd bear the newspaper twists
bulging fat with winkles
proudly home, like torches.

Paula Meehan (b.1955)

['Buying Winkles' was also chosen by Ferdia MacAnna in *Lifelines*.]

FRANK McCOURT 573

9 February 1997

Dear Ralph Croly, Caroline Dowling and Gareth McCluskey,

Thanks for the invitation to participate in Lifelines 3 *and accept my admiration for the work you're doing.*

Now to my (favourite?) favorite poem. It's Wilfred Owen's 'Anthem for Doomed Youth'. *It's a powerful anti-war poem from a man killed just before the 'Great War' ended. In it he fuses the sounds, images and rituals of war and religion so that the activity of war becomes its own requiem. Its diction is sombre and stately as a death march.*

I hope this helps.

Sincerely,
Frank McCourt

Anthem for Doomed Youth

What passing-bells for these who die as cattle?
   Only the monstrous anger of the guns.
   Only the stuttering rifles' rapid rattle
Can patter out their hasty orisons.
No mockeries now for them; no prayers nor bells,
   Nor any voice of mourning save the choirs, —
The shrill, demented choirs of wailing shells;
   And bugles calling for them from sad shires.

What candles may be held to speed them all?
   Not in the hands of boys, but in their eyes
Shall shine the holy glimmers of good-byes.
   The pallor of girls' brows shall be their pall;
Their flowers the tenderness of patient minds,
And each slow dusk a drawing-down of blinds.

Wilfred Owen (1893–1918)

LESLEY JOSEPH 574

3 February 1997

Dear All,

Thank you for your letter. My favourite poem is 'Felix Randal' by Gerard Manley Hopkins. I entered a competition for verse speaking when I was at school and spoke this poem — it got down to two of us who had to speak again. I won, and Jill Balcon awarded me a cup and my name was engraved. It's a beautiful poem — unusual and very satisfying to speak — wonderful rounded words.

Good luck.

Sincerely,
Lesley Joseph

Felix Randal

Felix Randal the farrier, O he is dead then? my duty all ended,
Who have watched his mould of man, big-boned and hardy-handsome
Pining, pining, till time when reason rambled in it and some
Fatal four disorders, fleshed there, all contended?

Sickness broke him. Impatient, he cursed at first, but mended
Being anointed and all; though a heavenlier heart began some
Months earlier, since I had our sweet reprieve and ransom
Tendered to him. Ah well, God rest him all road ever he offended!

This seeing the sick endears them to us, us too it endears.
My tongue had taught thee comfort, touch had quenched thy tears.
Thy tears that touched my heart, child, Felix, poor Felix Randal;

How far from then forethought of, all thy more boisterous years,
When thou at the random grim forge, powerful amidst peers,
Didst fettle for the great grey drayhorse his bright and battering sandal!

Gerard Manley Hopkins (1844–1889)

['Felix Randal' was the choice of Cyril Cusack in *Lifelines* and of Eamon Grennan in *Lifelines 2*.]

MICHAEL MULLEN   575

To my typewriter, on its 21st, and my 42nd, birthday

from a selfsufficient garden which I tend with pensive toil
I could bring you thyme and basil (what you'd really like is oil);
but some class of gallant gesture is certainly your due,
since you are 21 today, and I am 42.

what foolishness possessed me to lay it on the line
that you were all I needed for an assured career in rhyme?
in satire, prose and lyric I would earn a handsome screw —
and now you rust at 21, I'm broke at 42.

you were to be the instrument — of what? I sometimes wonder;
a sort of verbal music, but eschewing verbal thunder.
I never used you to tell lies, though you'd have typed them true
right from the time I was 21, and you were spanking new.

you've typed all kinds of drivel, some mercenary, some fine,
an experimental novel, play, and poems nine times nine.
I've read out the best you've given me from Lille to Kalamazoo;
you've jetted far for 21; I lag at 42.

a continental rival once made seductive sounds
with circumflex and umlauts — but lacked the sign for £s
and that's the vital signal and the universal key . . .
I'd like it working overtime before I'm 43.

we've worked out things in common like 'Dante was a Guelf'
and when I hit this kind of form you can end the lines yourself.
it's not that we've been idle, but not all one's dreams come true
— easy beans at 21, tough tit at forty-two.

when I go next to Galway (don't we both deserve a rest?)
I'll fetch you a lovely ribbon and type up 'all the best',
and 'happy birthday' 'RIP' — all slogans old and new
for we never more will double score — 21 to 42.

if I should find a new machine (but that might be a bore)
I'd hardly live to see us 42 & 84,
and the way they make 'em nowadays, I doubt if it would too
— so let's just stay as sweet as we are, 21 & 42.

Sydney Bernard Smith (b.1936)

There is a long tradition in both the English and Irish language for the elegy form. Usually the subjects are concerned with people, great houses and the great events of history. Sydney Bernard Smith is the first one to use this form to celebrate his typewriter. The typewriter is a metaphor for the passage of time, the disappointment that life brings, the ageing process both in poet and machine.

The poem has a caustic and wry humour which belies the underlying sadness which pervades it.

The poem is a dual-autobiography. We learn as much about the poet as we do of the typewriter.

The shape of the poem has always pleased me and the use of numbers rhyming with words is quite unique.

It is a very subtle emotion poem, filled with world weariness and is Roman in its stoic resignation.

But beyond all that, it is a poem made for the voice and has part of the ballad tradition built into it. It could easily be turned into a robust song.

It has always been a source of pleasure and reflection for me.

Best wishes in all your endeavours.
Michael Mullen

BERYL BAINBRIDGE 576

I have chosen 'Dover Beach' by Matthew Arnold because I used to recite it as a child while roaming the shore at Formby, Lancashire. The sadness and morbidity of the last verse appealed to me. It still does.

Beryl Bainbridge

Dover Beach

The sea is calm tonight.
The tide is full, the moon lies fair
Upon the straits — on the French coast the light
Gleams and is gone; the cliffs of England stand,
Glimmering and vast, out in the tranquil bay.
Come to the window, sweet is the night air!
Only, from the long line of spray
Where the sea meets the moon-blanched land,
Listen! you hear the grating roar
Of pebbles which the waves draw back, and fling,
At their return, up the high strand,
Begin, and cease, and then again begin,
With tremulous cadence slow, and bring
The eternal note of sadness in.

Sophocles long ago
Heard it on the Aegean, and it brought
Into his mind the turbid ebb and flow
Of human misery; we
Find also in the sound a thought,
Hearing it by this distant northern sea.

The Sea of Faith
Was once, too, at the full, and round earth's shore
Lay like the folds of a bright girdle furled.
But now I only hear
Its melancholy, long, withdrawing roar,
Retreating to the breath
Of the night wind, down the vast edges drear
and naked shingles of the world.

Ah, love, let us be true
To one another! for the world, which seems
To lie before us like a land of dreams,
So various, so beautiful, so new,
Hath really neither joy, nor love, nor light,
Nor certitude, nor peace, nor help for pain;
And we are here as on a darkling plain
Swept with confused alarms of struggle and flight,
Where ignorant armies clash by night.

Matthew Arnold (1822–1888)

['Dover Beach' was chosen by Mary O'Donnell in *Lifelines*.]

TONY KEILY

Dear Lifelines,

Thanks for the request for a poem.

I am choosing 'Border Sick Call' by John Montague.

John Montague's poetry is a question of stories built out of material from his own past and the past of the community. These stories are full of hard-edged detail but are at the same time dreams in that they contain something very important which can't ever be said literally. This added dimension means they demand to be read again and again. Put all of this poet's stories, or poems, together, and you have a kind of epic that is unique in contemporary writing, maybe in writing of any time.

The best of luck with your project.

Best wishes,
Tony Keily

Border Sick Call

FOR SEAMUS MONTAGUE, MD, MY BROTHER,
in memory of a journey in winter
along the Fermanagh–Donegal border.

Looks like, I'm breaking the ice! — Fats Waller

Weary, God!
of starfall and snowfall,
weary of north winter, and weary
of myself like this, so cold and thoughtful.
— Hayden Carruth

1
Hereabouts, signs are obliterated,
but habit holds.

We wave a friendly goodbye
to a Customs Post that has twice
leaped into the air
to come to earth again
as a makeshift, a battered trailer
hastily daubed green: *An Stad*.

The personnel still smile
and wave back,
their limbs still intact.

Fragments of reinforced concrete,
of zinc, timber, sag and glint in the hedge
above them, the roof and walls
of their old working place:

> *Long years in France,*
> *I have seen little like this,*
> *même dans le guerre Algerienne,*
> *the impossible as normal,*
> *lunacy made local,*
> *surrealism made risk.*

Along the glistening main road
snow plough-scraped, salt-sprinkled,
we sail, chains clanking,
the surface bright, hard, treacherous
with only one slow, sideways skid
before we reach the side road.

Along ruts ridged with ice
the car now rocks, until we reach
a gap walled with snow where
silent folk wait and watch
for our, for your, arrival.

The high body of a tractor
rides us a few extra yards
on its caterpillar wheels
till it also slips and slopes
into a hidden ditch
to tilt helpless, one large
welted tyre spinning.

2
Shanks' mare now, it seems,
for the middle-aged,
marching between hedges
burdened with snow,
low bending branches
which sigh to the ground
as we pass, to spring back.

And the figures fall back
with soft murmurs of
'on the way home, doctor?'
shades that disappear
to merge into the fields,
their separate holdings.

Only you seem to know
where you are going
as we march side by side,
following the hillslope
whose small crest shines
like a pillar of salt,
only the so solid scrunch
and creak of snow crystals
thick-packed underneath
your fur boots, my high
farmer's wellingtons.

Briefly we follow
the chuckling rush
of a well-fed stream
that swallows, and swells
with the still-melting snow
until it loses itself
in a lough, a mountain tarn
filmed with crisp ice
which now flashes sunlight,
a mirror of brightness,
reflecting, refracting
a memory, a mystery:

Misty afternoons in winter
we climb to a bog pool;
rushes fossilised in ice.
A run up, and a slide —
boots score a glittering
path, until a heel slips
and a body measures its length
slowly on ice, starred with
cracks like an old plate.

Into this wide, white world
we climb slowly higher,
no tree, or standing stone,
only cold sun and moorland,
where a stray animal,
huddled, is a dramatic event,
a gate a silvered statement,
its bars burred with frost,
tracks to a drinking trough,
rutted hard as cement:
a silent, islanded cottage,
its thatch slumped in,
windows cracked, through which,
instead of Christians, cattle
peer out, in dumb desolation.

And I remember how, in Fintona,
you devoured Dante by the fireside,
a small black World's Classic.
But no purgatorial journey
reads stranger than this,
our Ulster border pilgrimage
where demarcations disappear,
landmarks, forms, and farms vanish
into the ultimate coldness of an ice age,
as we march towards Lettercran,
in steelblue, shadowless light,
The Ridge of the Tree, the heart of whiteness.

3
We might be astronauts creak-
ing over the cold curve
of the moon's surface, as our boots
sink, rasp over crusted snow,
sluggish, thick, dreamlike,

until, for the first time
in half-an-hour, we see

a human figure, shrunken
but agile, an old, old man
bending over something, poking
at it furiously with a stick:
carcass of fox or badger?

'Hello,' we hallo, like strangers
on an Antarctic or arctic ice floe ⎯
Amunsen greeting a penguin! ⎯
each detail in cold relief.

Hearing us, the small figure halts,
turns an unbelieving face, then
takes off, like a rabbit or hare
with a wounded leg, the stick its pivot,
as it hirples along, vigorously
in the wrong, the opposite
direction, away from us,
the stricken gait of the aged
transformed into a hobble,
intent as a lamplighter.

We watch as our pathfinder,
our potential guide, dwindles
down the valley, steadily
diminishing until
he burrows,
bolts under,
disappears into,
a grove of trees.

'And who might that be,
would you say?' I ask my brother
as we plod after him
at half his pace. 'Surely
one of my most urgent patients,'
he says, with a wry smile,
'the sick husband gone to get
his sicker wife back to bed
before I arrive.' And he smiles
again, resignedly.

'And besides, he wants to tidy
the place up, before the Doctor
comes. Things will be grand
when we finally get there:
he just wasn't expecting anyone
to brave the storm.

'But there'll be a good welcome
when we come.'

And sure enough all is waiting,
shining, inside the small cottage.
The fire laughs on the hearth,
bellows flared, whilst the dog rises
to growl, slink, then wag its tail.

4
My brother is led into the bedroom.
Then himself, a large-eared, blue-eyed gnome,
still pert with the weight of his eighty years,
discourses with me before his hearth,
considerately, like a true host.

'Border, did you say,
how many miles to the border?
Sure we don't know where it starts
or ends up here, except we're lost
unless the doctor or postman finds us.

'But we didn't always complain.
Great hills for smuggling they were,
I made a packet in the old days,
when the big wars were rumbling on,
before this auld religious thing came in.

'You could run a whole herd through
between night and morning, and no one
the wiser, bar the B-Specials,
and we knew every mother's son
well enough to grease the palm,
quietlike, if you know what I mean.
Border be damned, it was a godsend.
Have you ever noticed, cows have no religion?'

Surefooted, in darkness,
stick-guiding his animals,
in defiance of human frontiers,
the oldest of Irish traditions,
the creach *or cattle raid,*
as old as the Táin.

Now, delighted with an audience,
my host rambles warmly on;
holding forth on his own hearth:

'Time was, there'd be a drop
of the good stuff in the house,'
the head cocked sideways
before he chances a smile,
'but not all is gone.
Put your hand in the thatch
there, left of the door,
and see what you find.'

Snug as an egg under a hen,
a small prescription bottle of colourless poteen.
'Take that medicine with you for the road home.
You were brave men to come.'

5
Downhill, indeed, is easier,
while there is still strong light,
an eerie late afternoon glow
boosted by the sullen weight
of snow on the hedges,
still or bowing to the ground
again, as we pass, an iceblue
whiteness beneath our steady tread;
a snow flurry, brief, diamond-hard,
under a frieze of horsetail cloud.

The same details of field, farm
unravelling once again, as the doctor
plods on, incongruous in his fur boots
(but goodness often looks out of place),
downhill, with the same persistence
in a setting as desolate as if
a glacier had just pushed off:

> *Thick and vertical*
> *the glacier slowly*
> *a green white wall*
> *grinding mountains*
> *scooping hollows*
> *a gross carapace*
> *sliding down the*
> *face of Europe*
> *to seep, to sink*
> *its melting weight*
> *into chilly seas;*
> *bequeathing us*
> *ridges of stone,*
> *rubble of gravel,*
> *eskers of hardness:*
> *always within us —*
> *a memory of coldness.*

Only one detail glints different.
On that lough, where the sun burns
above the silver ice, like a calcined stone,
a chilling fire, orange red,
a rowboat rests, chained in ice,
ice at gunwhale, prow and stern,
ice jagged on the anchor ropes;
still, frozen, 'the small bark of my wit',
la navicella del mio ingegno.
Why could I not see it on the way
up, only on the journey home,

I wonder as my brother briefly disappears
across the half-door of another house,
leaving me to wait, as glimmers gather
into the metallic blues of twilight,
and watch, as if an inward eye were opening,
details expand in stereoscopic brightness,
a buck hare, not trembling, unabashed,
before he bounds through the frozen grass,
a quick scatter of rabbits, while
a crow clatters to the lower wood,
above the incessant cries of the sheep herd.

6
When my brother returns, breath pluming,
although he risks only a swallow,
the fiery drink unleashes his tongue:
from taciturn to near-vision,

'I heard you chatting to old MacGurren,
but the real border is not between
countries, but between life and death,
that's where the doctor comes in.

'I have sat beside old and young
on their death beds, and have seen
the whole house waiting, as for birth,
everything scoured, spick-and-span,
footsteps tiptoeing around.

'But the pain is endless,
you'd think no one could endure it,
but still they resist, taste the respite,
until the rack tightens again
on the soiled, exhausted victim.'

> *But the poem is endless,*
> *the poem is strong as our weakness,*

*strong in its weakness,
it will never cease until it has said
what cannot be said.*

*The sighs and crying of someone
who is leaving this world
in all its solid, homely detail
for another they have only heard tell of,
in the hearsay called religion,
or glimpsed uneasily in dream.*

'People don't speak of it,
lacking a language for this terrible thing,
a forbidden subject, a daily happening,
pushed aside until it comes in.

I remember the first time I saw it
on my first post as a *locum*.'

(That smell in the sickroom —
stale urine and *faeces* —
the old man on the grey bed,
his wife crouched in darkness.

Many generations of family
lined up along the stairs
and out into the farmyard:
the youngest barely aware

of the drama happening inside
that unblinking frame of light;
but horseplaying, out loud.
Three generations, and the tree shaking.

He has lain still for months
but now his muscles tighten,
he lifts himself into a last
bout of prayers and imprecations.

The old woman also starts up
but there is no recognition,
only that ultimate effort, before
he falls back, broken,

The rosary lacing stiff fingers.
'I did not expect to witness
the process in such a rush:
it still happens in these lost places.')

7
Just as we think we are finally clear,
another shade steps out from the shadows
(out of the darkness, they gather to your goodness),
with its ritual murmured demand:
'Doctor, would you be so good to come in?
The wife is taken bad again.'

All the clichés of rural comedy
(which might be a rural tragedy),
as he leads us along a tangled path,
our clabbery *via smaritta*.

Briars tug at us, thorn and whin
jag us, we trudge along a squelching drain;
my brother and I land ankle-deep in slush,
a gap guttery as a boghole,
and he has to haul us out by hand,
abjectly, 'Sorry we've no back lane.'

In his house, where an Aladdin burns,
we step out of our boots, socks,
before the warm bulk of the Rayburn,
and my brother pads, barefooted,
into the back room, where a woman moans.

Nursing a mug of tea in the kitchen
I confer anxiously with her cowed man.
'She's never been right since the last wain,
God knows, it's hard on the women.'

Three ragged little ones in wellingtons
stare at the man from Mars,
suck their thumbs and say nothing.
There is a tinny radio but no television.
A slight steam rises where our socks hang.
At last my brother beckons him in.

When we leave, no more conversation;
the labourer stumbling before us,
his hand shielding a candle
which throws a guttering flame:
a sheltering darkness of firs, then,
spiked with icicles, a leafless thorn,
where the gate scringes on its stone.

When we stride again on the road,
there is a bright crop of stars,
the high, clear stars of winter,
the studded belt of Orion,
and a silent, frost-bright moon
upon snow crisp as linen
spread on death or bridal bed;
blue tinged as a spill of new
milk from the crock's lip.

8
Another mile, our journey is done.
The main road again. The snow-laden car
gleams strange as a space machine.

We thrust snow from the roof;
sit cocooned as the engine warms,
and the wipers work their crescents clean

With a beat steady as a metronome.
Brother, how little we know of each other!
Driving from one slaughter to another

Once, you turned on the car radio
to hear the gorgeous pounding rhythms
of your first symphony: Beethoven.

The hair on your nape crawled.
Startled by the joy, the energy,
the answering surge in your own body.

In the face of suffering, unexpected affirmation.
For hours we've been adrift from humankind,
navigating our bark in a white landlocked ocean.

Will a stubborn devotion suffice,
sustained by an ideal of service?
Will dogged goodwill solve anything?

Headlights carve a path through darkness
back through Pettigo, towards Enniskillen.
The customs officials wave us past again.

But in what country have we been?

John Montague (b.1929)

ANITA GROENER 578

9 January 1997

Dear Ralph, Caroline and Gareth,

Thank you for your invitation!

I send you a poem I love by the poet Rainer Maria Rilke.

Although Austrian, he has lived his life in Prague. There is a sense of displacement present in his work, sometimes suffocating, sometimes liberating but always from a longing to belong.

It may be because of my own 'alienation' in some ways that I like his work so much; between being a foreigner living in Ireland (having made it my home), and visiting my home country, The Netherlands (feeling at times more like a foreigner when I am there).

This particular poem to me is very visual and inspiring. It contains a stillness, a quiet sense of being in-between.

Wishing you well and every success with your book,

Sincerely yours,
Anita Groener

Abend

Der Abend wechselt langsam die Gewänder,
die ihm ein Rand von alten Bäumen hält;
du schaust: und von dir scheiden sich die Länder,
ein himmelfahrendes und eins, das fällt;

und lassen dich, zu keinem ganz gehörend,
nicht ganz so dunkel wie das Haus, das schweigt,
nicht ganz so sicher Ewiges beschwörend,
wie das, was Stern wird jede Nacht und steigt —

und lassen dir (unsäglich zu entwirrn)
dein Leben bang und riesenhaft und reifend,
so daß es, bald begrenzt und bald begreifend,
abwechselnd Stein in dir wird und Gestirn.

Evening

The sky puts on the darkening blue coat
held for it by a row of ancient trees;
you watch: and the lands grow distant in your sight,
one journeying to heaven, one that falls;

and leave you, not at home in either one,
not quite so still and dark as the darkened houses,
not calling to eternity with the passion
of what becomes a star each night, and rises;

and leave you (inexpressibly to unravel)
your life, with its immensity and fear
so that, now bounded, now immeasurable,
it is alternately stone in you and star.

Rainer Maria Rilke (1875–1926)

GLENN PATTERSON

19 January 1997

Dear Ralph, Caroline and Gareth,

Thank you for your letter. I enclose a brief paragraph (at least I hope it's brief enough) on my favourite poem, Louis MacNeice's 'Snow'.

May I take this opportunity to congratulate the three of you on your decision to take on this latest Lifelines *project and to wish you every success with its publication.*

Yours sincerely,
Glenn Patterson

Snow

The room was suddenly rich and the great bay-window was
Spawning snow and pink roses against it
Soundlessly collateral and incompatible:
World is suddener than we fancy it.

World is crazier and more of it than we think,
Incorrigibly plural. I peel and portion
A tangerine and spit the pips and feel
The drunkenness of things being various.

And the fire flames with a bubbling sound for world
Is more spiteful and gay than one supposes —
On the tongue on the eyes on the ears in the palms of one's
    hands —
There is more than glass between the snow and the huge roses.

Louis MacNeice (1907–1963)

I am torn between this and another MacNeice poem, Canto IV of the 'Autumn Journal' sequence. I settle for 'Snow' because it was the first poem that really got through to me, that worked on me as a poem and not as an object of study. I was in the lower sixth in a school in Belfast, in an English class displaced from its usual room to a large lecture theatre. Somewhere in the course of the lesson — I have always thought it was when we reached the lines 'I peel and portion / A tangerine and spit the pips and feel / The drunkenness of things being various' — I started to feel as though my eyes, or perhaps, more properly, my ears, were opening. My teacher of the time still tells me she remembers me saying, with a sort of awe, 'Oh, God, I see it.' An epiphany experienced while reading a poem describing an epiphany. These moments it seems to me, moments when everything appears to come together, are the moments most worth living for; certainly they are the moments most worth writing for. I think what happened the day I read 'Snow' was that I started wanting to be a writer.

['Snow' was also chosen by Andy O'Mahony in *Lifelines*.]

JESSIE LENDENNIE

Salmon Publishing Ltd

Dear Lifelines,

Many apologies for this delay. Thank you so much for including me!

'The Sound of Trees' by Robert Frost.

Here is what I think about this beautiful, rhythmically wonderful poem: Like all Frost's work, this poem is deceptively simple on the surface, but deeply complex. Its halting rhythm and reflective mood totally capture the conflicting thoughts inherent in the creative longing for movement and change; the desire to be other than what we are . . . the feeling that somewhere 'out there' is the real world. This feeling is skilfully contrasted with our envy of the permanence of the natural world. The sound of the trees speaks to the rootless American spirit, but the trees are also rooted as we can never be. We envy the trees' power to be whole in themselves: the trees still sway when we are gone, we have the choice to go . . . we are gone . . . we have 'less to say', but the trees are still in voice, calling and recalling our absence.

Thanks again for this opportunity to speak for one of my very favourite poems.

Yours,
Jessie Lendennie

The Sound of Trees

I wonder about the trees.
Why do we wish to bear
Forever the noise of these
More than another noise

So close to our dwelling place?
We suffer them by the day
Till we lose all measure of pace,
And fixity in our joys,
And acquire a listening air.
They are that that talks of going
But never gets away;
And that talks no less for knowing,
As it grows wiser and older,
That now it means to stay.
My feet tug at the floor
And my head sways to my shoulder
Sometimes when I watch trees sway,
From the window or the door.
I shall set forth for somewhere,
I shall make the reckless choice
Some day when they are in voice
And tossing so as to scare
The white clouds over them on.
I shall have less to say,
But I shall be gone.

Robert Frost (1874–1963)

STEPHEN PEARCE 581

19 June 1997

Dear Kidz,

I have thought about your request for a poem for the last few years and really wanted to respond except I don't know any poems. When I was at secondary school I had Irish poems and Shakespeare drummed into me in such a way that I have avoided Shakespeare and Irish ever since. I have also found in life that the more direct the language I use the more accurately I communicate. It's like I can say 'The bird shat on me' or 'O thou wondrous feathered friend who glides through the ethereal ethers spreading and sharing with me that with which nature has so bountifully filled thy delicate frame'. Gimme a break.

Anyway, if I am in doubt I ask my kids. So I asked my five-year-old daughter to tell me a poem, and here it is.

Greetings,
Stephen Pearce

Lipstick

Lipstick sticks as you lick,
when you kiss someone
and sometimes you kiss
when you are licking.

Mirin Pearce (b.1992)

FRANK McDONALD

The Irish Times
21 June 1997

Dear Editors,

Firstly, may I apologise for the very long delay in responding to your letter, but I'm afraid the newsroom in The Irish Times *is somewhat like Bedlam and my own desk bears close resemblance to a combat zone!*

I decided to select not a poem, but a letter, for this edition of Lifelines. *It is a most unusual letter, written by Chief Seattle of the Duwamish tribe in Washington State to the US President, Franklin Pierce, in 1854. In response to an offer from the federal government to purchase the Indian lands and relocate his tribe on a reservation.*

Chief Seattle's letter has its own lyricism and delivers a powerful message about how we all need to care for the natural world — our environment — particularly in its much-quoted phrases about how 'the Earth is sacred' and 'all things are connected'. There are some who may think, on reading it, that the Chief goes somewhat over the top in places, but I don't believe so.

'Continue to contaminate your bed, and you will one night suffocate in your own waste', he warned. Who could doubt the veracity of this metaphor for what we are doing to the world? It is, I'm afraid, all too true. We need to learn about treading softly on the Earth, as Chief Seattle clearly did, and try a little harder to pass on what we have inherited to succeeding generations of humanity in as close as possible to an uncontaminated state.

By the way, I also like a quote from Big Jim Larkin, who led the workers of Dublin during the 1913 lock-out. It is emblazoned on a bronze plaque on the plinth of Oisín Kelly's marvellous statue of Larkin in the middle of O'Connell Street and reads as follows: 'The great appear to be great because we are on our knees; let us rise.'

Yours sincerely,
Frank McDonald

The Earth Is Sacred

How can you buy or sell the sky, the warmth of the land? The idea is strange to us. If we do not own the freshness of the air and the sparkle of the water, how can you buy them?

Every part of this earth is sacred to my people. Every shining pine needle, every sandy shore, every mist in the dark woods, every clearing and humming insect is holy in the memory and experience of my people. The sap which courses through the trees carries the memories of the red man. The white man's dead forget the country of their birth when they go to walk among the stars. Our dead never forget this beautiful earth, for it is the mother of the red man. We are part of the earth and it is part of us. The perfumed flowers are our sisters; the deer, the horse, the great eagle, these are our brothers. The rocky crests, the juices in the meadows, the body heat of the pony, and man — all belong to the same family.

So, when the Great Chief in Washington sends word that he wishes to buy our land, he asks much of us. The Great Chief sends word he will reserve us a place so that we can live comfortable among our own people. He will be our Father and we will be his children. So we will consider your offer to buy our land. But it will not be easy. For this land is sacred to us. The shining water that moves in the streams and rivers is not just water but the blood of our ancestors. If we sell you the land, you must remember that it is sacred, and you must teach your children that each ghostly reflection in the clear water of the lakes tells of events and memories in the life of my people. The water's murmur is the voice of the father's father.

Kindness to the Rivers

The rivers are our brothers, they quench our thirst. The rivers carry our canoes, and feed our children. If we sell you our land, you must remember, and teach your children, that the rivers are our brothers, and yours, and you must henceforth give the rivers the kindness you would give a brother.

We know that the white man does not understand our ways. One portion of land is the same to him as the next, for he is a stranger who comes in the night and takes from the land whatever he needs. The Earth is not his brother, but his enemy, when he has conquered it, he moves on. He leaves his father's graves behind, and he does not care. He kidnaps the earth from his children, and he does not care. His father's graves, and his children's birthright, are forgotten. He treats his mother, the earth, and his brother, the sky, as things to be bought, plundered, sold like sheep or bright beads. His appetite will devour the earth and leave behind only a desert. I do not know. Our ways are different from yours. The sight of your cities pains the eyes of the red man. But perhaps it is because the red man is a savage and does not understand.

There is no quiet place in the white man's cities; no place to hear the unfurling of leaves in spring, or the rustle of the insect's wings. The clatter only seems to insult the ears. And what is there to life if a man cannot hear the lonely cry of the whippoorwill, or the argument of the frogs around a pond at night? The Indian prefers the soft sound of the wind darting over the face of a pond, and the smell of wind itself, cleansed by the midday rain, or scented with the pinon pine.

The Air Is Precious

The air is precious to the red man, for all things share the same breath — the beast, the tree, and the human. The white man does not seem to notice the air he breathes. Like a man dying for many days he is numb to the stench. But if we sell you our land you must remember that the air is precious to us, that the air shares its spirit with all the life it supports. The wind that gave our grandfather his first breath also receives his last sigh. And if we sell you our land, you must keep it apart and sacred, as a place where even the white man can go to taste the wind that is sweetened by the meadow's flowers.

All Things Are Connected

So we will consider your offer to buy our land. If we decide to accept, I will make one condition; the white man must treat the beasts of this land as his brothers. I have seen a thousand rotting buffaloes on the prairie, left by the white man who shot them from a passing train. I am a savage and I do not understand how the smoking iron horse can be more important than the buffalo that we kill only to stay alive. What is man without the beasts? If all the beasts were gone, man would die from great loneliness of spirit, for whatever happens to the beast also happens to man. All things are connected. Whatever befalls the earth befalls the sons of earth. The white man, too, shall pass — perhaps sooner than other tribes. Continue to contaminate your bed, and you will one night suffocate in your own waste. When the buffalo are all slaughtered, the wild horses all tamed, the secret corners of the forest heavy with scent of many men, and the view of ripe hills blotted by talking wires, where is the thicket? Gone. Where is the eagle? Gone. And what is it to say goodbye to the swift pony and the hunt? It is the end of living and the beginning of survival.

Chief Seattle (?1786–1866)

MARTIN McDONAGH

Dear All,

I think my favourite poem is 'The Raven' by Edgar Allan Poe. It has fantastic rhyme-schemes, cool alliteration and tells a weird little story brilliantly.

If that's already been chosen, there's a neat little Haiku poem that I heard on the radio once which goes . . .

> Reflected
> In the eye of a dragonfly
> Mountains.

. . . but I don't know who it's by. As well as being a neat image on its own, I like the way it suggests that even the most ugly and insignificant of creatures may have more importance than the most seemingly majestic and lasting.

All the best,
Martin McDonagh

The Raven

Once upon a midnight dreary, while I pondered, weak and
    weary,
Over many a quaint and curious volume of forgotten lore —
While I nodded, nearly napping, suddenly there came a
    tapping,
As of some one gently rapping, rapping at my chamber door.
''Tis some visitor,' I muttered, 'tapping at my chamber door —
        Only this and nothing more.'

Ah, distinctly I remember it was in the bleak December,
And each separate dying ember wrought its ghost upon the
    floor.
Eagerly I wished the morrow; — vainly I had sought to borrow
From my books surcease of sorrow — sorrow for the lost
    Lenore —
For the rare and radiant maiden whom the angels name
    Lenore –
        Nameless here for evermore.

And the silken sad uncertain rustling of each purple curtain
Thrilled me — filled me with fantastic terrors never felt before;
So that now, to still the beating of my heart, I stood repeating:
''Tis some visitor entreating entrance at my chamber door —
Some late visitor entreating entrance at my chamber door;
        This it is and nothing more.'

Presently my soul grew stronger; hesitating then no longer,
'Sir,' said I, 'or Madam, truly your forgiveness I implore;
But the fact is I was napping, and so gently you came rapping,
And so faintly you came tapping, tapping at my chamber door,
That I scarce was sure I heard you' — here I opened wide the door; —
                Darkness there and nothing more.

Deep into that darkness peering, long I stood there wondering, fearing,
Doubting, dreaming dreams no mortals ever dared to dream before;
But the silence was unbroken, and the stillness gave no token,
And the only word there spoken was the whispered word, 'Lenore!'
This I whispered, and an echo murmured back the word, 'Lenore!' —
                Merely this and nothing more.

Back into the chamber turning, all my soul within me burning,
Soon again I heard a tapping something louder than before.
'Surely,' said I, 'surely that is something at my window lattice;
Let me see, then, what thereat is, and this mystery explore —
Let my heart be still a moment , and this mystery explore; —
                'Tis the wind and nothing more.'

Open here I flung the shutter, when, with many a flirt and flutter,
In there stepped a stately Raven of the saintly days of yore.
Not the least obeisance made he; not a minute stopped or stayed he,
But, with mien of lord or lady, perched above my chamber door —
Perched upon a bust of Pallas just above my chamber door —
                Perched, and sat, and nothing more.

Then this ebony bird beguiling my sad fancy into smiling,
By the grave and stern decorum of the countenance it wore,
'Though thy crest be shorn and shaven, thou,' I said, 'art sure no craven,
Ghastly grim and ancient Raven wandering from the Nightly shore —
Tell me what thy lordly name is on the Night's Plutonian shore!'
                Quoth the Raven, 'Nevermore.'

Much I marvelled this ungainly fowl to hear discourse so plainly,
Though its answer little meaning — little relevancy bore;

For we cannot help agreeing that no living human being
Ever yet was blessed with seeing bird above his chamber
   door —
Bird or beast upon the sculptured bust above his chamber door,
                  With such name as 'Nevermore.'

But the Raven, sitting lonely on that placid bust, spoke only
That one word, as if his soul in that one word he did outpour.
Nothing farther then he uttered; not a feather then he
   fluttered —
Till I scarcely more than muttered: 'Other friends have flown
   before —
On the morrow *he* will leave me as my Hopes have flown
   before.'
              Then the bird said, 'Nevermore.'

Startled at the stillness broken by reply so aptly spoken,
'Doubtless,' said I, 'what it utters is its only stock and store,
Caught from some unhappy master whom unmerciful Disaster
Followed fast and followed faster till his songs one burden
   bore —
Till the dirges of his Hope that melancholy burden bore
              Of "Never — nevermore."'

But the Raven still beguiling all my sad soul into smiling,
Straight I wheeled a cushioned seat in front of bird and bust
   and door;
Then, upon the velvet sinking, I betook myself to linking
Fancy unto fancy, thinking what this ominous bird of yore —
What this grim, ungainly, ghastly, gaunt, and ominous bird of
   yore
              Meant in croaking 'Nevermore.'

This I sat engaged in guessing, but no syllable expressing
To the fowl whose fiery eyes now burned into my bosom's core;
This and more I sat divining, with my head at ease reclining,
On the cushion's velvet lining that the lamp-light gloated o'er,
But whose velvet violet lining with the lamp-light goating o'er
              She shall press, ah, nevermore!

Then, methought, the air grew denser, perfumed from an
   unseen censer
Swung by Seraphim whose foot-falls tinkled on the tufted
   floor.
'Wretch,' I cried, 'thy God hath lent thee — by these angels he
   hath sent thee
Respite — respite and nepenthe from thy memories of Lenore!
Quaff, oh quaff this kind nepenthe and forget this lost Lenore!'
              Quoth the Raven, 'Nevermore.'

'Prophet!' said I, 'thing of evil! — prophet still, if bird or
 devil! —
Whether Tempter sent, or whether tempest tossed thee here
 ashore,
Desolate, yet all undaunted, on this desert land enchanted —
On this home by Horror haunted, — tell me truly, I implore —
Is there — *is* there balm in Gilead? — tell me — tell me, I
 implore!'
            Quoth the Raven, 'Nevermore.'

'Prophet!' said I, 'thing of evil! — prophet still, if bird or devil!
By that heaven that bends above us — by that God we both
 adore —
Tell this soul with sorrow laden if, within the distant Aidenn,
It shall clasp a sainted maiden whom the angels name Lenore —
Clasp a rare and radiant maiden whom the angels name
 Lenore.'
            Quoth the Raven, 'Nevermore.'

'Be that word our sign of parting, bird or fiend!' I shrieked,
 upstarting —
'Get thee back into the tempest and the Night's Plutonian
 shore!
Leave no black plume as a token of that lie thy soul hath
 spoken!
Leave my loneliness unbroken! — quit the bust above my
 door!
Take thy beak from out my heart, and take thy form from off
 my door!'
            Quoth the Raven, 'Nevermore.'

And the Raven, never flitting, still is sitting, still is sitting
On the pallid bust of Pallas just above my chamber door;
And his eyes have all the seeming of a demon's that is
 dreaming,
And the lamp-light o'er him streaming throws his shadow on
 the floor;
And my soul from out that shadow that lies floating on the
 floor
            Shall be lifted — nevermore!

Edgar Allan Poe (1809–1849)

['The Raven' was also chosen by Julie Burchill in *Lifelines 2*.]

JEREMY CLARKSON   584

18 February 1997

Thank you for your letter to Jeremy Clarkson asking for his favourite poem.

He is away, but has asked me to let you know that it is Monty Python's Speverent Rooner poem — Jeremy's always been a huge Python fan.

Best wishes with your project.

Yours sincerely,
Francie Clarkson
(Jeremy's wife)

Port Shoem

I've a grouse and harden in the country,
An ace I call my plown,
A treat I can replace to
When I beed to knee alone
Catterfly and butterpillar
Perch on beafy lough
And I listen to the dats and cogs
As they mark and they biaow.
Yes, wature here is nunderful
There is no weed for nords,
While silling by my windowflutter
Biny little tirds.

Speverent Rooner

(from Monty Python's *Big Red Book*)

MICHAEL McDOWELL   585

Dáil Éireann
Baile Átha Cliath 2
14 February 1997

Dear Ralph, Caroline and Gareth,

I refer to your recent letter in relation to Lifelines.

My favourite poem is 'The Lady of Shalott' by Tennyson. I think it is a wonderful romantic story. A poem that once learnt by heart will be a powerful image for the rest of your life.

Yours sincerely,
Michael McDowell

The Lady of Shalott

Part I
On either side the river lie
Long fields of barley and of rye,
That clothe the wold and meet the sky;
And through the field the road runs by
    To many-towered Camelot;
And up and down the people go,
Gazing where the lilies blow
Round an island there below,
    The island of Shalott.

Willows whiten, aspens quiver,
Little breezes dusk and shiver
Through the wave that runs for ever
By the island in the river
    Flowing down to Camelot.
Four grey walls, and four grey towers,
Overlook a space of flowers,
And the silent isle imbowers
    The Lady of Shalott.

By the margin, willow-veiled,
Slide the heavy barges trailed
By slow horses; and unhailed
The shallop flitteth silken-sailed
    Skimming down to Camelot:
But who hath seen her wave her hand?
Or at the casement seen her stand?
Or is she known in all the land,
    The Lady of Shalott?

Only reapers, reaping early
In among the bearded barley,
Hear a song that echoes cheerly
From the river winding clearly,
    Down to towered Camelot:
And by the moon the reaper weary,
Piling sheaves in uplands airy,
Listening, whispers ''Tis the fairy
    Lady of Shalott.'

Part II
There she weaves by night and day
A magic web with colours gay.
She has heard a whisper say,
A curse is on her if she stay
    To look down to Camelot.

She knows not what the curse may be,
And so she weaveth steadily,
And little other care hath she,
    The Lady of Shalott.

And moving through a mirror clear
That hangs before her all the year,
Shadows of the world appear.
There she sees the highway near
    Winding down to Camelot:
There the river eddy whirls,
And there the surly village-churls,
And the red cloaks of market girls,
    Pass onward from Shalott.

Sometimes a troop of damsels glad,
An abbot on an ambling pad,
Sometimes a curly shepherd-lad,
Or long-haired page in crimson clad,
    Goes by to towered Camelot;
And sometimes through the mirror blue
The knights come riding two and two:
She hath no loyal knight and true,
    The Lady of Shalott.

But in her web she still delights
To weave the mirror's magic sights,
For often through the silent nights
A funeral, with plumes and lights
    And music, went to Camelot:
Or when the moon was overhead,
Came two young lovers lately wed;
'I am half sick of shadows,' said
    The Lady of Shalott.

Part III
A bow-shot from her bower-eaves,
He rode between the barley-sheaves,
The sun came dazzling through the leaves,
And flamed upon the brazen greaves
    Of bold Sir Lancelot.
A red-cross knight forever kneeled
To a lady in his shield,
That sparkled on the yellow field,
    Beside remote Shalott.

The gemmy bridle glittered free,
Like to some branch of stars we see
Hung in the golden Galaxy.
The bridle bells rang merrily
    As he rode down to Camelot:

And from his blazoned baldric slung
A mighty silver bugle hung,
And as he rode his armour rung,
    Beside remote Shalott.

All in the blue unclouded weather
Thick-jewelled shone the saddle leather,
The helmet and the helmet-feather
Burned like one burning flame together,
    As he rode down to Camelot.
As often through the purple night,
Below the starry clusters bright,
Some bearded meteor, trailing light,
    Moves over still Shalott.

His broad clear brow in sunlight glowed;
On burnished hooves his war-horse trode;
From underneath his helmet flowed
His coal-black curls as on he rode,
    As he rode down to Camelot.
From the bank and from the river
He flashed into the crystal mirror,
'Tirra Lirra,' by the river
    Sang Sir Lancelot.

She left the web, she left the loom,
She made three paces through the room,
She saw the water-lily bloom,
She saw the helmet and the plume,
    She looked down to Camelot.
Out flew the web and floated wide;
The mirror cracked from side to side;
'The curse is come upon me,' cried
    The Lady of Shalott.

Part IV
In the stormy east-wind straining,
The pale yellow woods were waning,
The broad stream in his banks complaining,
Heavily the low sky raining
    Over towered Camelot;
Down she came and found a boat
Beneath a willow left afloat,
And round about the prow she wrote
    The Lady of Shalott.

And down the river's dim expanse
Like some bold seer in a trance,
Seeing all his own mischance —
With a glassy countenance
    Did she look to Camelot.

And at the closing of the day
She loosed the chain, and down she lay;
The broad stream bore her far away,
    The Lady of Shalott.

Lying, robed in snowy white
That loosely flew to left and right —
The leaves upon her falling light —
Through the noises of the night
    She floated down to Camelot:
And as the boat-head wound along
The willowy hills and fields among,
They heard her singing her last song,
    The Lady of Shalott.

Heard a carol, mournful, holy,
Chanted loudly, chanted lowly,
Till her blood was frozen slowly,
And her eyes were darkened wholly,
    Turned to towered Camelot.
For ere she reached upon the tide
The first house by the water-side,
Singing in her song she died,
    The Lady of Shalott.

Under tower and balcony,
By garden-wall and gallery,
A gleaming shape she floated by,
Dead-pale between the houses high,
    Silent into Camelot.
Out upon the wharfs they came,
Knight and burgher, lord and dame,
And round the prow they read her name,
    The Lady of Shalott.

Who is this? and what is here?
And in the lighted palace near
Died the sound of royal cheer;
And they crossed themselves for fear,
    All the knights at Camelot:
But Lancelot mused a little space;
He said, 'She has a lovely face;
God in his mercy lend her grace,
    The Lady of Shalott.'

Alfred, Lord Tennyson (1809–1892)

['The Lady of Shalott' was also chosen by William Trevor in *Lifelines*.]

LOUIS DE PAOR 586

30 Aibreán 1997

Dear Ralph, Caroline and Gareth,

Míle buíochas as an gcuireadh chun dán a mholadh le haghaidh Lifelines 3 *agus tá súil agam go maithfidh sibh moill an mhéarfhadachais dom. Is é an dán atá roghnaithe agam ná* 'Hallaig' *le Somhairle MacGill-Eain. I still remember the strangeness and the absolute authority of Sorley Maclean's voice coming, it seemed, from another world beyond our own in a crowded basement in Cork in or about 1980. Throughout his work there is an overwhelming sense of an imagination charged with carrying the burden of a people's history, making present in words a world reduced to silence by the violent narrative of imperial history. His great achievement in* 'Hallaig' *and in many other poems is to redeem the submerged history of those cleared not only from their ancestral lands to make way for the laird's sheep and pine plantations but also from the unwritten pages of a people's memory. On their behalf MacGill-Eain has visited the Sabbath of the dead and brought time, the deer, to bay in the wood of Hallaig where the dead can still be seen alive.*

Guím gach rath ar an obair thábhachtach atá adir lámha agaibh le tamall a tharraingíonn an fhilíocht ar ais i dtreo an tsaoil mar a bhfuil a bhaile le ceart.

Le mórmheas,
Louis de Paor

Hallaig
'Tha tìm, am fiadh, an coille hallaig'

Tha bùird is tàirnean air an uinneig
troimh 'm faca mi an Aird an Iar
's tha mo ghaol aig Allt Hallaig
'na craoibh bheithe, 's bha i riamh

eadar an t-Inbhir's Poll a' Bhainne,
thall 's a bhos mu Bhaile-Chùirn:
tha i 'na beithe, 'na calltuinn,
'na caorunn dhìreach sheang ùir.

Ann an Screapadal mo chinnidh,
far robh Tarmad 's Eachunn Mór,
tha 'n nigheanan 's am mic 'nan coille
ag gabhail suas ri taobh an lóin.

Uaibhreach a nochd na coilich ghiuthais
ag gairm air mullach Cnoc an Rà,
dìreach an druim ris a' ghealaich —
chan iadsan coille mo ghràidh.

Fuirichidh mi ris a' bheithe
gus an tig i mach an Cárn,
gus am bi am bearradh uile
o Bheinn na Lice f' a sgàil.

Mura tig 's ann theàrnas mi a Hallaig
a dh' ionnsaigh sàbaid nam marbh,
far a bheil an sluagh a' tathaich,
gach aon ghinealach a dh' fhalbh.

Tha iad fhathast ann a Hallaig,
Clann Ghill-Eain 's Clann MhicLeòid,
na bh' ann ri linn Mhic Ghille-Chaluim:
Chunnacas na mairbh beò.

Na fir 'nan laighe air an lianaig
aig ceann gach taighe a bh' ann,
na h-igheanan 'nan coille bheithe,
díreach an druim, crom an ceann.

Eadar an Leac is na Feàrnaibh
tha 'n rathad mór fo chóinnich chiùin,
's na h-igheanan 'nam badan sàmhach
a' dol a Chlachan mar o thùs.

Agus a' tilleadh as a' Chlachan,
á Suidhisnis 's á tir nam beò;
a chuile té òg uallach
gun bhristeadh cridhe an sgeòil.

O Allt na Feàrnaibh gus an fhaoilinn
tha soilleir an dìomhaireachd nam beann
chan eil ach coimhthional nan nighean
ag cumail na coiseachd gun cheann.

A' tilleadh a Hallaig anns an fheasgar,
anns a' chamhanaich bhalbh bheò,
a' lìonadh nan leathadan casa,
an gàireachdaich 'nam chluais 'na ceò,

's am bòidhche 'na sgleò air mo chridhe
mun tig an ciaradh air na caoil,
's nuair theàrnas grian air cùl Dhùn Cana
thig peileir dian á gunna Ghaoil;

's buailear am fiadh a tha 'na thuaineal
a' snòtach nan làraichean feòir;
thig reothadh air a shùil 'sa' choille:
chan fhaighear lorg air fhuil ri m' bheò.

Somhairle MacGill-Eain (1911–1996)

Hallaig
'Time, the deer, is in the wood of Hallaig'

The window is nailed and boarded
through which I saw the West
and my love is at the Burn of Hallaig,
a birch tree, and she has always been

between Inver and Milk Hollow,
here and there about Baile-chuirn:
she is a birch, a hazel,
a straight, slender young rowan.

In Screapadal of my people
where Norman and Big Hector were,
their daughters and their sons are a wood
going up beside the stream.

Proud tonight the pine cocks
crowing on the top of Cnoc an Ra,
straight their backs in the moonlight —
they are not the wood I love.

I will wait for the birch wood
until it comes up by the cairn,
until the whole ridge from Beinn na Lice
will be under its shade.

If it does not, I will go down to Hallaig,
to the Sabbath of the dead,
where the people are frequenting,
every single generation gone.

They are still in Hallaig,
MacLeans and MacLeods,
all who were there in the time of Mac Gille Chaluim:
the dead have been seen alive.

The men lying on the green
at the end of every house that was,
the girls a wood of birches,
straight their backs, bent their heads.

Between the Leac and Fearns
the road is under mild moss
and the girls in silent bands
go to Clachan as in the beginning,

and return from Clachan
from Suisnish and the land of the living;
each one young and light-stepping,
without the heartbreak of the tale.

From the Burn of Fearns to the raised beach
that is clear in the mystery of the hills,
there is only the congregation of the girls
keeping up the endless walk,

coming back to Hallaig in the evening,
in the dumb living twilight,
filling the steep slopes,
their laughter a mist in my ears,

and their beauty a film on my heart
before the dimness comes on the kyles,
and when the sun goes down behind Dun Cana
a vehement bullet will come from the gun of Love;

and will strike the deer that goes dizzily,
sniffing at the grass-grown ruined homes;
his eye will freeze in the wood,
his blood will not be traced while I live.

Sorley MacLean (1911–1996)

WILLIAM WALL 587

13 January 1997

Many thanks for your letter. I feel honoured to be asked to contribute. My favourite poem is called 'They flee from me that sometime did me seek . . .' by Thomas Wyatt, a remarkable sixteenth-century poet.

Why? That is hard to say. I like the wit, the plaintive tone, the sensuality, the simple directness of it. Wyatt was an interesting man and I suppose I have as much affection for the man behind the poem as the poem itself. Many people could say the same, for example, about Seamus Heaney. Wyatt was first and foremost a diplomat as well as a poet of great skill and sensitivity. He was probably Anne Boleyn's lover before Henry set his cap at her and this may have got him into trouble. At any rate, he was eventually charged with adultery and though he was not executed he was imprisoned! Dangerous times! He died shortly after his release on his last diplomatic mission.

I hope this is helpful.

Best wishes,
William Wall

The Lover Showeth How He Is Forsaken of Such as He Sometime Enjoyed

They flee from me, that sometime did me seek
With naked foot stalking within my chamber.
Once have I seen them gentle, tame, and meek
That now are wild, and do not once remember
That sometime they have put themselves in danger
To take bread at my hand, and now they range,
Busily seeking in continual change.

Thankéd be fortune, it hath been otherwise,
Twenty times better; but once especial,
In thin array, after a pleasant guise,
When her loose gown did from her shoulders fall,
And she me caught in her arms long and small,
And therewithal, so sweetly did me kiss
And softly said: 'Dear heart, how like you this?'

It was no dream, for I lay broad awaking.
But all is turned now, through my gentleness,
Into a bitter fashion of forsaking.
And I have leave to go, of her goodness,
And she also to use newfangleness.
But since that I unkindly so am servéd,
How like you this, what hath she now deservéd?

Thomas Wyatt (1503–1542)

[This poem was also chosen by Andrew Motion in *Lifelines*.]

AUSTIN McQUINN 588

22 January 1997

Dear Ralph, Caroline and Gareth,

I am delighted and honoured to contribute to your worthy project, having enjoyed Lifelines *and* Lifelines 2 *so much.*

One of my favourite poems is 'In Memory of W B Yeats' *by W H Auden. It is many things: a generous tribute from one poet to another, a homage reflecting the poetic forms Yeats himself used, a lament which is both intimate and epic. But what moves me most is the poem's expression of belief in the sustaining power of art.*

With best wishes,
Yours sincerely,
Austin McQuinn

In Memory of W B Yeats
(died January 1939)

1
He disappeared in the dead of winter:
The brooks were frozen, the airports almost deserted,
And snow disfigured the public statues;
The mercury sank in the mouth of the dying day.
O all the instruments agree
The day of his death was a dark cold day.

Far from his illness
The wolves ran on through the evergreen forests,
The peasant river was untempted by the fashionable quays;
By mourning tongues
The death of the poet was kept from his poems.

But for him it was his last afternoon as himself,
An afternoon of nurses and rumours;
The provinces of his body revolted,
The squares of his mind were empty,
Silence invaded the suburbs,
The current of his feeling failed: he became his admirers.

Now he is scattered among a hundred cities
And wholly given over to unfamiliar affections;
To find his happiness in another kind of wood
And be punished under a foreign code of conscience.
The words of a dead man
Are modified in the guts of the living.

But in the importance and noise of tomorrow
When the brokers are roaring like beasts on the floor of the
    Bourse,
And the poor have the sufferings to which they are fairly
    accustomed,
And each in the cell of himself is almost convinced of his
    freedom;
A few thousand will think of this day
As one thinks of a day when one did something slightly
    unusual.
O all the instruments agree
The day of his death was a dark cold day.

2
You were silly like us: your gift survived it all;
The parish of rich women, physical decay,
Yourself; mad Ireland hurt you into poetry.
Now Ireland has her madness and her weather still,
For poetry makes nothing happen: it survives
In the valley of its saying where executives
Would never want to tamper; it flows south
From ranches of isolation and the busy griefs,
Raw towns that we believe and die in; it survives,
A way of happening, a mouth.

3
    Earth, receive an honoured guest;
    William Yeats is laid to rest:
    Let the Irish vessel lie
    Emptied of its poetry.

    Time that is intolerant
    Of the brave and innocent,
    And indifferent in a week
    To a beautiful physique,

    Worships language and forgives
    Everyone by whom it lives;
    Pardons cowardice, conceit,
    Lays its honours at their feet.

    Time that with this strange excuse
    Pardoned Kipling and his views,
    And will pardon Paul Claudel,
    Pardons him for writing well.

    In the nightmare of the dark
    All the dogs of Europe bark,
    And the living nations wait,
    Each sequestered in its hate;

    Intellectual disgrace
    Stares from every human face,
    And the seas of pity lie
    Locked and frozen in each eye.

    Follow, poet, follow right
    To the bottom of the night,
    With your unconstraining voice
    Still persuade us to rejoice;

With the farming of a verse
Make a vineyard of the curse,
Sing of human unsuccess
In a rapture of distress;

In the deserts of the heart
Let the healing fountain start,
In the prison of his days
Teach the free man how to praise.

W H Auden (1907–1973)

PAUL CARSON

3 June 1997

Dear Ralph, Caroline and Gareth,

Thank you very much for your letter and in particular thank you for asking me to contribute to Lifelines 3.

In medicine, aspiring students have to make decisions early in their secondary education which subjects they wish to study. Unfortunately, this tends to force many towards science as opposed to the arts. Consequently, many doctors have little exposure to poetry, apart from what must be learned for examinations.

There is one poem I recall vividly and which I enjoyed. It is by William Butler Yeats, 'He Wishes for the Cloths of Heaven'. It is particularly apt in medicine because so many of our patients are so unwell they have nothing left but their dreams.

I hope that this is useful for you in your new book and thank you again for inviting me to take part.

Yours sincerely,
Paul Carson
Dr Paul Carson

He Wishes for the Cloths of Heaven

Had I the heavens' embroidered cloths,
Enwrought with golden and silver light,
The blue and the dim and the dark cloths
Of night and light and the half-light,
I would spread the cloths under your feet:
But I, being poor, have only my dreams;
I have spread my dreams under your feet;
Tread softly because you tread on my dreams.

W B Yeats (1865–1939)

['He Wishes for the Cloths of Heaven' was chosen by Brian Boydell, Judith Woodworth, Michael Mortell and Brian Leyden in *Lifelines 2*.]

SEAMUS HOSEY 590

RTÉ
23 January 1997

Dear Ralph, Caroline and Gareth,

Congratulations on keeping the Lifelines *flag flying and keeping up the spirit of adventure, concern and enterprise started back in 1985 by your fellow Wesley students.*

I am delighted to nominate 'On Raglan Road' by Patrick Kavanagh as a favourite poem of mine. Like so many of Kavanagh's poems it manages to combine simplicity with profundity. This, I think, is a great love poem and I can never read it without hearing the voice of Luke Kelly bringing it so dramatically to life to the air of 'The Dawning of the Day'. This poem by Patrick Kavanagh seems to me a perfect exposition of Joyce's line which says it all: 'We lived and loved and laughed and left.'

Good luck with such a worthwhile venture and may Lifelines 3 *give as much pleasure as the previous volumes.*

Yours sincerely,
Seamus Hosey

On Raglan Road

On Raglan Road on an autumn day I met her first and knew
That her dark hair would weave a snare that I might one day rue;
I saw the danger, yet I walked along the enchanted way,
And I said, let grief be a fallen leaf at the dawning of the day.

On Grafton Street in November we tripped lightly along the ledge
Of the deep ravine where can be seen the worth of passion's pledge,
The Queen of Hearts still making tarts and I not making hay —
O I loved too much and by such by such is happiness thrown away.

I gave her gifts of the mind I gave her the secret sign that's known
To artists who have known the true gods of sound and stone
And word and tint. I did not stint for I gave her poems to say.
With her own name there and her own dark hair like clouds over fields of May.

On a quiet street where old ghosts meet I see her walking now
Away from me so hurriedly my reason must allow
That I had wooed not as I should a creature made of clay —
When the angel woos the clay he'd lose his wings at the dawn of day.

Patrick Kavanagh (1904–1967)

TOM GARVIN

Department of Politics
University College Dublin
16 January 1997

Dear Caroline, Gareth and Ralph,

Thank you very much for asking me to contribute to Lifelines 3. *I have many favourite poems, among them Coleridge's 'The Rime of the Ancient Mariner', rather too long for your purposes, I think.*

I would like to nominate 'On Raglan Road', by Patrick Kavanagh. It has many resonances for me, not least that of watching Luke Kelly sing it in Dublin thirty years ago. The poem evokes the city as it was in the 1950s in its use of familiar placenames. It is an urban ballad, and a love song. I like it also because of its descent from Irish tradition. My grandfather, John Daly of Clonakility, West Cork, born about 1870, sang its ancestor as his favourite song ('The Dawning of the Day'). He taught it to me as a child. As a boy in Ring College, County Waterford, I was taught the eighteenth-century Kerry version, 'Fáinne Geal an Lae'.

'On Raglan Road' symbolises a continuity of singing tradition over two centuries, from Irish to English and from rural to urban. All three versions are about a man's love for a woman.

Wishing you the best of luck with your anthology (I have the first two!) and a happy new year,

Tom Garvin

PS Good luck to all of you, Fifth Form Pupils, in your big exam in, I think, 1998.

The Dawning of the Day

At early dawn I once had been,
Where Lene's blue waters flow,
When summer bid the groves be green,
The lamp of light to glow,
As on by bow'r and town and tow'r,
And wide spread fields I stray,
I met a maid in the green-wood shade,
At the dawning of the day.

Her feet and beauteous head were bare,
No mantle fair she wore,
But down her waist fell golden hair
That swept the tall grass o'er,
With milking pail she sought the vale,
And bright her charms display,
Outshining far the morning star,
At the dawning of the day.

Beside me sat that maid divine,
Where grassy banks outspread,
'Oh! let me call thee ever mine,
Dear maid,' I gently said,
A blush o'er-spread her lily cheek,
She rose and sprang away,
The sun's first light pursued her flight
At the dawning of the day.

Anonymous

Fáinne Geal an Lae

Maidin moch do ghabhas amach,
Ar bhruach Locha Léin;
An Samhradh 'teacht 's an chraobh len' ais,
Is lonradh te ón ngréin,
Ar thaisteal dom trí bhailte poirt is bánta míne réidhe,
Cé a gheobhainn le m'ais ach an chúileann deas,
Le fáinne geal an lae.

Ní raibh bróg ná stoca, caidhp ná clóc;
Ar mo stóirín óg ón spéir,
Ach folt fionn órga síos go troigh,
Ag fás go barr an fhéir.
Bhí calán crúite aici ina glaic,
'S ar dhrúcht ba dheas a scéimh,
Do rug barr gean ar Bhéineas deas,
Le fáinne geal an lae.

Do shuigh an bhrídeog sios le m'ais,
Ar bhinse glas den fhéar,
Ag magadh léi, bhíos dá maíomh go pras,
Mar mhnaoi nach scarfainn léi.
'S é dúirt sí liomsa, 'imigh uaim,
Is scaoil ar siúl mé a réic,'
Sin iad aneas na soilse ag teacht,
Le fáinne geal an lae.

Anonymous

PATRICIA McKENNA

Offices of the European Parliament
Dublin 2
23 January 1997

Dear Ralph, Caroline and Gareth,

Thanks a million for your letter requesting details of my favourite poem: 'On Raglan Road' by Patrick Kavanagh. I hope that you will bend the rules a tiny bit for me, as most people think of this work as a song, rather than a poem.

Best of luck with the new edition of Lifelines. *The previous editions were extremely impressive and I look forward to seeing the fruits of your work.*

Le gach dea-ghuí,
Patricia McKenna

'On Raglan Road' *is one of the most beautiful things ever written. So many people's experiences of life and love are contained in the lines:*

> I saw the danger, yet I walked along the enchanted way,
> And I said, let grief be a fallen leaf at the dawning of the day.

I always thought that nobody could come even close to Luke Kelly's version of this song, but I was proven wrong when I heard Sinéad O'Connor's haunting rendition recently.

Like myself, Kavanagh grew up in Monaghan and then moved to Dublin, where his finest poems were written. His poems, especially the ones he wrote on the banks of the Grand Canal, show that you can find serenity and peace amid the hustle and bustle of Dublin life and highlight how everything must be done to preserve the capital's heritage.

['On Raglan Road' was chosen by Ken Bourke in *Lifelines* and by Jimmy Murphy in *Lifelines 2*. It was also chosen by Tom Garvin and Seamus Hosey in this volume.]

RICHARD WILSON   593

9 February 1997

Dear Ralph,

Thank you very much for your letter. My favourite poem is 'To a Mouse' by Robert Burns. It's a poem that shows Burns at his best — the language has great lyrical grace and it illustrates beautifully Burns's compassion for his fellow creatures. I only wish some more farmers could exhibit the same compassion to their animals!

Best wishes,
Richard Wilson

['To a Mouse' was also chosen by Alex Ferguson. The poem can be found on page 33.]

NORA OWEN   594

Oifig an Aire Dlí agus Cirt
Baile Átha Cliath
Office of the Minister for Justice
Dublin
17 January 1997

'When You Are Old' *and* 'A Drinking Song' *by W B Yeats.*

W B Yeats manages to paint a picture with his words and in his words you feel he has actually lived out the occasions he's describing!

Nora Owen

A Drinking Song

Wine comes in at the mouth
And love comes in at the eye;
That's all we shall know for truth
Before we grow old and die.
I lift the glass to my mouth,
I look at you, and I sigh.

W B Yeats (1865–1939)

['When You Are Old' was also chosen by Tony Roche in this volume. The poem can be found on page 169.]

MARY FINAN 595

Wilson Hartnell Public Relations Ltd
18 February 1997

'When You Are Old' by W B Yeats is a translation of Ronsard's poem 'Quand Tu Sera Vieille'. I have always felt that it was one of the most beautiful love poems ever written. Everyone wants to be loved for the kind of person they are, rather than who they are or how they look. Lines such as

> But one man loved the pilgrim soul in you,
> And loved the sorrows of your changing face.

I find I get fonder of this poem as the decades pass by. Rather like Agatha Christie who, when asked what it was like being married to an archaeologist, replied 'Wonderful, darling, the older I get the more interesting he finds me!'

Mary Finan
Managing Director

['When You Are Old' was chosen by Anthony Clare in Lifelines, by Eilís Ní Dhuibhne in Lifelines 2 and by Tony Roche and Nora Owen in this volume. The poem is on page 169.]

MICHAEL PARKINSON 596

10 March 1997

Dear Ralph, Caroline and Gareth,

Michael Parkinson has asked me to write and thank you for your letter.

His favourite poem is 'Dulce Et Decorum Est' by Wilfred Owen, about the horror of war. He believes it to be one of the greatest poems of its sort ever written.

With kind regards,
Yours sincerely,
Kathleen Coleman
Michael Parkinson's Office

Dulce Et Decorum Est

Bent double, like old beggars under sacks,
Knock-kneed, coughing like hags, we cursed through sludge,
Till on the haunting flares we turned our backs
And towards our distant rest began to trudge.
Men marched asleep. Many had lost their boots
But limped on, blood-shod. All went lame; all blind;
Drunk with fatigue; deaf even to the hoots
Of tired, outstripped Five-Nines that dropped behind.

Gas! GAS! Quick, boys! — An ecstasy of fumbling,
Fitting the clumsy helmets just in time;
But someone still was yelling out and stumbling
And flound'ring like a man in fire or lime . . .
Dim, through the misty panes and thick green light,
As under a green sea, I saw him drowning.

In all my dreams, before my helpless sight,
He plunges at me, guttering, choking, drowning.

If in some smothering dreams you too could pace
Behind the wagon that we flung him in,
And watch the white eyes writhing in his face,
His hanging face, like a devil's sick of sin;
If you could hear, at every jolt, the blood
Come gargling from the froth-corrupted lungs,
Obscene as cancer, bitter as the cud
Of vile, incurable sores on innocent tongues, —
My friend, you would not tell with such high zest
To children ardent for some desperate glory,
The old Lie: *Dulce et decorum est
Pro patria mori.*

Wilfred Owen (1893–1918)

JONATHAN RHYS MEYERS

Ralph, Caroline, Gareth — Hi,

Thank you for your wonderful offer to submit poems for Lifelines. *I hope I'm not too late.*

In the slaughterhouse of love they kill
Only the best, none of the weak or deformed.
Don't run away from this dying
Whoever is not killed for love is dead meat.

Mevlana Jalaluddin Rumi (1207–1273)

The room is open to the turquoise blues
No space: coffers and chests
Outside the wall is full of birthwork
Where the gums of elves vibrate.

These are really the plottings of genie —
This expense and this futile disorder!
It is the African fairy who furnishes
The blackberry, and the hornets in the corners.

Arthur Rimbaud (1854–1891)

Yours,
Jonathan Rhys Meyers

PAULINE QUIRKE 598

Birds of a Feather

Good luck with your production of Lifelines. *My favourite poem, 'Don't Quit', got me through some difficult times in my life.*

Don't Quit

When things go wrong, as they sometimes will,
When the road you're trudging seems all uphill,
When the funds are low, and the debts are high,
And you want to smile, but you have to sigh,
Don't quit.
When care is pressing you down a bit,
Rest if you must, but don't you quit.
Life is queer with its twists and turns,
As everyone of us sometimes learns,
And many a failure turns about,
When he might have won had he stuck it out;
Don't give up though the pace seems slow,
You may succeed, with another blow.
Success is failure turned inside out,
The silver tint of the clouds of doubt,
And you never can tell how close you are,
It may be near when it seems so far;
So stick to the fight when you're hardest hit
It's when things seem worse, that you must not quit.

Anonymous

PHILIP CASTLE 599

Villefranche-sur-mer
France
12 January 1997

Dear Ralph Croly, Caroline Dowling and Gareth McCluskey,

Thank you for your letter.

Nonsense verse is my choice, and the three little pieces by Belloc, Lear and Sitwell I've picked give me the most pleasure. Lear lived in my part of the world and although he painted superb architectural views of Mediterranean cities, occasionally to be seen in Partridge Fine Arts, Bond Street, he is only remembered for his verse.

Sitwell voices the cynical abstract fantasies of a trained mind unleashed on its fellows.

Belloc is the social sniper who reduces convention to anarchy.

Buildings are my obsession. I draw them and then dream them into the phantasmagoric, preserving some of their original character to contrast the fantasy with the reality. Working through subjects as diverse as Maltese Romanesque to Whitehall Spanish Rococo, itself a parody, I revel in computer Gothic, the machine-made madness in stainless steel and glass of the modern financial centres.

What of the future? Swift knew the way, turning nonsense into voyages of adventure. For him it was the crossing of the oceans to lands of midgets and giants. For me it is the crossing of the heavens to planets of non-Euclidean space where circular triangles contain six right angles.

I hope this will be of some use to you.

Every good wish for 1997,

Sincerely,
Philip Castle

There was an old person of Dundalk,
Who tried to teach fishes to walk;
When they tumbled down dead, he grew weary, and said,
'I had better go back to Dundalk!'

Edward Lear (1812–1888)

Trio for Two Cats and a Trombone

Long steel grass —
The white soldiers pass —
The light is braying like an ass.
See
The tall Spanish jade
With hair black as nightshade
Worn as a cockade!
Flee
Her eyes' gasconade
And her gown's parade
(as stiff as a brigade).
Tee-hee!
The hard and braying light
Is zebra'd black and white
It will take away the slight
And free
Tinge of the mouth-organ sound
(Oyster-stall notes) oozing round
Her flounces as they sweep the ground.
The
Trumpet and the drum
And the martial cornet come
To make the people dumb —
But we
Won't wait for sly-foot night
(Moonlight, watered milk-white, bright)
To make clear the declaration
Of our Paphian vocation
Beside the castanetted sea
Where stalks Il Capitaneo
Swaggart braggadocio
Sword and moustachio —
He
Is green as a cassada
And his hair is an armada.
To the jade 'Come kiss me harder'
He called across the battlements as she
Heard our voices thin and shrill
As the steely grasses' thrill
Or the sound of the onycha
When the phoca has the pica
In the palace of the Queen Chinee!

Edith Sitwell (1887–1964)

Lord Lundy
(Second Canto)

It happened to Lord Lundy then,
As happens to so many men:
Towards the age of twenty-six,
They shoved him into politics;
In which profession he commanded
The income that his rank demanded
In turn as Secretary for
India, the Colonies, and War.
But very soon his friends began
To doubt if he were quite the man:
Thus, if a member rose to say
(As members do from day to day),
'Arising out of that reply . . . !'
Lord Lundy would begin to cry.
A Hint at harmless little jobs
Would shake him with convulsive sobs.

While as for Revelations, these
Would simply bring him to his knees,
And leave him whimpering like a child.
It drove his Colleagues raving wild!
They let him sink from Post to Post,
From fifteen hundred at the most
To eight, and barely six — and then
To be Curator of Big Ben! . . .
And finally there came a Threat
To oust him from the Cabinet!

The Duke — his aged grand-sire — bore
The shame till he could bear no more.
He rallied his declining powers,
Summoned the youth to Brackley Towers,
And bitterly addressed him thus —
'Sir! you have disappointed us!
We had intended you to be
The next Prime Minister but three:
The stocks were sold; the Press was squared;
The Middle Class was quite prepared.
But as it is! . . . My language fails!
Go out and govern New South Wales!'

The Aged Patriot groaned and died:
And gracious! how Lord Lundy cried!

Hilaire Belloc (1870–1953)

ANTONIA LOGUE 600

21 July 1997

Hi,

Thanks a million for asking me for my favourite poem for Lifelines 3 *— I've definitely to earn my spurs yet, but it's an honour being asked.*

I got stuck between two poems — I love both of them for such different reasons and in the end I couldn't make up my mind . . . they're 'Little Girl Wakes Early' *by Robert Penn Warren and* 'As I Walked Out One Evening' *by W H Auden.* 'Little Girl Wakes Early' *is the most tender poem I've ever read. There is an unbearable sadness in the last lines, and I think only the luckiest or hardiest people could read them and not nod, even slightly. I had such a deeply happy childhood, but eventually nothing innoculates you against the feelings in those last lines.*

Auden's 'As I Walked Out One Evening' *is a savage poem, but within it are twelve lines [stanzas 3–5] of the most beautiful, daft love poetry. I was given them as an inscription once inside a book, and those twelve lines have vied with* 'Little Girl Wakes Early' *ever since as the lines that move me most, but for much nicer reasons . . .*

I really hope Lifelines 3 *works out brilliantly for you all — like lots of others, I've spent Stephen's Day curled up with* Lifelines, *and it's such a pleasure to contribute to it.*

Take care,

With warmest wishes,

Antonia Logue

Little Girl Wakes Early

Remember when you were the first one awake, the first
To stir in the dawn-curdled house, with little bare feet
Cold on boards, every door shut and accurst,
And behind shut doors no breath perhaps drew, no heart beat.

You held your breath and thought how all over town
Houses had doors shut, and no whisper of breath sleeping,
And that meant no swinging, nobody to pump up and down,
No hide-and-go-seek, no serious play at housekeeping.

So you ran outdoors, bare feet from the dew wet,
And climbed the fence to the house of your dearest friend,
And opened your lips and twisted your tongue, all set
To call her name — but the sound wouldn't come in the end,

For you thought how awful, if there was no breath there
For answer. Tears start, you run home, where now mother,
Over the stove, is humming some favorite air.
You seize her around the legs, but tears aren't over,

And won't get over, not even when she shakes you —
And shakes you hard — and more when you can't explain.
Your mother's long dead. And you've learned that when
    loneliness takes you
There's nobody ever to explain to — though you try again and
    again.

Robert Penn Warren (1905–1988)

As I walked out one Evening

As I walked out one evening,
    Walking down Bristol Street,
The crowds upon the pavement
    Were fields of harvest wheat.

And down by the brimming river
    I heard a lover sing
Under an arch of the railway:
    'Love has no ending.

'I'll love you, dear, I'll love you
    Till China and Africa meet,
And the river jumps over the mountain
    And the salmon sing in the street.

'I'll love you till the ocean
    Is folded and hung up to dry
And the seven stars go squawking
    Like geese about the sky.

'The years shall run like rabbits
    For in my arms I hold
The Flower of the Ages,
    And the first love of the world.'

But all the clocks in the city
    Began to whirr and chime:
'O let not Time deceive you,
    You cannot conquer Time.

'In the burrows of the Nightmare
    Where Justice naked is,
Time watches from the shadow
    And coughs when you would kiss.

'In headaches and in worry
　　Vaguely life leaks away,
And Time will have his fancy
　　Tomorrow or today.

'Into many a green valley
　　Drifts the appalling snow;
Time breaks the threaded dances
　　And the diver's brilliant bow.

'O plunge your hands in water,
　　Plunge them in up to the wrist;
Stare, stare in the basin
　　And wonder what you've missed.

'The glacier knocks in the cupboard,
　　The desert sighs in the bed,
And the crack in the tea-cup opens
　　A lane to the land of the dead.

'Where the beggars raffle the banknotes
　　And the Giant is enchanting to Jack,
And the Lily-white Boy is a Roarer
　　And Jill goes down on her back.

'O look, look in the mirror,
　　O look in your distress;
Life remains a blessing
　　Although you cannot bless.

'O stand, stand at the window
　　As the tears scald and start;
You shall love your crooked neighbour
　　With your crooked heart.'

It was late, late in the evening,
　　The lovers they were gone;
The clocks had ceased their chiming
　　And the deep river ran on.

W H Auden (1907–1973)

Notes on the contributors (in alphabetical order)

Myrtle Allen (p 183) — Cookery expert and author (*The Ballymaloe Cookbook*); **Brian Ashton** (p 202) — Irish rugby coach and former international rugby scrum-half; **Michael Aspel** (p 3) — Television broadcaster (presenter of *This Is Your Life*) and memoir writer (*Polly Wants a Zebra*); **Kate Atkinson** (p 190) — Novelist (*Behind the Scenes at the Museum*; *Human Croquet*); **R J Ayling** (p 159) — Director of British Airways; **Ivy Bannister** (p 27) — playwright and short story writer (*Magician and Other Stories*); **Beryl Bainbridge** (p 216) — Novelist (*The Dressmaker*; *The Bottle Factory Outing*; *Injury Time*; *Every Man for Himself*); **Eileen Battersby** (p 13) — *Irish Times* staff arts journalist, broadcaster and critic; **Gerard Beirne** (p 117) — poet (*Digging My Own Grave*) and fiction writer and winner of the Hennessy overall Best Writer award 1994; **Niamh Bhreathnach** (p 30) — Labour politician, former Minister for Education; **Mary Rose Binchy** (p 148) — Artist; **Tony Blair** (p 204) — Politician, leader of the Labour Party, became British Prime Minister on 2 May 1997; **John Boland** (p 53) — Journalist and critic; **Dermot Bolger** (p 44) — Novelist (*Nightshift,The Journey Home*; *Father's Music*), playwright (*Lament for Arthur Cleary*), poet, journalist and editor; **Betty Boothroyd** (p 62) — Speaker in the House of Commons; first woman ever elected to the position; **Pat Boran** (p 143) — Poet (*The Unwound Clock*; *Familiar Things*; *The Shape of Water*) and short story writer (*Strange Bedfellows*); **Angela Bourke** (p 46) — short story writer (*By Salt Water*), critic, broadcaster and lecturer; **Paul Brady** (p 37) — Singer, songwriter; **Melvyn Bragg** (p 180) — Novelist (*The Hired Man*; *Kingdom Come*; *Josh Lawton*; *The Maid of Buttermere*; *Credo*), broadcaster, Head of the Arts Department at London Weekend Television, editor of *The South Bank Show* and presenter of *Start the Week* on BBC Radio 4; **Stephen Brennan** (p 5) — Actor; **John Burnside** (p 7) — Scottish poet (*The Hoop*; *Common Knowledge*; *Feast Days*; *Swimming in the Flood*; *A Normal Skin*) and novelist (*The Dumb House*); **Catherine Byrne** (p 111) — Actor on stage (*Dancing at Lughnasa*; *Molly Sweeney*; *Give Me Your Answer Do!*) and television (*Upwardly Mobile*); **Hayden Carruth** (p 199) — American poet (*The Bloomingdale Papers*; *Brothers, I Have Loved You All*; *Selected Poems*; *The Sleeping Beauty*) and writer of essays and reviews (*Effluences from the Sacred Caves*); **Paul Carson** (p 251) — Novelist (*Scalpel*), author of books for children, writer (*How to Cope with Your Child's Allergies*; *Coping Successfully with Your Hyperactive Child*; *Coping Successfully with Your Child's Asthma*) and medical doctor; **Kevin Casey** (p 52) — Novelist (*The Sinner's Bell*; *A Sense of Survival*; *Dreams of Revenge*) and short story writer; **Philip Casey** (p 64) — Novelist (*The Fabulists*), poet and playwright (*Cardinal*); **Barry Castle** (p 177) — Artist, writer and illustrator (*Cooking for Cats*); **Philip Castle** (p 260) — Artist; **Patrick Chapman** (p 125) — Poet (*Jazztown*; *The New Pornography*); **Jeremy Clarkson** (p 239) — Journalist and newspaper columnist, television presenter (*Motorworld*) and author (*Clarkson on Cars*; *Jeremy Clarkson's Motorworld*); **Harry Clifton** (p 19) — Poet (*The Walls of Carthage*; *Office of the Salt Merchant*; *Comparative Lives*; *The Liberal Cage*; *Night Train Through the Brenner* and selected poems, *The Desert Route*); **Dame Catherine Cookson** (p 185) — Novelist (*The Round Tower*; *The Blind Miller*; *Colour Blind*; *The Gillyvors*); **Ronnie Corbett** (p 104) — Comedian; **Andrea Corr** (p 77) — Singer/musician, member of The Corrs; **Tom Courtenay** (p 174) — Actor on stage (*Art*) and screen (*The Dresser*); **Roz Cowman** (p 82) — Poet (*The Goose Herd*) and winner of the Patrick Kavanagh Award 1985; **Elaine Crowley** (p 204) — Novelist (*Dream of Other Days*; *The Petunia-Coloured Coat*; *The Ways of Women*; *A Family Cursed*) and writer (*Cowslips and Chainies: A Memoir of Dublin in the 1930s*); **Michael Curtin** (p 198) — Novelist (*The Self-Made Men*; *The Replay*; *The League Against Christmas*; *The Plastic Tomato Cutter*; *The Cove Shivering Club*); **Philip Davison** (p 11) — Novelist

(*The Book-Thief's Heartbeat; Twist and Shout; The Illustrator; The Crooked Man*) and playwright (*The Invisible Mending Company*); **Richard Dawkins** (p 189) — Scientist and writer (*River Out of Eden*); **John F Deane** (p 66) — Poet (*Stalking After Time; High Sacrifice; Winter in Meath; Road with Cypress and Star; The Stylized City; Walking on Water*), short-story writer (*Free Range*) and novelist (*One Man's Place*), also founder of Poetry Ireland and founder of Dedalus Press; **Eamon Delaney** (p 176) — Novelist (*The Casting of Mr O'Shaughnessy*) and journalist; **Matthew Dempsey** (p 197) — Journalist and editor of *The Farmers Journal*; **Louis de Paor** (p 244) — Poet (*Próca Solais is Luatha; 30 Dán; Aimsir Bhreicneach / Freckled Weather; Seo, Siúd agus Uile*); **Roddy Doyle** (p 91) — Novelist (*The Commitments; The Snapper; The Van; Paddy Clarke Ha Ha Ha; The Woman Who Walked Into Doors*) and playwright (*Brownbread; War*); **Martin Drury** (p 158) — Director of The Ark; **Robert Dunbar** (p 211) — Lecturer, editor, writer and critic; **Terry Eagleton** (p 105) — Professor of English at Oxford, critic and writer (*Criticism and Ideology; Marxism and Literary Criticism; The Rape of Clarissa; Literary Theory: An Introduction; The Function of Criticism*), novelist (*Saints and Scholars*) and playwright (*Saint Oscar*); **Brian Fallon** (p 83) — Chief critic of the *Irish Times*; **Sebastian Faulks** (p 126) — Novelist (*Birdsong; A Trick of the Light; The Girl at the Lion D'Or*) and writer of non-fiction (*The Fatal Englishman: Three Short Lives*); **Alex Ferguson CBE** (p 33) — Manager of The Manchester United Football Club plc; **Mary Finan** (p 257) — Director of Wilson Hartnell Public Relations Ltd; **Fr Aengus Finucane** (p 157) — Founder of Concern; **Penelope Fitzgerald** (p 78) — English novelist (*Offshore* — Booker prize 1979, *The Beginning of Spring; The Gate of Angels; The Blue Flower*); **Marie Foley** (p 81) — Artist; **Aisling Foster** (p 128) — Novelist (*Safe in the Kitchen*), playwright and critic; **Mildred Fox** (p 197) — Politician, Independent TD; **Tom Garvin** (p 253) — Professor of Politics at University College Dublin, writer (*Nationalist Revolutionaries in Ireland, 1858–1928; The Evolution of Irish Nationalist Politics; 1922: The Birth of Irish Democracy*); **Mary Gordon** (p 101) — Novelist (*Final Payments; The Company of Women; Men and Angels; Temporary Shelter; The Other Side*) and writer (*Good Boys and Dead Girls; The Shadow Man*); **Michael Gorman** (p 187) — Poet (*Postcards from Galway; Waiting for the Sky to Fall; Up She Flew*); **Lady Valerie Goulding** (p 18) — Co-founder of the Central Remedial Clinic; **Anita Groener** (p 228) — Artist; **Andrew Hamilton** (p 172) — Composer; **Charles Handy** (p 200) — Business consultant, author (*The Empty Raincoat: Making Sense of the Future; Age of Unreason; Hungry Spirit*) **Kerry Hardie** (p 115) — Poet (*A Furious Place*) and winner of the 1996 Friends Provident National Poetry Competition; **Dr John W Harris** (p 209) — Principal of Wesley College and former Special Adviser to three Ministers for Education; **Rolf Harris** (p 194) — Australian songwriter, performer and artist; **Josephine Hart** (p 21) — Novelist (*Damage; Sin; Obsession*); **Lara Harte** (p 62) — Novelist (*First Time*); **Michael Hartnett** (p 184) — Poet (*Anatomy of a Cliché; The Hag of Beare; Gipsy Ballads; A Farewell to English; Culu Ide: The Retreat of Ita Cagney; Inchicore Haiku; Poems to Younger Women; The Killing of Dreams*); **Anne Haverty** (p 173) — Novelist (*One Day as a Tiger*), biographer (*Constance Markievicz*), poet and winner of the Rooney Prize 1997; **Katy Hayes** (p 165) — Short story writer (*Forecourt*) and novelist (*Curtains*); **Dermot Healy** (p 35) — Novelist (*Banished Misfortune; Fighting with Shadows; A Goat's Song*), poet (*The Ballyconnell Colours*) and memoir writer (*The Bend for Home*); **Marie Heaney** (p 136) — Writer (*Over Nine Waves: A Book of Irish Legends*), broadcaster and critic; **Oscar Hijuelos** (p 22) — American novelist (*Our House in the Last World; The Mambo Kings Play Songs of Love; The Fourteen Sisters of Emilio Montez O'Brien; Mr Ives' Christmas*); **Selima Hill** (p 110) — Poet (*The Accumulation of Small Acts of Kindness; Saying Hello at the Station; My Darling Camel; Little Book of Meat; Violet*); **Tobias Hill** (p 26) — Poet (*Year of the Dog*) and short story writer (*Skin*); **Seamus**

NOTES ON THE CONTRIBUTORS

Hosey (p 252) — Broadcaster, producer and editor (*Speaking Volumes*); **Brendan Howlin** (p 39) — Labour politician, former Minister for the Environment; **Declan Hughes** (p 196) — Playwright (*I Can't Get Started; Digging For Fire; Love and a Bottle; New Morning; Halloween Night; Philip Newman's Weekend*); **John Hughes** (p 134) — Poet (*The Something in Particular; Negotiations with the Chill Wind; The Devil Himself*); **Kathleen Jamie** (p 60) — Scottish poet (*The Way We Live; The Autonomous Region* — with Sean Mayne Smith) and travel writer (*The Golden Peak*); **Elizabeth Jolley** (p 15) Australian novelist, born in England (*The Newspaper of Claremont Street; The Well; The Sugar Mother; Cabin Fever*); **Lesley Joseph** (p 214) — Actor (*Birds of a Feather*); **Fergal Keane** (p 188) — Broadcaster with the BBC and writer (*Letter to Daniel*); **Tony Keily** (p 217) — Novelist (*The Shark Joke; 37 Heartbeats Per Minute*) and short story writer; **John Kelly** (p 175) — Broadcaster (presenter of *The Eclectic Ballroom* on Radio Ireland), radio and television producer, novelist (*Grace Notes and Bad Thoughts*), poet and writer (*Cool About the Ankles*); **Frank Kermode** (p 89) — Professor of English, critic and writer (*Not Entitled: A Memoir*); **Marian Keyes** (p 65) — Novelist (*Watermelon; Lucy Sullivan Is Getting Married*); **Tony Kushner** (p 190) — American playwright (*A Bright Room Called Day; Angels In America — I — Millennium Approaches, II — Perestroika*); **Soinbhe Lally** (p 111) — Writer of children's books (*The Green Room; Song of the River*); **Eugene Lambert** (p 94) — Puppeteer and writer; **Eamonn Lawlor** (p 208) — Journalist and broadcaster; **Jessie Lendennie** (p 230) — Poet (*Daughter*) and founder of Salmon Publishing; **Denise Levertov** (p 67) — English-born American poet (*The Double Image; Relearning the Alphabet; Life in the Forest; Evening Train*) and critic (*The Poet in the World; Light up the Cave*); **Gary Lineker** (p 87) — Sports star and television presenter; **Antonia Logue** (p 263) — Novelist (*The Shadow Box*) and journalist; **P J Lynch** (p 2) — Illustrator of children's books (*The Snow Queen; The King of Ireland's Son; The Christmas Miracle of Jonathan Toomey*) and writer (*East o' the Sun and West o' the Moon*); **Colum McCann** (p 8) — Short story writer (*Fishing the Sloe-Black River*) and novelist (*Songdogs; Underground Snow*) and winner of the 1994 Rooney Prize; **Molly McCloskey** (p 193) — Short story writer (*Solomon's Seal*); **Mike McCormack** (p 181) — Short story writer (*Getting It in the Head*) and winner of the 1996 Rooney Prize; **Frank McCourt** (p 213) — Writer (*Angela's Ashes*) and performer with his brother Malachy in a musical review about their Irish youth (*A Couple of Blaguards*); **Martin McDonagh** (p 235) — Playwright (*The Beauty Queen of Leenane; The Cripple of Inishmaan; The Lieutenant of Inishmore; A Skull in Connemara; The Lonesome West; The Pillowman*); **Frank McDonald** (p 232) — Environment Correspondent of the *Irish Times*, author (*The Destruction of Dublin; Saving the City*) and co-author — with Peigín Doyle — (*Ireland's Earthen Homes*); **Michael McDowell** (p 239) — Former politician and TD for Progressive Democrats, barrister; **Declan McGonagle** (p 98) — Director of The Irish Museum of Modern Art; **Iggy McGovern** (p 118) — Poet and Associate Professor of Physics at Trinity College, Dublin; **Tom Mac Intyre** (p 179) — Poet, novelist, short story writer and dramatist (*The Bearded Lady; Rise up Lovely Sweeney; Dance For Your Daddy; Good Evening Mr Collins*); **Patricia McKenna** (p 255) — Politician and MEP; **Susan McKenna-Lawlor** (p 207) — Professor of Experimental Physics at St Patrick's College, Maynooth, Managing Director of Space Technology (Ireland) Ltd, member of the International Academy of Astronautics, received the Russian Tsiokovsky Gold Medal for contributions to cosmonautics; **Pauline McLynn** (p 146) — Actor (roles include Mrs Doyle in *Father Ted*); **Conor McPherson** (p 205) — Playwright (*The Good Thief; This Lime Tree Bower; St Nicholas; The Weir*) and screenwriter (*I Went Down*); **Austin McQuinn** (p 248) — Artist; **Brenda Maddox** (p 90) — Journalist, broadcaster and author (*Beyond Babel: New Directions in Communications; The Half-Parent: Living with Other People's Children;*

Married and Gay; *Who's Afraid of Elizabeth Taylor*; *Nora: The Real Life of Molly Bloom*); **John Major** (p 55) — Politician, former leader of the British Conservative Party and former Prime Minister; **Aidan Mathews** (p 79) — Short story writer (*Adventures in a Bathyscope*; *Lipstick on the Host*), playwright (*Exit/Entrance*), poet (*Windfalls*; *Minding Ruth*) and novelist (*Muesli at Midnight*); **Orla Melling** (p 119) — Pseudonym of G V Whelan, Irish-Canadian writer and critic, writer of children's books (*The Druid's Tune*; *The Singing Stone*; *The Hunter's Moon*); **Arthur Miller** (p 1) — Playwright (*Death of a Salesman*; *The Crucible*; *A View from the Bridge*; *The American Clock*); **Lia Mills** (p 122) — Novelist (*Another Alice*); **Michael Mortell** (p 145) — President of University College Cork; **Michael Mullen** (p 215) — Novelist (*Kelly*; *Festival of Fools*; *The Hungry Land*; *Rites of Inheritance*) and children's writer (*Sea Wolves from the North*; *The Flight of the Earls*); **Bríd Óg Ní Bhuachalla** (p 63) — Broadcaster, journalist and writer (*Kids Day Out*); **Fionnuala Ní Chiosáin** (p 169) — Artist; **Áine Ní Ghlinn** (p 99) — Poet (*An Cheim Bhriste*; *Gairdín Pharthais*; *Deora Nar Caoineadh*), writer (*Mna as an Gnath*; *Deithe Is Daoine*), journalist and broadcaster; **Betty Ann Norton** (p 50) — Drama teacher and Director of the Betty Ann Norton School of Drama; **Joyce Carol Oates** (p 171) — American novelist (*Them*; *With Shuddering Fall*; *Marya: A Life*), short story writer, poet and critic; **Miriam O'Callaghan** (p 131) — Broadcaster and journalist, presenter of *Prime Time* on RTE; **Brendan O'Carroll** (p 168) — Comedian, playwright (*Grandad's Sure Lilly's Still Alive*), novelist (*The Mammy*; *The Chiseller*; *The Granny*) and television presenter; **Bernard O'Donoghue** (p 201) — Poet (*Poaching Rights*; *The Absent Signifier*; *The Weakness*; *Gunpowder*) and writer on medieval English; **Desmond O'Grady** (p 136) — Poet (*Chords and Orchestrations*; *Reilly*; *The Dark Edge of Europe*; *Off Licence*; *The Dying Gaul*; *Sing Me Creation*); **Nora Owen** (p 256) — Politician; **Michael Parkinson** (p 257) — Broadcaster; **Siobhán Parkinson** (p 116) — Children's writer (*All Shining in the Spring*; *Amelia*; *No Peace for Amelia*; *Sisters — No Way!*; *Off We Go — The Country Adventure*; *Off We Go — The Dublin Adventure*) and editor (*Home: An Anthology of Modern Irish Writing*); **Glenn Patterson** (p 229) — Novelist (*Burning Your Own*; *Fat Lad*); **Stephen Pearce** (p 231) — Potter; **Harold Pinter** (p 131) — English playwright (*The Birthday Party*; *The Caretaker*; *Ashes to Ashes*; *One for the Road*; *Mountain Language*); **Andy Pollak** (p 71) — Journalist, Education Correspondent with the *Irish Times*; **Terry Prone** (p 135) — Short story writer (*Blood Brothers, Soul Sisters*), novelist (*Racing the Moon*), broadcaster, media consultant and Managing Director of Carr Communications Ltd; **Ita Quilligan** (p 124) — Artist; **Eimear Quinn** (p 203) — Singer and musician, singer of the winning song in the 1996 Eurovision Song Contest; **Feargal Quinn** (p 97) — Managing Director of Superquinn; **Justin Quinn** (p 113) — Poet (*The 'O'o'a'a' Bird*) and co-editor of *Metre*; **Pauline Quirke** (p 259) — Actor (*Birds of a Feather*); **Jane Ray** (p 28) — Illustrator (*The Story of the Creation*; *The Story of Christmas*; *Noah's Ark*; *A Balloon for Grandad*; *The Happy Prince*; *The Orchard Book of Magical Tales*) and designer; **Peter Reading** (p 206) — Poet (*For the Municipality's Elderly*; *Stet*; *Shitheads: New Poems*; *Collected Poems I* and *II*); **Jonathan Rhys Meyers** (p 258) — Actor and winner of the inuagural Guinness Award for Outstanding Young Actor (*A Man of No Importance*; *The Disappearance of Finbar*; *Michael Collins*; *B Monkey*); **Rodney Rice** (p 121) — Broadcaster and journalist, presenter of *Saturday View* on RTE Radio 1; **Anne Robinson** (p 92) — Newspaper columnist and television presenter (BBC's *Points of View* and *Watchdog*); **Tim Robinson** (p 146) — Map-maker and writer (*The Stones of Aran: Pilgrimage*; *The Stones of Aran: Labyrinth*; *The View from the Horizon*); **Anthony Roche** (p 168) — Lecturer, broadcaster, critic and writer (*Contemporary Irish Drama*); **Frank Ronan** (p 88) — Novelist and short story writer (*The Men who Loved Evelyn Cotton*; *A Picnic in Eden*; *The Better Angel*; *Dixie Chicken*; *Handsome Men Are Slightly Sunburnt*; *Lovely*); **James Ryan** (p 85) —

NOTES ON THE CONTRIBUTORS

Novelist (*Home from England*; *Dismantling Mr Doyle*); **Mary Ryan** (p 156) — Novelist (*Whispers in the Wind*; *Glenallen*; *Into the West*); **Trevor Sargent** (p 76) — TD for the Green Party / Comhaontas Glas; **Michael Schmidt** (p 107) — Poet (*Bedlam and the Oak Wood*; *The Love of Strangers*; *New and Selected Poems*) and founder of Carcanet Press, Manchester, and Poetry Nation; **Michael Scott** (p 114) — Children's writer (*Windlord*; *Earthlord*; *Firelord*; *The Seven Treasures: The Quest of the Sons of Tuireann*); **Sir Harry Secombe** (p 96) — Singer and comedian; **Will Self** (p 155) — Novelist (*Cock and Bull*; *The Sweet Smell of Psychosis*; *Great Apes*) and journalist; **Carol Shields** (p 8) — American-born Canadian novelist (*The Box Garden*; *Small Ceremonies*; *Mary Swann*; *Happenstance*; *The Republic of Love*; *The Stone Diaries*); **Jon Silkin** (p 31) — English poet (*The Peaceable Kingdom*; *The Re-ordering of the Stones*; *Nature with Man*; *Amana Grass*; *The Little Time-Keeper*); **Peter Sirr** (p 73) — Poet (*Marginal Tones*; *Talk, Talk*; *Ways of Falling*; *The Ledger of Fruitful Exchange*) and Director of the Irish Writers' Centre; **Dave Smith** (pseudonym of David Jeddie) (p 40) — American poet (*The Roundhouse Voices*; *Cuba Night*), novelist (*Onliness*) and critic; **Michael Smurfit** (p 149) — Businessman; **Gordon Snell** (p 17) — Children's writer (*Cruncher Sparrow, High Flyer*; *The Mystery of Monk Island*; *The Tex and Sheelagh Omnibus*) and critic; **Pauline Stainer** (p 170) — Poet (*The Honeycomb*; *Sighting the Slave Ship*); **Sir Tom Stoppard** (p 163) — Playwright (*Rosencrantz and Guildenstern Are Dead*; *The Real Inspector Hound*; *The Dog it Was that Died*; *Indian Ink*); **Eamonn Sweeney** (p 12) — Novelist (*Waiting for the Healer*), critic, journalist and broadcaster; **Marilyn Taylor** (p 54) — Children's writer (*Could I Love a Stranger?*; *Could This Be Love I Wondered?*; *Call Yourself a Friend?*); **Melanie Rae Thon** (p 149) — American novelist (*Meteors in August*; *Iona Moon*) and short story writer (*Girls in the Grass*; *First Body*); **Colm Tóibín** (p 9) — Novelist (*The South*; *The Heather Blazing*; *The Story of the Night*) and writer (*Walking Along the Border*; *Homage to Barcelona*); **Barbara Trapido** (p 106) — Novelist (*Brother of the More Famous Jack*; *Noah's Ark*; *Temples of Delight*; *Juggling*); **Joanna Trollope** (p 1) — Novelist (*The Rector's Wife*; *The Choir*; *A Village Affair*; *A Passionate Man*; *The Men and the Girls*), writer (*Britannia's Daughters*) and author of historical romantic period sagas using the pseudonym Caroline Harvey; **William Wall** (p 247) — Poet, winner of the Patrick Kavanagh Award 1996 (*Mathematics*) and short story writer; **Jill Paton Walsh** (p 29) — Novelist (*Lapsing*; *A School for Lovers*; *Knowledge of Angels*) and children's writer; **Robert Welch** (p 109) — Professor of English at the University of Ulster at Coleraine, poet (*Muskerry*), novelist (*The Kilcolman Notebook*), writer (*Irish Poetry from Moore to Yeats*; *Changing States*) and editor (*The Oxford Companion to Irish Literature*); **David Wheatley** (p 61) — Poet and co-editor of *Metre*; **Katharine Whitehorn** (p 103) — Journalist with the *Observer*; **David Whyte** (p 38) — Poet (*The House of Belonging*), writer (*Heart Aroused: Poetry and the Preservation of the Soul at Work*) and scientist; **Susan Wicks** (p 153) — Poet (*Underwater Singing*), novelist (*The Key*) and writer (*Driving My Father*); **A N Wilson** (p 140) — Novelist (*The Sweets of Pimlico*; *The Healing Art*; *Who Was Oswald Fish?*; *Wise Virgin*; *A Bottle in the Smoke*), biographer (*Sir Walter Scott*; *Milton*; *Belloc*; *Tolstoy*; *C S Lewis*; *Jesus*; *Paul: The Mind of the Apostle*), broadcaster, journalist and critic; **Richard Wilson** (p 256) — Comedian, actor (*One Foot in the Grave*); **Barbara Windsor** (p 178) — Actor (star of many 'Carry On' films; plays Babs in *Eastenders*).

Index of poets and their works

	page
Anonymous	
Don't Quit	259
Fáinne Geal an Lae	254
Frankie and Johnny	35
The Dawning of the Day	253
The Maidens Came	170
Westron wynde when wyll thow blow	110
William Allingham (1824–1889)	
The Fairies	100
Matthew Arnold (1822–1888)	
Dover Beach	216
W H Auden (1907–1973)	
As I walked out one Evening	264
In Memory of W B Yeats	249
Lullaby	17
Musée des Beaux Arts	135
The Shield of Achilles	101
The Wanderer	55
Minnie Aumonier	
This Is My Prayer	186
Richard Harris Barham (1788–1845)	
The Jackdaw of Rheims	57
Samuel Beckett (1906–1989)	
Roundelay	176
Hilaire Belloc (1870–1953)	
Lord Lundy	262
The Winged Horse	52
Wendell Berry (b.1934)	
A Meeting	9
Sujata Bhatt (b.1956)	
Swami Anand	20
Bible (Authorised King James)	
Psalm 51	80
Elizabeth Bishop (1911–1979)	
In the Waiting Room	47
Questions of Travel	107
Eavan Boland (b.1944)	
The Pomegranate	123
Richard Brautigan (1933–1984)	
On the Elevator Going Down	198
Rupert Brooke (1887–1915)	
The Soldier	204
Robbie Burns (1759–1796)	
To a Mouse	33

INDEX OF POETS AND THEIR WORKS

John Burnside (b.1955)
September Evening — 115

Raymond Carver (1938–1988)
Hummingbird — 188
Late Fragment — 194

G K Chesterton (1874–1936)
The Donkey — 77

Amy Clampitt (1920–1994)
Iola, Kansas — 12

Austin Clarke (1896–1974)
The Planter's Daughter — 202

Michael Coady (b.1939)
Though There Are Torturers — 159

David Croft (b.1964)
The Things You Never See — 125

Anthony Cronin (b.1928)
For a Father — 124

E E Cummings (1894–1962)
somewhere i have never travelled,gladly beyond — 11

Celia de Fréine
Rupert the Bear — 63

Emily Dickinson (1830–1886)
Tell all the Truth but tell it slant — — 8

Ernest Dowson (1867–1900)
Even Now — 29

Robert Duncan (1919–1988)
My Mother Would Be a Falconress — 191

T S Eliot (1888–1965)
Four Quartets — an excerpt — 22

James Elroy Flecker (1884–1915)
A Ship, an Isle, a Sickle Moon — 146

Padraic Fiacc (b.1924)
Storm Bird — 121

Robert Frost (1874–1963)
After Apple-Picking — 171
Fragmentary Blue — 106
Stopping by Woods on a Snowy Evening — 98
The Sound of Trees — 230

Patrick Galvin (b.1927)
Message to the Editor — 92

Louise Glück (b.1943)
The White Lilies — 148

Oliver Goldsmith (?1730–1774)
The Deserted Village — an excerpt ... 158

Michael Gorman (b.1952)
The People I Grew Up With Were Afraid ... 146

W S Graham (1918–1986)
I Leave This at Your Ear ... 131

Kerry Hardie (b.1951)
May ... 117

Thomas Hardy (1840–1928)
God's Funeral ... 141
Heredity ... 205
When I Set out for Lyonesse ... 114

Tony Harrison (b.1937)
Long Distance II ... 196

Michael Hartnett (b.1941)
The Night Before Patricia's Funeral ... 184

Francis Harvey
Vulture ... 111

Robert Hayden (1913–1980)
Those Winter Sundays ... 187

Seamus Heaney (b.1939)
At the Wellhead ... 112
Digging ... 97
Requiem for the Croppies ... 40
The Diviner ... 1
The Flight Path ... 160
The Railway Children ... 39

George Herbert (1593–1633)
Mortification ... 134

John Hewitt (1907–1987)
After the Fire ... 145
The Scar ... 121

Friedrich Hölderlin (1770–1843)
Brot und Wein (translated by Michael Hamburger) ... 61

Miroslav Holub (b.1923)
Brief Reflection on Accuracy (translated by Ewald Osers) ... 118

Gerard Manley Hopkins (1844–1889)
Felix Randal ... 214
Heaven-Haven ... 2
No worst, there is none ... 206
Spring and Fall ... 29
The Windhover ... 138

Horace (65BC–8BC)
Ode VII, Book 4 (translated by A E Housman) ... 83

INDEX OF POETS AND THEIR WORKS

A E Housman (1859–1936)
A Shropshire Lad — an excerpt 189
Last Poems 173

Ted Hughes (b.1930)
The Horses 86

Pearse Hutchinson (b.1927)
Málaga 10
Until 65

Biddy Jenkinson (b.1949)
Geallúint 180

Attila József (1905–1937)
The Seventh (translated by John Batki) 144

Patrick Kavanagh (1904–1967)
A Star 176
Dear Folks 20
On Raglan Road 252

John Keats (1795–1821)
To Autumn 183

Omar Khayyám (?1048–1122)
The Rubáiyát (translated by Edward FitzGerald) 156

Rudyard Kipling (1865–1936)
If 56

Maxine Kumin (b.1925)
Woodchucks 28

Walter Savage Landor (1775–1864)
His Painters 85

Philip Larkin (1922–1985)
And Now the Leaves Suddenly Lose Strength 14
Love Songs in Age 53
The Whitsun Weddings 163

Edward Lear (1812–1888)
There was an old person of Dundalk . . . 260

Francis Ledwidge (1887–1917)
A Little Boy in the Morning 45

Denise Levertov (b.1923)
A Tree Telling of Orpheus 68
Heron I 67

Norman Lindsay (1879–1969)
The Tale of a Despicable Puddin' Thief 194

Henry Wadsworth Longfellow (1807–1882)
The Children's Hour 185
The Day Is Done 4

Michael Longley (b.1939)
Household Hints 7

Robert Lowell (1917–1977)
For the Union Dead   126

Catherine Phil MacCarthy (b.1954)
Rag Doll   64

Frank McGuinness (b.1953)
A Woman Untouched   132

Sorley MacLean (Somhairle MacGill-Eain) (1911–1996)
Hallaig   244

Louis MacNeice (1907–1963)
Dublin   50
Snow   229
Valediction   128

Nina Malinovski
Pure Praise   120

Don(ald) Marquis (1878–1937)
mehitabel in the catacombs   24

John Masefield (1878–1967)
Sea Fever   87

Paula Meehan (b.1955)
Buying Winkles   212

Czeslaw Milosz (b.1911)
Encounter (translated by Milosz and Lillian Vallee)   60

John Milton (1608–1674)
Paradise Lost (lines 242–270)   182
Paradise Lost (lines 704–722)   203
Sonnet XXIII   205

Adrian Mitchell (b.1932)
especially when it snows . . .   2

John Montague (b.1929)
Border Sick Call   218
The Trout   209

Thomas Moore (1779–1852)
Oft, in the stilly night . . .   199

Nuala Ní Dhomhnaill (b.1952)
Ceist na Teangan (translated by Paul Muldoon)   49
Gan Do Chuid Éadaigh   165

Christopher Nolan (b.1966)
Christopher Nolan's Tribute to a Friend   19

Brendan O'Carroll
In Praise of Women   168

Desmond O'Grady (b.1935)
Professor Kelleher and the Charles River   139

INDEX OF POETS AND THEIR WORKS

Ono No Komachi (834–880)
Hana no ira wa   170

Seán Ó Ríordáin (1916–1977)
Ní Ceadmhach Neamhshuim   76

Wilfred Owen (1893–1918)
Anthem for Doomed Youth   213
Dulce Et Decorum Est   258

Mirin Pearce (b.1992)
Lipstick   232

Pádraig Pearse (1879–1916)
The Wayfarer   66

Sylvia Plath (1932–1963)
By Candlelight   154

Edgar Allan Poe (1809–1849)
The Raven   235

Jacques Prévert (1900–1977)
Alicante   203

Rainer Maria Rilke (1875–1926)
Abend   228
Durch den sich Vögel werfen   81
Liebes-Lied (translated by Andy Gaus)   37

Arthur Rimbaud (1854–1891)
The room is open to the turquoise blues . . .   259

Theodore Roethke (1908–1963)
I Knew a Woman   155

Speverent Rooner [Monty Python]
Port Shoem   239

Isaac Rosenberg (1890–1918)
Dead Man's Dump   31

Mevlana Jalaluddin Rumi (1207–1273)
In the slaughterhouse of love they kill   258
Quatrain 1078 (translated by Moyne and Banks)   26
Unmarked Boxes (translated by Moyne, Banks, Arberry and Nicholson)   26

Saint Geraud (Bill Knott) (b.1940)
Poem   149

Siegfried Sassoon (1886–1967)
Base Details   91
Concert-Interpretation   210

Chief Seattle (?1786–1866)
The Earth Is Sacred   233

Harry Secombe (b.1921)
On Growing Old   96

William Shakespeare (1564–1616)
Fear No More the Heat o' the Sun 200
Sonnet XXIX 88
Sonnet LVI 175
Sonnet LXXIII 103

Percy Bysshe Shelley (1792–1822)
Ozymandias 115

Edith Sitwell (1887–1964)
Trio for Two Cats and a Trombone 261

Christopher Smart (1722–1771)
Jubilate Agno 73

Dave Smith (b.1942)
The Roundhouse Voices 42

Stevie Smith (1902–1971)
Come, Death (II) 178
Every Lovely Limb's a Desolation 177

Sydney Bernard Smith (b.1936)
To my typewriter, on its 21st, and my 42nd, birthday 215

Wallace Stevens (1879–1955)
The Plain Sense of Things 113

Robert Louis Stevenson (1850–1894)
Dedication 104

Alfred, Lord Tennyson (1809–1892)
The Lady of Shalott 240

Dylan Thomas (1914–1953)
Lament 5

Edward Thomas (1878–1917)
Old Man 105

David Wagoner (b.1926)
The Poets Agree to Be Quiet by the Swamp 118

Derek Walcott (b.1930)
Love after Love 201

Robert Penn Warren (1905–1988)
Little Boy and Lost Shoe 41
Little Girl Wakes Early 263

John Greenleaf Whittier (?1807–1892)
Kind Words 179

Oscar Wilde (1854–1900)
The Ballad of Reading Gaol — an excerpt 150

William Wordsworth (1770–1850)
I Wandered Lonely as a Cloud 181
It is a beauteous Evening, calm and free 173
The Prelude — an excerpt 15

INDEX OF POETS AND THEIR WORKS

Thomas Wyatt (1503–1542)
The Lover Showeth How He Is Forsaken of Such as He Sometime Enjoyed	248

W B Yeats (1865–1939)
A Drinking Song	256
Byzantium	109
He Wishes for the Cloths of Heaven	251
The Circus Animals' Desertion	90
The Cold Heaven	89
The Host of the Air	72
The Stare's Nest by My Window	78
The Stolen Child	94
The White Birds	82
To a Wealthy Man Who Promised a Second Subscription to the Dublin Municipal Gallery if it Were Proved the People Wanted Pictures	207
When You Are Old	169

Index of titles

	page
A Drinking Song	256
A Little Boy in the Morning	45
A Meeting	9
A Ship, an Isle, a Sickle Moon	146
A Shropshire Lad	189
A Star	176
A Tree Telling of Orpheus	68
A Woman Untouched	132
After Apple-Picking	171
After the Fire	145
Alicante	203
And Now the Leaves Suddenly Lose Strength	14
Anthem for Doomed Youth	213
As certain as color . . .	170
As I walked out one Evening	264
At the Wellhead	112
Base Details	91
Border Sick Call	218
Bread and Wine	61
Brief Reflection on Accuracy	118
Brot und Wein	61
Buying Winkles	212
By Candlelight	154
Byzantium	109
Ceist na Teangan	49
Christopher Nolan's Tribute to a Friend	19
Come, Death (II)	178
Concert-Interpretation	210
Dead Man's Dump	31
Dear Folks	20
Dedication	104
Digging	97
Don't Quit	259
Dover Beach	216
Dublin	50
Dulce Et Decorum Est	258
Durch den sich Vögel werfen	81
Encounter	60
Especially When It Snows	2
Even Now	29
Evening	228
Every Lovely Limb's a Desolation	177
Fáinne Geal an Lae	254
Fear no more the heat o' the sun	200
Felix Randal	214
For a Father	124
For the Union Dead	126
Four Quartets	22
Fragmentary Blue	106
Frankie and Johnny	35
Gan Do Chuid Éadaigh	165

INDEX OF TITLES

Geallúint	180
God's Funeral	141
Hallaig	244
Hana no ira wa	170
He Wishes for the Cloths of Heaven	251
Heaven-Haven	2
Heredity	205
Heron I	67
His Painters	85
Household Hints	7
Hummingbird	188
I Knew a Woman	155
I Leave This at Your Ear	131
I Wandered Lonely as a Cloud	181
If	56
In Memory of W B Yeats	249
In Praise of Women	168
In the slaughterhouse of love they kill	258
In the Waiting Room	47
Iola, Kansas	12
It is a beauteous Evening, calm and free . . .	173
Jubilate Agno	73
Kind Words	179
Lament	5
Last Poems	173
Late Fragment	194
Liebes-Lied	37
Lipstick	232
Little Boy and Lost Shoe	41
Little Girl Wakes Early	263
Long Distance II	196
Lord Lundy	262
Love after Love	201
Love Songs in Age	53
Lovesong	38
Lullaby	17
Málaga	10
May	117
mehitabel in the catacombs	24
Message to the Editor	92
Mortification	134
Musée des Beaux Arts	135
My Mother Would Be a Falconress	191
Ní Ceadmhach Neamhshuim	76
No worst, there is none . . .	206
Ode VII, Book 4	83
Oft, in the stilly night . . .	199
Old Man	105
On Growing Old	96
On Raglan Road	252
On the Elevator Going Down	198
Ozymandias	115
Paradise Lost (lines 242–270)	182
Paradise Lost (lines 704–722)	203

Poem	149
Port Shoem	239
Professor Kelleher and the Charles River	139
Psalm 51	80
Pure Praise	120
Quatrain 1078	26
Questions of Travel	107
Rag Doll	64
Requiem for the Croppies	40
Roundelay	176
Rupert the Bear	63
Sea Fever	87
September Evening	115
Snow	229
somewhere i have never travelled . . .	11
Sonnet XXIII (Milton)	205
Sonnet XXIX (Shakespeare)	88
Sonnet LVI (Shakespeare)	175
Sonnet LXXIII (Shakespeare)	103
Spring and Fall	29
Stopping by Woods on a Snowy Evening	98
Storm Bird	121
Swami Anand	20
Tell all the Truth but tell it slant —	8
The Ballad of Reading Gaol	150
The Children's Hour	185
The Circus Animals' Desertion	90
The Cold Heaven	89
The Dawning of the Day	253
The Day Is Done	4
The Deserted Village	158
The Diviner	1
The Donkey	77
The Earth Is Sacred	233
The Fairies	100
The Flight Path	160
The Horses	86
The Host of the Air	72
The Jackdaw of Rheims	57
The Lady of Shalott	240
The Language Issue	49
The Lover Showeth How He Is Forsaken of Such as He Sometime Enjoyed	248
The Maidens Came	170
The Night Before Patricia's Funeral	184
The People I Grew Up With Were Afraid	146
The Plain Sense of Things	113
The Planter's Daughter	202
The Poets Agree to Be Quiet by the Swamp	118
The Pomegranate	123
The Prelude	15
The Railway Children	39
The Raven	235
The room is open to the turquoise blues	259
The Roundhouse Voices	42

INDEX OF TITLES

The Rubáiyát	156
The Scar	121
The Seventh	144
The Shield of Achilles	101
The Soldier	204
The Sound of Trees	230
The Stare's Nest by My Window	78
The Stolen Child	94
The Tale of a Despicable Puddin' Thief	194
The Things You Never See	125
The Trout	209
The Wanderer	55
The Wayfarer	66
The White Birds	82
The White Lilies	148
The Whitsun Weddings	163
The Windhover	138
The Winged Horse	52
There was an old person of Dundalk	260
This Is My Prayer	186
Those Winter Sundays	187
Though There Are Torturers	159
To a Mouse	33
To a Wealthy Man Who Promised a Second Subscription to the Dublin Municipal Gallery if it Were Proved the People Wanted Pictures	207
To Autumn	183
To my typewriter, on its 21st, and my 42nd, birthday	215
Trio for Two Cats and a Trombone	261
Unmarked Boxes	26
Until	65
Valediction	128
Vulture	111
Westron wynde when wyll thow blow	110
What birds plunge through . . .	81
When I Set out for Lyonesse	114
When You Are Old	169
Without Your Clothes	166
Woodchucks	28

Index of first lines

	page
A Caucasian gets on at	198
A little word in kindness spoken	179
A puddin'-thief, as I've heard tell	194
A sheepman in the Mournes observed it first	111
A ship, an isle, a sickle moon	146
Aber Freund! wir kommen zu spät. Zwar leben die Götter	61
About suffering they were never wrong	135
After a night when sky was lit with fire	145
After the leaves have fallen, we return	113
And did you get what	194
And now the leaves suddenly lose strength	14
As a man and woman make	148
As certain as color	170
As I walked out one Evening	264
At early dawn I once had been	253
Beauty was that	176
Bent double, like old beggars under sacks	258
Beside yon straggling fence that skirts the way	158
Between my finger and my thumb	97
Between the dark and the daylight	185
But, my friend, we have come too late	61
By the name of all the living stubborn	120
Cuirim mo dhóchas ar snámh	49
Cut from the green hedge a forked hazel stick	1
Der Abend wechselt langsam die Gewänder	228
Diffugere nives, redeunt iam gramina campis	83
Don't grieve. Anything you lose comes round	26
Doom is dark and deeper than any sea-dingle	55
Durch den sich Vögel werfen	81
especially when it snows	2
Even now, the fragrance of your hair	29
Fear no more the heat o' the sun	200
Felix Randal the farrier, O he is dead then? my duty all ended	214
First bring me Raphael, who alone hath seen	85
Fish	118
Flat on the bank I parted	209
For I will consider my Cat Jeoffry	73
For the long nights you lay awake	104
Frankie and Johnny were lovers	35
From far, from eve and morning	189
from a selfsufficient garden which I tend with pensive toil	215
Gassing the woodchucks didn't turn out right	28
'Geall dom gean síoraí'	180
Grey brick upon brick	50
Had I the heavens' embroidered cloths	251
Have mercy upon me, O God, according to thy loving kindness	80
He disappeared in the dead of winter	249
He will not come, and still I wait	45
Hereabouts, signs are obliterated	218
How can you buy or sell the sky, the warmth of the land?	233
How should I keep my soul in bounds, that it	38

INDEX OF FIRST LINES

How soon doth man decay!	134
I am flying to California on Virgin Airlines	132
I am the family face	205
I caught this morning morning's minion, kingdom of daylight's dauphin, dapple-dawn-drawn Falcon, in his riding	138
I climbed through woods in the hour-before-dawn dark	86
I feel a mortal isolation	177
I feel ill. What can the matter be?	178
I have desired to go	2
I knew a woman, lovely in her bones	155
I leave this at your ear for when you wake	131
I met a traveller from an antique land	115
I must abjure the Balm of Life, I must	156
I must go down to the seas again, to the lonely sea and the sky	87
I place my hope on the water	49
I saw a slowly-stepping train	141
I sought a theme and sought for it in vain	90
I wandered lonely as a cloud	181
I want the mornings to last longer	96
I will seek Beauty all my days	186
I wonder about the trees	230
I would that we were, my beloved, white birds on the foam of the sea!	82
If I should die, think only this of me	204
If I were fierce, and bald, and short of breath	91
If you can keep your head when all about you	56
If you set out in this world	144
In a dream I meet	9
In full flare of sunlight I came here, man-tall but thin	42
In Kosbad during the monsoons	20
In the slaughterhouse of love they kill	258
In Worcester, Massachusetts	47
Is fearr liom tú	165
'Is this the region, this the soil, the clime'	182
It happened to Lord Lundy then	262
It is a beauteous Evening, calm and free	173
It's ten years ago today you turned me out o' doors	52
I've a grouse and harden in the country	239
Just a line to remind my friends that after much trouble	20
Lay your sleeping head, my love	17
Lipstick sticks as you lick	232
Long steel grass	261
Maidin moch do ghabhas amach	254
Márgarét, are you gríeving	29
Methought I saw my late espousèd saint	205
My comings and goings	121
My long two-pointed ladder's sticking through a tree	171
My mother would be a falconress	191
My mother would spare me sixpence and say	212
Níl cuil, níl leamhan, níl beach	76
No worst, there is none. Pitched past pitch of grief	206
O'Driscoll drove with a song	72
Oft, in the stilly night	199
Old clothes have hearts, livers that last longer	7
Old Man, or Lad's-love, — in the name there's nothing	105

on all that strand	176
On either side the river lie	240
On Raglan Road on an autumn day I met her first and knew	252
Once upon a midnight dreary, while I pondered, weak and weary	235
paris france	24
Remember when you were the first one awake, the first	263
Riding all night, the bus half empty, toward the interior	12
Season of mists and mellow fruitfulness	183
She kept her songs, they took so little space	53
She looked over his shoulder	101
She used to have the same nightmare	63
She utters the screech at the birth of my life	168
Sir —	92
Slowly, slowly, slowly	19
So spake the grisly Terror, and in shape	203
somewhere i have never travelled,gladly beyond	11
St Simon Heron	67
Straw-haired. Patchworked. I am	64
Suddenly I saw the cold and rook-delighting heaven	89
Sundays too my father got up early	187
Suppose I say	188
Sweet love, renew thy force; be it not said	175
Tell all the Truth but tell it slant —	8
Tha bùird is tàirnean air an uinneig	244
That time of year thou mayst in me behold	103
That Whitsun, I was late getting away	163
The audience pricks an intellectual Ear . . .	210
The beauty of the world hath made me sad	66
The bees build in the crevices	78
The blessèd stretch and ease of it	117
The Charles river reaps here like a sickle. April	139
The chestnut casts his flambeaux, and the flowers	173
The day is done, and the darkness . . .	4
The dove descending breaks the air	22
The first fold first, then more foldovers drawn	160
The Jackdaw sat on the Cardinal's chair!	57
The little boy lost his shoe in the field	41
The maidens came	170
The marmalade cat, sitting by your patio door	125
The mind of Man is fram'd even like the breath	15
the night before Patricia's funeral in 1951	184
The old South Boston Aquarium stands	126
The only legend I have ever loved is	123
The only response	149
The people I grew up with were afraid	146
The plunging limbers over the shattered track	31
The pockets of our great coats full of barley	40
The room is open to the turquoise blues	259
The room was suddenly rich and the great bay-window was	229
The scent of unseen jasmine on the warm night beach	10
The sea is calm tonight	216
The sky puts on the darkening blue coat	228
The snows are fled away, leaves on the shaws	84
The time will come	201

INDEX OF FIRST LINES

The unpurged images of day recede	109
The way an old man from his window looks out at the beauty	65
The window is nailed and boarded	246
Their verdure dare not show . . . their verdure dare not show . . .	128
There are too many waterfalls here; the crowded streams	107
There is no chapel on the day	150
There was an old person of Dundalk	260
There's not a chance now that I might recover	121
They flee from me, that sometime did me seek	248
They hold their hands over their mouths	118
Think that you're gliding out from the face of a cliff	26
This is winter, this is night, small love	154
Though I much prefer you	166
Though my mother was already two years dead	196
Though there are torturers in the world	159
Une orange sur la table	203
Up the airy mountain	100
We were riding through frozen fields in a wagon at dawn	60
Wee, sleekit, cow'rin' tim'rous beastie	33
Westron wynde when wyll thow blow	110
What birds plunge through is not the intimate space	81
What passing-bells for these who die as cattle?	213
When fishes flew and forests walked	77
When I set out for Lyonesse	114
When I was a windy boy and a bit	5
When, in disgrace with Fortune and men's eyes	88
When night stirred at sea	202
When they talk about angels in books	115
When things go wrong, as they sometimes will	259
When we climbed the slopes of the cutting	39
When you are old and grey and full of sleep	169
Where dips the rocky highland	94
White dawn. Stillness. When the rippling began	68
Whose woods these are I think I know	98
Why make so much of fragmentary blue	106
Wie soll ich meine Seele halten, daß	37
Wine comes in at the mouth	256
With the exact length and pace of his father's stride	124
You gave, but will not give again	207
Your songs, when you sing them with your two eyes closed	112

Contributors to the first Lifelines

Fleur Adcock, Darina Allen, Sir Kingsley Amis (deceased), Martin Amis, Lord Jeffrey Archer, Simon Armitage, Margaret Atwood, Robert Ballagh, Mary Banotti, MEP, John Banville, Lynn Barber, Julian Barnes, Gerald Barry, Sebastian Barry, John Bayley, Mary Beckett, Emmet Bergin, Sara Berkeley, Pauline Bewick, Maeve Binchy, Kenneth Blackmore, Michael Blumenthal, Eavan Boland, Ken Bourke, Clare Boylan, Alicia Boyle, Kenneth Branagh, Richard Branson, Séamus Brennan, TD, Noel Browne (deceased), Helen Lucy Burke, Barbara Bush, A S Byatt, CBE, Gay Byrne, Ollie Campbell, Noelle Campbell-Sharp, Bunny Carr, Amy Clampitt (deceased), Anthony Clare, Adam Clayton, Don Cockburn, Shane Connaughton, Jilly Cooper, Elizabeth Cope, Wendy Cope, Anthony Cronin, William Crozier, Dorothy Cross, Cyril Cusack (deceased), Niamh Cusack, Cardinal Cahal Daly, Ita Daly, Derek Davis, Treasa Davison, Seamus Deane, Greg Delanty, Dame Judi Dench, Thomas Docherty, Patricia Donlon, Theo Dorgan, Anne Doyle, Maria Doyle, Margaret Drabble, CBE, Alan Dukes, TD, Myles Dungan, Eileen Dunne, Paul Durcan, Archbishop Robin Eames, Lauris Edmond, Felim Egan, Ben Elton, Peter Fallon, Brian Farrell, Desmond Fennell, Anne Fine, Mr Justice Thomas A Finlay, Garret FitzGerald, Mary FitzGerald, Theodora FitzGibbon (deceased), T P Flanagan, Bob Gallico, Sir John Gielgud, Ellen Gilchrist, Larry Gogan, Patrick Graham, Victor Griffin, Hugo Hamilton, Eithne Hand, Mary Harney, TD, Charles Haughey, Isabel Healy, Seamus Heaney, Margaret Heckler, Chaim Herzog (deceased), Tom Hickey, Rita Ann Higgins, Desmond Hogan, Alan Hollinghurst, Michael Holroyd, Miroslav Holub, Patricia Hurl, Jeremy Irons, Glenda Jackson, MP, Jennifer Johnston, Rónán Johnston, John Kavanagh, John B Keane, Richard Kearney, Sr Stanislaus Kennedy, Brendan Kennelly, Pat Kenny, Declan Kiberd, Benedict Kiely, Galway Kinnell, Thomas Kinsella, Mick Lally, Barry Lang, Mary Lavin, Sue Lawley, David Leavitt, Louis Le Brocquy, Laurie Lee (deceased), Mary Leland, Brian Lenihan, TD (deceased), Hugh Leonard, Doris Lessing, Rosaleen Linehan, David Lodge, Michael Longley, Seán Lucy, Joe Lynch, Ferdia MacAnna, Joan McBreen, Nell McCafferty, Mr Justice Niall McCarthy (deceased), Thomas McCarthy, Tom McCaughren, Margaret MacCurtain (Sr Benvenuta), Mary McEvoy, Michael McGlynn, Medbh McGuckian, Frank McGuinness, Sir Ian McKellen, Bernard MacLaverty, Bryan MacMahon, Sean McMahon, Flo McSweeney, Jimmy Magee, Alice Maher, Derek Mahon, Thelma Mansfield, Augustine Martin (deceased), Maxi, Paula Meehan, Maire Mhac an tSaoi, Sue Miller, John Montague, Mary Mooney, Brian Moore, Christy Moore, Andrew Motion, Dame Iris Murdoch, Mike Murphy, Richard Murphy, Tom Murphy, Kevin Myers, Doireann Ní Bhriain, Eilean Ní Chuilleanáin, Nuala Ní Dhomhnaill, David Norris, Conor Cruise O'Brien, Julie O'Callaghan, Eilis O'Connell, Joseph O'Connor, Ulick O'Connor, Mary O'Donnell, Dennis O'Driscoll, Cardinal Tomás Ó Fiaich (deceased), Emer O'Kelly, Sharon Olds, Michael O'Loughlin, Andy O'Mahony, Tony O'Malley, Liam Ó Murchú, Joseph O'Neill, Hilary Orpen, Micheal O'Siadhail, Fintan O'Toole, Lord David Owen, Geraldine Plunkett, James Plunkett, Maureen Potter, Kathy Prendergast, Sir V S Pritchett (deceased), Deirdre Purcell, Marian Richardson, Christopher Ricks, Vivienne Roche, Neil Rudenstine, Patricia Scanlan, Anna Scher, Fiona Shaw, Antony Sher, James Simmons, Archbishop George Otto Simms (deceased), Maria Simonds-Gooding, Ailbhe Smyth, Camille Souter, Michele Souter, Alan Stanford, Amelia Stein, Francis Stuart, Alice Taylor, Mother Teresa, Sue Townsend, William Trevor, Gerrit van Gelderen (deceased), Helen Vendler, Michael Viney, Martin Waddell, Kathleen Watkins, Padraic White, Macdara Woods.

Contributors to Lifelines 2

Bertie Ahern, TD, Paul Andrews, SJ, John Arden, Neil Astley, Vincent Banville, Leland Bardwell, Ben Barnes, Kevin Barry, Bibi Baskin, John Behan, Ciaran Benson, Steven Berkoff, Agnes Bernelle, Wendell Berry, Harold Bloom, Seoirse Bodley, Veronica Bolay, Brian Bourke, Brian Boydell, Charles Brady (deceased), Conor Brady, Cecily Brennan, Rory Brennan, Joseph Brodsky (deceased), Denis Brown, Terence Brown, John Bruton TD, Julie Burchill, Donald Caird, Ciana Campbell, Moya Cannon, John Carey, Eithne Carr, Ciaran Carson, Charles Causley, Jung Chang, Siobhán Cleary, Michael Coady, Paddy Cole, Michael Colgan, Evelyn Conlon, Marita Conlon-McKenna, Róisín Conroy, Barrie Cooke, Emma Cooke, Art Cosgrove, Ingrid Craigie, John Creedon, Jeananne Crowley, Margrit Cruikshank, Pádraig J Daly, Brian D'Arcy, Michael Davitt, Gerald Dawe, Éamon de Buitléar, Eilís Dillon (deceased), Brian Dobson, Terry Dolan, Emma Donoghue, Katie Donovan, Mary Dorcey, Avril Doyle, Rose Doyle, Carol Ann Duffy, Joe Duffy, Anne Dunlop, Helen Dunmore, Sean Dunne (deceased), Alison Dye, Desmond Egan, Conor Fallon, Bernard Farrell, Eithne Fitzgerald, Gabriel Fitzmaurice, Christopher Fitz-Simon, Roy Foster, Maureen Gaffney, Tess Gallagher, Trevor Geoghegan, Máire Geoghegan-Quinn, Allen Ginsberg (deceased), Louise Glück, Richard Gorman, Tim Goulding, Bernadette Greevy, Eamon Grennan, Vona Groarke, Donald Hall, Daniel Halpern, James Hanley, Nigel Hawthorne, Michael D Higgins, Kathryn Holmquist, Nick Hornby, Kevin Hough, Sean Hughes, Ted Hughes, Gemma Hussey, Garry Hynes, Neil Jordan, Jenny Joseph, Mark Joyce, Madeleine Keane, Brian Keenan, Eamon Kelly, Maeve Kelly, Jim Kemmy, Anne Kennedy, Brian P Kennedy, Mary Kennedy, Jean Kennedy Smith, Philip King, Penelope Leach, Hermione Lee, Anne Le Marquand Hartigan, Brian Leyden, Edna Longley, Seán Lysaght, Sam McAughtry, Eugene McCabe, Patrick McCabe, Catherine Phil MacCarthy, Moy McCrory, Steve MacDonogh, Eleanor McEvoy, Barry McGovern, Jamie McKendrick, John MacKenna, Liz McManus, Ciarán Mac Mathúna, Deirdre Madden, Anne Madden Le Brocquy, David Malouf, David Marcus, Jim Mays, Leonard Michaels, Áine Miller, Mary Morrissey, Michael Mortell, Paul Muldoon, Jimmy Murphy, Gloria Naylor, Eilís Ní Dhuibhne, Christopher Nolan, Sharon O'Brien, Conor O'Callaghan, Gwen O'Dowd, Proinnsías Ó Duinn, Macdara Ó Fátharta, Colm O'Gaora, Fionn O'Leary, Olivia O'Leary, Jane O'Malley, Mary O'Malley, Brendan O'Reilly, Emily O'Reilly, Cathal Ó Searcaigh, Micheál Ó Súilleabháin, Seán Ó Tuama, Jay Parini, Don Paterson, Tom Paulin, Tim Pigott-Smith, Robert Pinsky, E Annie Proulx, John Quinn, Richard W Riley, Lilian Roberts Finlay, Michèle Roberts, Adi Roche, Gabriel Rosenstock, Carol Rumens, James Scanlon, Vikram Seth, John Shinnors, Jo Slade, Art Spiegelman, Dick Spring, Niall Stokes, Eithne Strong, Imogen Stuart, Matthew Sweeney, R S Thomas, Carl Tighe, Maura Treacy, Charles Tyrrell, Jean Valentine, Edward Walsh, Dolores Walshe, John Waters, Fay Weldon, Hugo Williams, Judith Woodworth, Charles Wright, Nancy Wynne-Jones.

Acknowledgements

A note from the editor and compilers
Thank you to Kate Bateman, Carolyn Bowden, Alison Brennan, Frank Cinnamond, Mary Clayton, Kevin Costello, Graham Darlington, Linda Deacon, Brian Delaney, Greg Delanty, Rolly Dingle, Caroline Filgas, Sue Flanagan, Malachi Friel, Roislinn Gallagher, Gloria Greenwood, John Harris, Frank Hughes, Mavis Johnson, Marybeth Joyce, Suzanne Kinkade, Sonja Kinlan, Cormac Kinsella, Ross Lauder, Harold Leech, John Leeson, Ray Lynn, Stuart McCoy, Iain McMillan, Fidelma Meehan, Simon Miller, Trudy Moynan, Edna Nash, Sharon O'Brien, Kate O'Carroll, Dennis O'Driscoll, Craig Petrie, Michael Renehan, Joseph Tsang, William Villiers-Tuthill, Ann Walsh, Sarah Willis, Garry Wynne and Treasa Coady and everyone at Town House for their help with the production of Lifelines 3.

For permission to reprint copyright material, the compilers, editor and publishers are grateful to the following:

Blackstaff Press for 'After the Fire' and 'The Scar' by John Hewitt and 'Storm Bird' by Padraic Fiacc; Calder Publications Ltd for 'Roundelay' by Samuel Beckett; Carcanet Press Ltd for 'Swami Anand' by Sujata Bhatt from *Brunizem* by Sujata Bhatt and 'Encounter' by Czeslaw Milosz from *Bells in Winter* by Czeslaw Milosz; R Dardis Clarke, 21 Pleasants Street, Dublin 8, for 'The Planter's Daughter' by Austin Clarke; Cork University Press for 'Message to the Editor' by Patrick Galvin; David Croft for 'The Things You Never See'; Celia de Fréine for 'Rupert the Bear'; Anthony Cronin for 'For a Father'; David Higham Associates for 'The Closing Album', 'Dublin' and 'Valediction' by Louis MacNeice from *Collected Poems* by Louis MacNeice, published by Faber and Faber, and 'Lament' by Dylan Thomas from *The Poems* by Dylan Thomas, published by J M Dent; Ecco Press for 'The White Lilies' by Louise Glück from *The Wild Iris*, © 1992 by Louise Glück; Faber and Faber Ltd for 'Little Gidding IV' by T S Eliot from *Four Quartets* by T S Eliot, 'Love Songs in Age' and 'The Whitsun Weddings' by Philip Larkin from *Collected Poems* by Philip Larkin, 'Requiem for the Croppies' by Seamus Heaney from *Door into the Dark* by Seamus Heaney, 'At the Well Head' and 'Flight Path' by Seamus Heaney from *The Spirit Level* by Seamus Heaney, 'The Railway Children' by Seamus Heaney from *Station Island* by Seamus Heaney, 'The Diviner' and 'Digging' by Seamus Heaney from *Death of a Naturalist* by Seamus Heaney, 'The Horses' by Ted Hughes from *The Hawk in the Rain* by Ted Hughes, 'As I Walked Out One Evening', 'In Memory of W B Yeats', 'Musée des Beaux Arts' and 'The Shield of Achilles' by W H Auden from *Collected Poems* by W H Auden, 'I Knew a Woman' by Theodore Roethke from *The Collected Poems of Theodore Roethke* by Theodore Roethke, 'For the Union Dead' by Robert Lowell from *For the Union Dead* by Robert Lowell, 'The Plain Sense of Things' by Wallace Stevens from *The Collected Poems of Wallace Stevens* by Wallace Stevens, 'Love after Love' by Derek Walcott from *Collected Poems 1948–1984* by Derek Walcott, 'Iola, Kansas' by Amy Clampitt from *Westward* © by Amy Clampitt 1990; Farrar, Straus & Giroux Inc for 'In the Waiting Room' and 'Questions of Travel' by Elizabeth Bishop from *The Complete Poems: 1927–1979* by Elizabeth Bishop, © 1979, 1983 by Alice Helen Methfessel; Gallery Press for 'Buying Winkles' by Pamela Meehan from *The Man Who Was Marked by Winter* (1991), 'Málaga' by Pearse Hutchinson from *Selected Poems* (1982) and 'Until' by Pearse Hutchinson from *Barnsley Main Seam* (1995) by Pearse Hutchinson, 'May' by Kerry Hardie from *A Furious Place* (1996) by Kerry Hardie, 'Border Sick Call' and 'The Trout' by John Montague from

ACKNOWLEDGEMENTS

Collected Poems (1995) by John Montague, 'Though There Are Torturers' by Michael Coady from *Two for a Woman, Three from a Man* and 'Ceist na Teangan' and 'Gan do Chuid Éadaigh' by Nuala Ní Dhomhnaill from *Pharaoh's Daughter* (1990); Michael Gorman for 'The People I Grew up with Were Afraid'; Mrs Nessie Graham for 'I Leave this at Your Ear by' W S Graham; Tony Harrison for 'Long Distance II'; Harvill Press for 'Late Fragment' and 'Hummingbird' by Raymond Carver from *A New Path to the Waterfall* published in Britain by Collins Harvill, © 1989 by Tess Gallagher; Henry Holt & Company Inc for 'The Sound of Trees' by Robert Frost; Biddy Jenkinson for 'Geallúint' from *Dán na hUidhre*; Catherine Phil MacCarthy for 'Rag Doll' from *This Hour of the Tide*, published by Salmon Poetry, 1994; James MacGibbon for 'Every Lovely Limb's a Desolation' and 'Come Death II' by Stevie Smith from *The Collected Poems of Stevie Smith* published by Penguin, © 1975 James MacGibbon; Frank McGuinness for his poem 'A Woman Untouched'; New Directions Publishing Corporation for 'My Mother Would Be a Falconress' by Robert Duncan from *Bending the Bow*, © 1968 by Robert Duncan, 'Heron' by Denise Levertov from *Evening Train*, © 1992 by Denise Levertov, 'A Tree Telling of Orpheus' by Denise Levertov from *Poems 1968–1972*, © 1970 by Denise Levertov, 'As Certain as Color' by Ono No Komachi from *One Hundred Poems from the Japanese* by Kenneth Rexroth; New Island Books/Raven Arts Press for 'To my typewriter, on its 21st and my 42nd birthday' by Sydney Bernard Smith and 'A Little Boy in the Morning' by Francis Ledwidge; Brendan O'Carroll for 'In Praise of Women'; Desmond O'Grady for 'Professor Kelleher and the Charles River'; Peters Fraser & Dunlop Group Ltd for 'The Winged Horse' and 'Lord Lundy' by Hilaire Belloc; Poetry Northwest/David Wagoner for 'The Poets Agree to Be Quiet by the Swamp' by David Wagoner; Random House UK Ltd for 'After Apple-Picking' by Robert Frost from *The Poems of Robert Frost* by Edward Connery Latham (ed), published by Jonathan Cape, and 'Household Hints' by Michael Longley; George Sassoon for 'Base Details' and 'Concert-Interpretation' by Siegfried Sassoon; Dave Smith for 'The Roundhouse Voices'; Society of Authors for V from *More Poems* by A E Housman, IX from *Last Poems* by A E Housman, XXXII from *A Shropshire Lad* by A E Housman and 'Sea Fever' by John Masefield; Ianthe Brautigan Swenson for 'On the Elevator Going Down' by Richard Brautigan from *June 30th, June 30th*, © 1978 by Richard Brautigan; William Morris Agency Inc on behalf of the Author's estate for 'Little Boy and Lost Shoe' by Robert Penn Warren from *Or Else*, © 1976 by Robert Penn Warren; W W Norton & Company Inc for 'Woodchucks' by Maxine Kumin from *Selected Poems 1960–1990*, © 1992 by Maxine Kumin.

Every effort has been made to trace copyright holders. The pubishers would be grateful to be notified of any additions that should be incorporated into any future printings of this volume.